TEACHING AND LEARNING PRIMARY SCIENCE

THE AUTHOR

After graduating in Physics at Oxford, Wynne Harlen taught in schools and colleges for a number of years and has subsequently been engaged in research, curriculum development and evaluation with particular reference to primary science since 1965. She gained a PhD through research into evaluation procedures at Bristol University and her first book, 'Science 5/13 : A Formative Evaluation', was published in 1973. For four years at Reading University she led the team which produced the 'Match and Mismatch' materials for use in teachers' courses for primary and middle school science. During this time she edited 'Evaluation and the Teachers' Role' for the Schools Council and contributed to a number of other publications on curriculum evaluation, including 'Values and Evaluation' and 'Evaluation Roles'. Later, as deputy director of the APU science project at the Centre for Science and Mathematics Education, Chelsea College, University of London, she was responsible for the national surveys and reports on the performance of primary children in science. She is also author of 'Assessment in Schools: Science'.

She has worked for regular short periods abroad, particularly in developing countries, and was invited by UNESCO to edit the first volume of 'New Trends in Primary School Science Education'. Her particular concern in work both at home and abroad is to encourage the kind of learning where children use the processes of science to develop their conceptual understanding and scientific attitudes. Recently appointed as Professor of Science Education in the University of Liverpool, her aim is to promote research, teaching methods, classroom activities and teacher training courses which advance this kind of learning at all stages of schooling.

TEACHING AND LEARNING
PRIMARY SCIENCE

Wynne Harlen

Teachers College, Columbia University
New York

ISBN 0-8077-2865-9

Typeset by Burns & Smith, Derby.
Printed and bound by Butler & Tanner Ltd, Frome and London.

CONTENTS

Acknowledgements

During the writing of this book initial plans and first drafts of chapters have been reviewed by two expert primary teachers, Ian Bennett and Carys Griffiths. I am most grateful to them for their constructive comments and for supplying ideas and material which have been included in later drafts of this book.

In addition there are many others who have contributed to this book less consciously; for although I have written down the words, the ideas are the product of exchanges and experience of working with others over the past 20 years or so. I am therefore indebted to many people (including Juliet) whose ideas have influenced mine through informal discussions, sympathetic listening or just a chance remark, as well as to those whose writings have been informative and stimulating and are listed in the references.

I am grateful to the following individuals and publishers for permission to quote copyright material:

Romola Showell

The director of education, County of Avon

The acting director of education, Cheshire County Council

The editors of Research in Science Education

The Schools Curriculum Development Committee

The Open University

Macdonald and Co (Publisher) Ltd

Oliver and Boyd

Harper and Row Ltd

My thanks are also due to Peggy Walker for combining patience and expertise in word processing the manuscript.

INTRODUCTION

This book is about science education in the first 7 or 8 years of school: from when children enter school to the age of 12 or 13 years. The past decade has seen a widespread acceptance that, in principle, science has a role to play in this early phase of education, yet practice in very many schools does not match up to what this role demands. In some schools science may be on the timetable or scheme of work and yet children may not be learning science; in others the reverse may be the case. It all depends, of course, on what we mean by 'learning science'. Views about this vary with regard to science in primary education as they do with regard to science at later phases of education.

The particular views of learning, of science and of learning science taken in this book are based as far as possible on existing evidence from research and reflection on experience. But it has to be acknowledged that, since primary science is relatively young, there is no great volume of research and tradition of scholarship in this area as there is for secondary science education. This neglect is a pity, since the first 8 years of school are not only in quantity a highly significant proportion of children's education (in many countries of the world it constitutes all of the education of the majority of children) but these years have perhaps even greater significance in occupying the formative period when a foundation of basic skills, concepts and attitudes is created. The situation has to be accepted, however. We are at a point in time where there is still much to find out about children's learning in science but also much to be gained by bringing together the ideas and information at present available into some coherent whole so that further developments in theory and practice may take place in step with each other. The present book is offered as a contribution to this progress.

Underlying the book is the view that decisions about the curriculum and everything relating to teaching should be based on a clear view of the kind of learning that is intended. The notion of 'kind of learning' embraces both the way children learn and what they learn, the two being interdependent aspects of learning. The way children learn the concepts and skills that will help them make sense of the world around them is described here as a process of trying out existing, or given, ideas against experience and modifying or accepting the ideas in the light of the result. Whether the result is modification, acceptance or rejection of ideas depends on the way they are related to experience as well as on what the experience is. So, for learning about the world, skills of selecting, applying and testing ideas are necessary as well as access to a range of useful ideas. These skills are described in this book as the process skills of science. Process skills are involved in connecting ideas with experience and attempting to make sense of the experience. They include skills of gathering information (observation), attempting to explain observations by applying existing ideas (hypothesizing), testing out ideas (raising questions, devising investigations, interpreting information) and communication. There is no invariant order in which these skills will be deployed, it will depend on the familiarity and nature of the experiences.

In plain terms, then, the way children learn is by making their own sense of the world, selecting or working out for themselves what are useful ways of thinking and useful ideas. What they learn as a result will depend on how they do this selecting and working out. An idea that is tested in a scientific manner by prediction and subsequent investigation of the validity of the prediction may be found wanting and rejected in favour of an alternative which stands up better to the test. The same idea, however, if tested with less rigour, may well be accepted in the face of the same evidence. (Some illustrative examples are given in Chapter 3.) Taking this view of learning seriously means giving children the opportunity to develop ideas through using science process skills and the chance to develop their process skills so that their ideas will help them make better sense of the world around them. We therefore give a great deal of attention in this book to the notion of progress in process skills and the teacher's role in this progress.

At the primary level of education the distinctive nature of science is not always apparent. We have spoken so far of science as 'making sense of the world' but this could be said to describe the whole of the curriculum. What, then, is particular to science and what does it share with other subject areas? A great deal of a so-called 'scientific' approach is equally good practice in studying the world around from a historical, social or scientific perspective. Many of the process skills, attitudes and concepts defined as aims of science (in Chapter 2) would overlap with aims of mathematics, English, art, etc. In the primary school the precise definition of boundaries matters less than at the secondary level where subjects are taught separately. Nevertheless, even though science experiences may be integrated with other experiences in topic work or broad areas of work such as environmental studies, it is important for the teacher to be aware of the specifically scientific experiences that are necessary, for these can so easily be neglected in an integrated approach.

Science is essentially about understanding things through interacting with them, finding out by enquiring of the things themselves. Thus skills relating to the testing of hypotheses by experiment are particularly significant. (This point is further developed on p. 70.) Some concepts that emerge from the experimental investigation or observation of the world are also particular to science. Those relating to the physical characteristics or observed behaviour of things, such as that living things share certain features or that gases expand when heated, are different in the ways in which they are arrived at from concepts such as 'justice', 'power' or 'beauty'. In the case of attitudes it is more difficult to distinguish any that are specific to scientific activity since by definition they are generalized aspects of behaviour. While not relevant only to science, 'respect for evidence' and 'critical reflection' can be seen as particularly important to this type of activity.

The relation between science and technology is one that is of growing interest at the primary level as much as at other levels. Again the label is less important than the appreciation of the nature of each activity. Both are relevant in the education of young children but one should not be mistaken for the other. Technology is about solving problems by designing and making some artifact, whereas science is about understanding. They are, however, more closely related than this simple statement seems to suggest. In the pursuit of scientific activity, problems are often encountered which require technology, as for example in devising ways of observing (a microscope results from the application of technology to such a problem) or in handling data (a computer). At the same time the solution of problems by technology involves the application of concepts arrived at through science (the understanding of reflection and refraction of light in the case of the microscope, for instance). Technology is also involved in the solving of problems in other areas of the curriculum outside science.

While closely related, even at the primary level, science and technology are quite distinct. There is more to science than solving practical problems and more to technology than applying science concepts. In this book the focus is on scientific activity and while there is much that is relevant to technology there is no pretence to discuss its nature and possible role in the primary curriculum.

About the book

The book falls into two roughly equal parts. The first five chapters are about children's learning: how learning in science may take place, what aims are appropriate for the under-thirteens and how opportunities for learning can be evaluated and improved. Chapters 6–10 focus on various aspects of making provision for this learning: the kinds of activities appropriate as children develop, the role of the teacher in these activities, the assessment of progress, the curriculum planning at various levels and the provision of resources. The following outlines of each chapter may help the reader to locate the parts of the book where particular topics are aired.

1.   Science as an essential part of children's education

Reference is made at the start to the present generally poor state of primary science and to the obstacles perceived by teachers as preventing implementation of science. The case for including science in the primary curriculum is then examined and some recent and urgent reasons are added to those generally cited. These are that children are developing ideas about the world around whether or not they are taught science but that these ideas are likely to be 'non-scientific' and unhelpful if not challenged, that the development of intellectual skills and of concepts are interconnected and that the early development of attitudes toward science should be based on experience of scientific activity not on hearsay and myths about 'white-coated scientists'. The nature of scientific activity for young children is then considered, involving a preliminary examination of the interaction of process skills and concepts. The chapter concludes with an extended example of 'children and science in action' in the form of transcribed discussions among groups involved in a scientific investigation. References are made to this example in later chapters.

2.   Areas of scientific development

The function of this chapter is to go into more detail about the process skills, attitudes and concepts which can be developed through science activities. Process skills are identified under six main headings, the nature of each then being discussed in subsequent sections. Similarly, five groups of attitudes relating to science activities are proposed and discussed. Concepts are discussed briefly at the end of the chapter as a preliminary to a more extended treatment in Chapter 4.

3. Changing children's ideas and ways of thinking

This chapter presents some ideas about how children use existing ideas and process skills in attempting to make sense of the world around and some speculations about the origin of these ideas. This 'model', relating ideas to experience, is then used to suggest how school activities may, and may not, affect the children's ideas and ways of thinking. The function of language in assisting children in developing and evaluating hypotheses is emphasized. Finally, implications of this theorizing are brought out in terms of direct relevance to teaching.

4. The question of content

In this chapter the relation between concepts and content is discussed before taking up the subject of concepts from where it was left at the end of Chapter 2. Criteria for identifying basic concepts are introduced and applied to produce a list of concepts which primary-school children might achieve through their science activities. Three examples are given to show how the concepts children may have differ from those which are the accepted scientific view. Once the concepts are selected there is still a wide range from which the content of activities relating to these concepts can be chosen and other criteria have to be applied. Relevance to things around children, their interests and the opportunity to use process skills are the additional criteria introduced.

5. Evaluating opportunities for learning science

The purpose of this chapter is to present a case for teachers evaluating the opportunities they provide for their children and to suggest ways of doing this. Three examples of classrooms are the starting point for raising questions about the provision being made for children's learning and how it might be improved. It is suggested that answering these questions involves clarifying the purpose of the evaluation, selecting criteria, deciding on the relevant information to gather, collecting the information and then applying the criteria in making a judgement. Some methods of collecting information are outlined. Suggested criteria are applied to the information given about the three classrooms to illustrate the diagnostic value that evaluation can have for the teacher.

6. Providing opportunities for learning science

This chapter marks the beginning of the part of the book concerned with the practical day-to-day matters of teaching science. Learning opportunities depend on the content of activities, the way the children interact with the content and the teacher's role. The teacher is responsible for selecting and arranging all of these and in doing so has to consider the match between what is provided and children's development. Matching involves both providing activities within the broad range suitable for the children as a group and 'fine tuning' to individuals. The characteristics of pupils in the age ranges 5–7, 7–9, 9–11 and 11–13 years are used as a basis for suggesting the broad range of content and types of activity relevant in each case.

7. The teacher's role

The theme of the previous chapter is continued in discussing the teacher's role in determining the opportunities for using and developing the various science process skills, in fostering scientific attitudes and forming science concepts. The introduction of 'scientific' words is one of the issues mentioned. Activities which provide these opportunities require careful planning which is not just a matter of selecting content but requires an organization and structure which will enable children to exchange ideas, check their ideas against evidence and prompt the critical review of their own procedures and reasoning.

8. Assessing children's progress

The concern in this chapter is for teachers to obtain information about their children which will help in keeping track of progress and can be used in matching demands to the children's developing abilities. The nature of the information required for this purpose is discussed and various ways of assessing children are reviewed. The most practical suggestion that emerges is for teachers to gather information about individual children's process skills, attitudes and concepts using developmental criteria applied to observations made during the children's activities. Examining some difficulties that may be encountered in doing this leads to the conclusion that the skills needed for gathering information about children by observation are the same as those required by teachers for helping children learn in the way proposed in this book. The chapter ends with a short section on the recording and use of the results of assessment.

9. Curriculum organization for continuity and progress

Decisions have to be taken by someone or some persons as to what to teach; but at what levels in the educational system should the different curricular decisions that are involved be made? This question is addressed from the point of view of a decentralized system where the locus of responsibility for the schools is at the local authority level and where detailed decisions about teaching are made at the school level. The main issue is the nature and extent of support that is appropriately provided at the local education authority (LEA) level, leaving schools the maximum freedom that is in the children's interests, but at the same time providing for teachers useful information and guidance in producing their own policies. Examples of LEA guidelines and of school policies are used in discussing these points and others concerning assigning responsibility for science in the school and the review and evaluation of the school policy on science.

10. Resources for teaching and learning science

This final chapter discusses the range of materials, equipment and aids which can be used in helping children's learning in science. Topics covered include the planning and provision of equipment in the school and the school grounds, the use of out-of-school resources through visits, written materials of various kinds and the use of radio, television and microcomputers. A necessary condition for effective science education is the efficient provision, organization and use of such resources.

CHAPTER 1

SCIENCE AS AN ESSENTIAL PART OF CHILDREN'S EDUCATION

Resistance to science at the primary level

It is well known, though not well understood, that, despite a great deal of effort and enthusiasm devoted to the cause of primary science in the past 20 years, the science experience of the majority of children up to the end of the primary-school years is minimal. Enquiries carried out to discover the reasons for what can only be described as resistance to science have come up with a now familiar list. The schools consider themselves as lacking equipment, storage space, expertise in managing group work in practical activities, time, guidance and support from outside the school, background knowledge and, above all, confidence in teaching science. However, when particular causes are studied in more depth (e.g. Davis, 1983) it is found that sometimes many of these reasons have little substance. Schools often have more equipment, books and teachers' guides available than teachers in the school realize; teachers who claim not to be able to handle the demands of group work in science can be observed to handle equally demanding group work in mathematics, craft work or English; time is found for whole mornings or afternoons to be spent in preparing assemblies, or for lengthy journeys to the swimming baths; LEA guidelines or policy statements, often giving detailed schemes of work and lists of sources of equipment, are not used and in some cases their existence is unknown.

This is not to say that the reasons given for not teaching science are not genuinely felt. There is no doubt that the majority of primary-school teachers *do* feel the need for more equipment, time, help, confidence, etc. But it is also undeniable that means exist in the system as a whole for meeting these felt needs and there must be a deeper reason why they are not being used. Such a reason is indicated by Norman Thomas, in discussing the HMI primary science survey (Thomas, 1980):

> The difficulty that primary school teachers have had in taking on and adapting the various primary science projects of the last two decades suggests that teachers in general are not convinced of the worth of this kind of work, or that they find it extremely difficult to organise, or that they feel too unsure of themselves to undertake it.
>
> (p. 10)

The first of the three reasons suggested here appears to underpin the other two and, indeed, the many other reasons which can be given. The valuable role of science as part of primary education is not understood. This lack of understanding exists not just (perhaps least of all) in schools but perhaps more importantly among teacher educators, LEA committee members and administrators and parents. If pre-service teacher courses ensured that all primary school teachers were as well prepared for teaching science as they are for teaching mathematics, language, physical education, etc., then lack of knowledge and confidence would be a far smaller problem. If LEAs provided more inservice time and more advisory teachers in science, then the need for support both within the school and outside it would be better met. If parents and governors insisted on science being part of the curriculum, adequate time would be found for it.

For all these things to happen there would have to be a much greater and more widespread appreciation of the value of science as a basic part of primary education. Without such appreciation change on the scale required is unlikely to take place. It is therefore in the conviction that there is a strong case for teaching primary science, and that a great deal depends on this case being understood, that this first chapter is devoted to explaining the importance and nature of early science education.

Role of science in primary education

A broad statement of the purpose of education is given in the Plowden Report (DES, 1967): 'to fit children for the society into which they will grow up'. The same source goes on to mention, still in very broad terms, some of the skills, attitudes and understanding which children need for the rapidly changing society they will encounter. The report avoided giving a definitive list of aims since it was acknowledged that these are often little more than platitudes and may bear a rather slight relation to what actually goes on in schools. However, if we are to justify the place of science, or any other subject, in education it is necessary to have a rather more detailed idea of what that education is intended to do. Such a statement was provided in the 'Green Paper' entitled *Education in Schools. A Consultative Document* (DES, 1977). It refers not to any particular age group, but the school education as a whole:

(i) to help children develop lively enquiring minds; giving them the ability to question and to argue rationally and to apply themselves to tasks;
(ii) to instil respect for moral values, for other people and for oneself, and tolerance of other races, religions and ways of life;
(iii) to help children understand the world in which we live and the interdependence of nations;
(iv) to help children to use language effectively and imaginatively in reading, writing and speaking;
(v) to help children to appreciate how the nation earns and maintains its standard of living and properly to esteem the essential role of industry and commerce in this process;
(vi) to provide a basis of mathematical, scientific and technical knowledge, enabling boys and girls to learn the essential skills needed in a fast-changing world of work;
(vii) to teach children about human achievement and aspirations in the arts and sciences, in religion and in the search for a more just social order;
(viii) to encourage and foster the development of the children whose social or environmental disadvantages cripple their capacity to learn, if necessary by making additional resources available to them.
(DES, 1977; para. 1.19)

It is accepted that science at the secondary level can make a valuable contribution toward achievement of these aims. Indeed, far from questioning it, recent proposals (DES, 1982) are for all pupils to experience a broad and relevant science programme right up to the age of 16 years without the choice of opting out, as happens at present.

What about the contribution of science when these aims are considered at the primary level? If it is assumed that all these aims do hold at the primary level, though perhaps with altered priorities compared with aims at the secondary level, then the case for science must be strong.

The problem at the infant and junior levels is often seen as one of striking the right balance between developing in children the basic skills of literacy and numeracy on the one hand and on the other providing a wide range of experiences relating to all the aims listed above. The HMI survey of 1978 found that a high priority is given in schools to the basic skills (taken as reading, writing and learning arithmetic) but also found that 'The basic skills are more successfully learnt when applied to other subjects ... there is no evidence in the survey to suggest that a narrower curriculum enabled children to do better in the basic skills.' It thus appears to be unproductive to consider basic-skill development separately from other subjects.

It is equally unproductive to use the other subjects as mere vehicles for learning basic skills. To treat them in this way would no doubt defeat the purpose in terms of basic skill development, for they might then be seen merely as subterfuges, as when children come to hate school trips if they always have to write about them afterwards. But such treatment would also be an obstacle to planning coherent experiences for the development of skills, attitudes and understanding relating to other subject areas.

So, although it clearly would be very simple to justify the inclusion of science in the primary curriculum in terms of its contribution to mathematics and to language development, it would not be productive to do so in these terms alone. There is no doubt that, as the HMI survey report's evidence confirms, the understanding of numbers, order of magnitude and the process of measurement is greatly helped by application in real problems such as children undertake in their science activities. Similarly, science activities place children in situations which they want to talk about, where they have to use new words and to choose words precisely, where they may speculate, plan, sequence their ideas, keep records and use sources of information. There is plentiful evidence of the contribution of such experiences to children's language development. But to think of the value of science *only* in these terms would be to diminish the importance of all except the fourth of the eight aims above.

Justifications for science

The contribution to mathematics and language development was only part of a wider justification for the inclusion of science in primary education which emerged at a UNESCO meeting on the incorporation of science and technology in the primary-school curriculum:

- science can help children to think in a logical way about everyday events and to solve simple practical problems. Such intellectual skills will be valuable to them wherever they live and whatever job they do;
- science, and its applications in technology, can help to improve the quality of people's lives. Science and technology are socially useful activities with which we would expect young children to become familiar;
- as the world is increasingly becoming more scientifically and technologically oriented, it is important that future citizens should be equipped to live in it;
- science, well taught, can promote children's intellectual development;
- science can positively assist children in other subject areas, especially language and mathematics;

— primary school is terminal for many children in many countries and this is the only opportunity they may have to explore their environment logically and systematically;

— science in the primary school can be real fun. Children everywhere are intrigued by simple problems, either contrived or real ones from the world around them. If science teaching can focus on such problems, exploring ways to capture children's interest, no subject can be more appealing or exciting to young children.

(UNESCO 1983)

Very similar points have been made in the publications of the ASE (e.g. 1966, 1971) and in the rationale of various sets of classroom materials (e.g. Brown & Young, 1982). Although plausible and well borne out by the experience of individual cases, it has to be admitted that they are not proven nor do they seem to have carried much weight in convincing teachers and others that science should be taught at the primary level.

Some of these claims reflect the glowing enthusiasm for curriculum reform in the 1960s. They were aspirations rather than substantiated findings, but it was part of the optimism of the time not to question them. Since then disenchantment with the effects of the attempts to change society by changing schools, coupled with the effects of 30% reduction in the school population (from 9 million in 1979 to 8 million in 1983 and to an estimated 7.5 million by 1989) (DES, 1981C) is associated with a scepticism about unsubstantiated claims.

Three important points that were not included in the list above should now be mentioned. They may well be taken more seriously, partly because they derive from recent and well-established research work and partly because they fit in with the current willingness to reconsider the whole structure of the science curriculum. Stated briefly they are:

● Children's ideas of the world around them are being built up during the primary years, whether or not they are taught science; without a scientific approach in their exploration of the world the ideas the children develop are 'everyday' or non-scientific which obstruct learning in science at the secondary level.

● The development of concepts and knowledge is not independent of the development of intellectual skills; unless children are helped to expand their ways of gathering and processing information then a 'scientific approach' is difficult to achieve.

● Children's attitudes to science are formed earlier than are their attitudes to most other subjects; without experience of scientific activity many children develop unhelpful attitudes, through hearsay and the mass media, which affect their performance in secondary science.

The mention in two of these statements of secondary science may make them unacceptable in the eyes of some primary school educators. Certainly the primary science curriculum projects of the 1960s and 1970s would not have wished to emphasize the role of primary science as a foundation for secondary science. 'Primary science' was seen as something quite distinct from 'secondary science' and the less contact between the two the better. The fear was that the secondary science curriculum would 'take over' or dictate the primary science curriculum given the slightest opportunity and each side felt that the other misunderstood its aims and methods. There is now some weakening of this stance and hopefully some opportunity for genuine dialogue and collaboration at transition points in schooling.

Challenging non-scientific ideas

The research which has led to the first of the points above has investigated children's understanding of some key science concepts in the early years of the secondary school. Groups in the USA, Canada, UK, France, Australia and New Zealand, some working independently and some in collaboration, have reached remarkably similar conclusions about children's own ideas. Because these ideas differ from the accepted scientific ideas they have been called 'misconceptions' or 'alternative frameworks'. The term 'children's own ideas' seems preferable, since this implies no right or wrong conception nor whether the child's ideas or the introduced scientific ones are regarded as 'alternative'. The findings of the groups working in New Zealand exemplify what has been uncovered by interviewing pupils and observing them in science lessons (Osborne & Freyberg, 1982). Their three main findings can be summarized as follows:

● Children approach the topics in their science lessons with quite firmly held ideas of their own, not with empty minds ready to fill with new ideas from their teacher.

● The children's ideas are often different from the scientific ideas used by their teachers and might well make better sense and seem more useful to children (for example, the scientific principle that moving objects continue in motion unless there is a force acting to stop them seems a less useful way of explaining daily observations than the idea that moving objects stop unless there is a force to keep them going).

● Formal science lessons at the secondary school often leave children's own ideas untouched and therefore much of what is presented to them makes little sense.

We shall come back later (Chapter 3) to the question of how children's own ideas are formed and how, once formed, they may be changed, but the immediate point is that there is a role for primary science in reducing this gap between the ideas children have and the ones that would enable them to benefit more from their later science education.

Combining processes and concept development

The second point, about the interaction of processes and concepts emerges from detailed studies of what children do and say during their activities in groups. Some evidence of this kind is presented later in this chapter. Such evidence questions the assumption that what children investigate is unimportant compared with how they investigate it. Such was the claim of the Nuffield Junior Science Project (1967), for example, and the basis for assuming that science can be learned without specifically scientific activities being encountered. 'But you're doing it all the time' was a reassurance given to teachers who showed anxiety about the thought of teaching science. What this meant was 'there is potential in all that you do for teaching science' but it did not mean that the potential was exploited or that no extra provision need be made to exploit it.

The realization that the ways in which children use and develop process skills in their current investigations depends on their existing ideas challenges the assumption that the subject matter of activities is unimportant. This is not to suggest that children cannot think and enquire scientifically in a social project or in a topic about local history, but that their scientific thinking will not develop if these are the only kinds of topics they encounter. As well as the more general skills, such as observation and interpretation of data, there are more specifically scientific skills to be developed and these require more specifically scientific activities. To some limited extent the scientific approach can be engendered in the methods used across the curriculum but the skills of enquiry cannot be fully developed unless children's activities include investigation of their physical and natural surroundings from an early age.

Fostering positive attitudes

The third point, about developing more positive attitudes toward science, is based on research (Ormerod & Duckworth, 1975) which has shown that children's interest in science is established at an early age. Already in 1959 research into the factors affecting secondary school pupils to choose science at the age of 13 years found that 'the scientists had long-standing stable attitudes favourable to science which were formed more than two years earlier, whilst non-scientists did not make up their mind until nearer the time of choice' (Kelly, 1959). Duckworth (1972), confirming this, found in addition that the attributes which favour the selection of science in the secondary school are evident in girls even earlier than in boys.

Although there is understandable concern to increase the number of scientists and technologists passing from school to higher education (which has in fact declined during the period of rapid technological expansion), the more important concern is with the attitudes to science of the population as a whole. Whether they choose to study science or not, our pupils should emerge from school with responsible attitudes to scientific activity. It appears that there is much less chance of this happening if science is encountered only at the secondary school, for attitudes and interests will already have begun to be set.

The reason for this may be the greater public exposure of science as a subject of debate in the media than is the case for other school subjects (there are many more television programmes, for example, about science than about history or mathematics; the BBC has several 'science' correspondents, but no 'geography' correspondent). But it is also likely to be linked with the point about children's own ideas. If children's first encounter with the subject called 'science' is one in which ideas are presented which are different from their own and do not seem to make sense in terms of everyday experience it is not surprising that a negative attitude is established fairly generally. Clearly, one step toward preventing this is to ensure that children's first encounter with science activities is not of this kind (which has implications for both secondary and primary science), but another is to make sure that science has some real first-hand meaning for them from an early age as something that can be enjoyable and useful.

It is perhaps worth emphasizing that the concern here is not for the minority who go on to study science, but for the education of the majority. The level of general skills of analytical and critical thinking, to which science makes an important but not unique contribution, required of everyone in the era of information technology is much higher than in the past. Further, there is a danger of a gulf opening up between those who understand and operate complex scientific technology and those whose lives are governed by it, unless there is a higher degree of scientific understanding throughout society. In preventing this damaging rift science education has a unique part to play. Thus there are important societal needs which have to be met by ensuring that both the general process skills and the specifically scientific ones are developed by everyone. This cannot be done if science education begins only at the secondary level.

Main contributions of primary science

These various points about the role of primary science in children's education can be drawn together under four main headings. There is a need for science in primary education because it can:

(i) Make a contribution to children's understanding of the world around them; understanding is seen as a developing mental structure which changes in response to children's broadening experience.

(ii) Develop ways of finding things out, checking ideas and using evidence; it is the way in which children interact with the things around them which will assist their learning not only in science but in other subjects also.

(iii) Build up ideas that will help rather than hinder later learning in science; this does not mean beginning to learn secondary science concepts in the primary school, but exploring and investigating in such a manner that children's own ideas can be put to the test.

(iv) Engender more positive and thoughtful attitudes toward science as a human activity; instead of unthinking reaction to the popular image of science, children need to experience science activity for themselves at a time when attitudes toward it are being formed which may have an influence for the rest of their lives.

Nature of early science activity

No claim is made in the summary list just given that there would be an automatic rise in the level of children's skills, concepts and attitudes consequent on introducing primary science activities. It has, however, been argued that these activities can have a unique and important role. Whether or not this role is taken depends on what is done and how it is done. The rest of the book is concerned with discussing these complex matters and can only make suggestions. As yet there is no evidence as to the efficacy of the approaches proposed here nor of other approaches; research aimed at providing such evidence is urgently needed. Even more urgent, however, is that teachers are able to find the help they need to make a start; without this no research can be carried out except in very artificial circumstances.

It has been seen that the contribution which primary science activities can make is in terms of developing ways of finding out and dealing with evidence, attitudes toward such activities and the understanding of the world around, both for present living and for future learning. What is involved here is a mixture of what are often described as the processes and the products of science. Although it is useful to discuss these separately, it is one of the main principles of this book that they are not separable in learning. Arguments as to whether primary science should be concerned with processes or products can be put aside as irrelevant; it has to be concerned with both.

Inductive and deductive reasoning

The reason for the earlier separation can readily be understood. The primary-science curriculum projects of the 1960s were anxious to make a clean break from the type of science typified by the 'object lesson' in which children were merely told about things and not given opportunity to gather and use evidence and to think things out for themselves. The Nuffield Junior Science Project (1967) made the distinction very clear: 'At this level we are concerned more with the development of an enquiring mind than with the learning of facts.' This was echoed by Science 5/13 (1972–1975) in defining the main aim as 'development of an enquiring mind and a scientific approach to problems.' It was recognized that in achieving this children would be 'developing basic concepts and logical thinking' and 'acquiring knowledge and learning skills' as well as skills and attitudes. However, the knowledge and concepts were treated as if they were a by-product of the processes and not as an integral part of the processes.

This is an inductive view of science which sees knowledge as coming from observations and evidence, by using processes such as inference and the search for patterns and relations. Consideration of the particular leads to statements or hypotheses about the general. The inductive view can be contrasted with the deductive one, which leads from the general to the particular, from cause to effect. A deductive view of science starts with a principle or theory and seeks evidence to test it or uses it to explain observations. A science programme based on an inductive view of science tends, like Science 5/13, to see its aims in the development of skills relating to the processes of science (process skills); a programme based on a deductive view expresses its aims in terms of knowledge of major concepts and principles of science.

The view taken here is that scientific activity is neither purely inductive nor deductive but must involve both inductive and deductive reasoning. To avoid overgeneralization of the point, the arguments for this are related to primary science. Stated simply they are that process skills cannot be used and developed independently of concepts and knowledge and conversely that concepts and knowledge cannot be learned with understanding without the use of process skills.

To take the first of these, it is not difficult to show that existing knowledge and concepts affect processes. For example, when children observe something they are not taking in through their senses all the information that is there. They make a selection:

> Take the example of the teacher who was hoping to show a group of children that a candle under a jar would burn for longer the larger the jar. He had three jars of different size and explained to the boys how to put them over three burning candles all at the same time. It worked well. So when the teacher asked them what differences they saw between the jars he was disappointed in their reply. 'Nothing. It was the same for all of them. All the candles went out.' None of the boys had observed what the teacher hoped they would notice — the difference in time of burning in each jar, a difference quite large enough to be noticed by someone looking for it. The teacher might easily have assumed that because the difference was observable it therefore had been observed.
> (Harlen & Symington, 1985)

Similarly, earlier experience influences children's search for patterns in observations and their planning and performance of investigations. (These interactions are illustrated in the example which comes later in this chapter.)

Two things follow from this. The first is that if process skills are limited by existing ideas in this way, then it is essential that ideas are developed if children's ways of exploring and investigating are to be extended. The second is that the process skills themselves have to be developed so that they can overcome the constraint of existing ideas. As will be seen in the next chapter, process skills gradually develop and one of the indications of development is the recognition that often in a situation there are different observations to be made, different ways of interpreting them, different hypotheses and approaches to testing them. Development in these directions means that process skills are less restricted by particular viewpoints and theories, though they may not ever be unbounded by existing ideas for the average person.

The claim that concept and knowledge acquisition cannot be independent of process skills is made on the basis of a particular view of concept development. This view is that children's ideas are forming all the time as they attempt to make sense of their experience. They do not wait to be told what to think about a particular phenomenon but work something out as best they can from previous experience and new observations. They may have to change initial ideas in the light of further information, but if they see for themselves the need to change they will not be confused. If, however, others tell them to adopt different ideas, yet they find no reason for this in their own thinking, the result is very likely to be confusion. The research of Osborne and Freyberg (1985) mentioned above is typical of the plentiful evidence which exists that children have their own ideas. Development of their ideas cannot take place from outside, but only from inside, children's minds. In rearranging their ideas they have to reinterpret information, draw different inferences, test out alternative ideas: in other words, they have to use process skills. This is part of a continuous progression which goes on throughout life. Adults, like children, readily forget ideas that do not make sense to them, however much sense they make to other people.

There are two comments to make about concepts which to some extent echo those about process skills. In the first place if concept development depends on process skills, as suggested, then it is important to give attention to process skills at the same time as concepts. Secondly, if children base their ideas on existing knowledge and ways of dealing with it (both necessarily limited by experience), then their ideas will often be different from those of adults and from accepted scientific views. This should not be a matter for concern as long as current concepts are seen in a developmental context. At any time children's ideas should be consistent with their experience and their ways of dealing with that experience. As either or both of these change, so will their ideas and indeed it is the function of school science to make sure that existing ideas are developed and gradually changed into more powerful and widely useful ones.

Science for primary children is therefore activity which provides opportunity for children:
● to explore the natural and man-made world around them
● to test out the ideas they have and develop them so that they become more useful in explaining what they find in their exploration
● to develop skills and attitudes required to gather and use evidence in forming and testing ideas.

As mentioned before, in science all these things are likely to happen at the same time, for they depend on one another and one cannot be carried out alone. The following example illustrates this and at the same time provides a bridge to the next chapter which is more specific about the particular skills, attitudes and concepts with which primary science is concerned.

Children and science in action : an example

The following are transcripts of the conversations of several of the groups within one class of 11-year-olds all working on the same problem. Each group was given four blocks of varnished wood of similar size and shape but different density and labelled A, B, C and D, a bowl of water, spring balance, ruler and an activity sheet as follows:

---

1. Float your blocks on the water
Look carefully at the way they are floating
What do you notice that is *the same* about the way all the blocks float?
What do you notice that is *different* between one block and another about the way they float?

Get one person to write down what you notice, or make a drawing to show how the blocks are floating

Check that you all agree that the record shows what you see

Put the blocks in order from best floater to worst floater

2. What other things are the same about the blocks?
What other things are different?
Think about their size, their mass, colour and anything else
Weigh and measure them
Make sure you keep a record of what you find

3. Now discuss all the things that are the same about the blocks
Get one person to put down a list of things that are the same
Now discuss all the things that are different and make a list of them

For each thing that is *different* about the blocks you should put down what you found about each block
Discuss with your group the best way to do this

4. Now look at your results of things that are different
Do you see any patterns in the differences?

Write down any pattern you find

The first group of five will be called group 1. They are all girls and have begun to digest the task.

Jenny   : Yes, one person to write down ...
Anya   : I know why — it's the varnish
Cheryl   : Just a minute! How do you know it's the varnish when we haven't even looked at it?

Anya	:	Yes, but look, they ...
Felicia	:	That one
		(putting block A into the water) Does it float?
		(all bend down to have a good look at the floating blocks)
Manjinder	:	Yes, half and half
Others	:	Half and half
Jenny	:	(Beginning to write this down) Right!
		(Felicia, Manjinder and Anya each pick up one of the remaining blocks)
Felicia	:	Shall I put B in?
Manjinder	:	I'll put C in
Anya	:	I'll put D in
Cheryl	:	Leave this A in there
Jenny	:	Now put B in there

Meanwhile a second group of four boys (Ahmed, Richard, Pete and Femi) and one girl (Rachel) have started in a similar way, putting one block in at a time and so far A, B and C are floating on the water. Five heads are crowded round the bowl and before D is put in one of the boys says:

Ahmed	:	C's nearly all gone, so D must sink
Richard	:	D must sink
		(block D is then put in and floats very high in the water)
Pete	:	Ah, D's floating on the top
Femi	:	D's the best floater
Pete	:	Now why is D the best floater?
Ahmed	:	Got more air in it
Richard	:	Got more air
Femi	:	...air bubbles
		(Ahmed takes block D out of the water to look more closely at it)
Ahmed	:	It's lighter
Richard	:	It's the lightest
Rachel	:	It's balsa wood
Pete	:	(taking the block from Ahmed) Yes, that *is* balsa wood
Rachel	:	Balsa (taking block and putting it back in the water)
		(meanwhile Ahmed picks up the spring balance as if to suggest weighing but puts it down again as the attention of the group turns again to the other blocks in the water)
Pete	:	Now which is floating the worst?
Richard	:	This one — C
		(he picks C out of the water and hands it to Femi)
		Now feel that one
Femi	:	That's
Richard	:	That's terribly heavy
Pete	:	That's why it's still floating — all wood floats — but, if — the heavier it is the lower it floats
Femi	:	Yes
Richard	:	Yes, but it still floats

Femi	:	(taking B out of the water)
		B's pretty heavy
Pete	:	(picking up pencil to begin making a record) So A ...
Rachel	:	— A is sort of —
Femi	:	A is half-way down, and B's ...
Richard	:	B sort of flops. It's half way —
Rachel	:	— down at one side
Pete	:	(concerned to have an agreed record) So how shall we describe the way A floats?
Rachel	:	A equals about half
Ahmed	:	A sinks half way and floats half way
Femi	:	I think ...
Pete	:	(writing) A is medium weight. Block A
Rachel	:	No, A block —
Ahmed	:	(to Pete) Yes, block A
Pete	:	(speaking as he writes) Block A ...
		(Ahmed turns to Richard while Pete writes and points to blocks B and C)
Ahmed	:	(to Richard) They're both the same
Richard	:	(to Ahmed) They're not, that one's lopsided
Pete	:	(speaking as he writes) ...is medium ...
Femi	:	(joining in with Richard and Ahmed) It's probably because of the varnish it's got on it
Rachel	:	(also joining in) Right
Pete	:	(summarizing what he has written) So, block A is medium weight and so ...
Femi	:	B
Richard	:	B's lopsided
Pete	:	(still writing) ... and so it ...
Femi	:	Yes, B's the worst one
Richard	:	No, C's the worst one
Pete	:	(reading what he has written and regaining the attention of the others) ... so it floats with half the wood under the water
Femi	:	Yes — about that
		(there is a pause, they all look again, putting their heads as low as possible to place their eye level near the water level)
Femi	:	Use a ruler — are you sure?
		(he goes to fetch a ruler)
Femi	:	Here's a ruler

Before going any further there is enough here in these children's activity to illustrate several points about the children's own ideas, mental skills and attitudes as they explore the material given to them. Right at the start Anya throws in what appears to be a wild hypothesis: 'It's the varnish'. There is no evidence for this, as Cheryl immediately points out to her, but it does show a desire to explain. In this case the 'explanation' is a low-level one, stated in terms of an observed feature (the varnish) without any attempt to propose a link between the supposed cause and its effect. Cheryl's intervention indicates an attitude of willingness to use evidence. They then proceed to gather that evidence by putting the blocks in the water systematically. Their first 'result' is a rough one, 'half and half', but it is recorded at the time.

The second group is also making statements ahead of observation at the start of the quoted extract. They have already put three blocks in the water and noticed a pattern (quite accidental) that each one floated lower in the water than the last. Block C has been observed to be 'nearly all gone' and they predict 'so D must sink'. They accept the evidence when they see it, however, and find that D floats higher than any other block. So they are quite willing to change their ideas in the light of evidence. Immediately there is some further hypothesizing as to why block D floats best. The initial hypothesis, about air inside it, is overtaken by one taken up by the group, that D is lighter. (Perhaps to the children these are not alternative hypotheses but different ways of saying the same thing: things with more air in them are lighter than things with less air.) They also use their previous knowledge to identify block D as balsa wood.

At the point where the floating of block D seems to have been explained by its being 'the lightest' there is in fact no evidence of this at all. The children have not even 'weighed' the blocks in their hands in any way which would have allowed comparisons to be made. The process of interpreting observations is clearly way ahead of actually making the observations in this case. But a realization of the lack of evidence for their statement may be what makes Ahmed pick up the spring balance. He does not persist at this point, sensing that the group interest has passed on to other things, but much later (in the continuation, to come) he is the one who does introduce the balance and initiates the weighing of the blocks.

The hypothesis about the weight of the blocks of wood being related to the way they float seems to direct the next section of their work. Notice how Richard, when he identifies block C as the worst floater, hands it to Femi and says 'Now feel that one'. He is referring to 'feeling' the weight and the observations he is making about the wood are clearly focused and narrowed down by the idea he has in mind. Pete puts the suggested relation clearly 'the heavier it is the lower it floats', after reminding himself, from previous knowledge, that 'all wood floats'. Pete then directs his attention to writing down what they have found (he is the recorder). But is it what they have found? What he writes is 'Block A is medium weight and so it floats with half the wood under the water.' Their observation was about the floating not about the weight; in fact they have no evidence about how the weight of A compares with that of other blocks. The statement recorded seems to have given an assumption the status of an observation and made their observation (of the floating) into an explanation for it. The ideas they have, based apparently on no more than jumping to conclusions, have influenced the process of gathering information. But they are still exploring the blocks, the water and the equipment and as long as the real things are in front of them there is the opportunity for them to reconsider and test out their ideas.

While Femi was explaining to Rachel why a ruler was needed, Richard was looking closely at block B floating in the water.

Richard	:	I can't understand why this is lopsided
Rachel	:	Well, look, see, it goes down that side
Richard	:	Yes, that's what I mean, I can't understand it
Pete	:	(who has not noticed this lopsided debate, having been busy writing the record, finishes writing about A) Now how is B?
Richard	:	Lopsided
Ahmed	:	Lopsided (taking B out of the water) Now B is ...
Rachel	:	Hang on a minute (she takes block B from Pete)
Pete	:	Now is B heavier than A, or lighter?
Rachel	:	Let's see if it's ... (she uses the ruler to measure the thickness of the block at all four corners; all the others close round to see what she is doing)
Richard	:	(answering Pete's earlier question) Sort of lopsided, Pete
Femi	:	Lopsided
Rachel	:	(after finishing the measuring of B) Yes, it's the same length all the way down, but it's lopsided
Pete	:	(picks up blocks A and B, weighing them in his hands) Now which one is heavier, do you reckon?
Ahmed	:	(reaches for the spring balance again) Try this
Pete	:	(picks up the pan to use with the spring balance) If we try this, we can use this — who knows how to set up something like this?
Femi	:	Well, you put it on the hook ... (he hooks the pan onto the spring balance) ... now you can weigh something on it
Richard	:	(who has put blocks A and B back in the water and is looking at block B) Lopside, in'it?
Pete	:	(picking block A out of the water) Now shake all the water off. Try A first (Rachel holds the spring balance while Pete puts block A on the pan)
Rachel	:	Just put it on

Pete   : Now what's it come up to?
               (he ducks under Rachel's arm so that he can put his eye right in front of
               the scale)
Femi   : (also closing one eye and peering at the scale)
               ... about sixty
Richard   : (also trying to look) ... about sixty-three
Pete   : Is there something we can hang it on, 'cos if you hang it on your hand
               you're likely to bounce it about

They then seek and find a way of steadying the spring balance. In the course
of this they notice the zero adjustment, take the block off and use the zero
adjustment and then discuss the reading of the divisions of the scale. From
this point their investigation takes on a much more business-like air. They are
not content with the rough 'feel' of the weight nor with describing the floating
as 'half way' for they begin to measure the parts of the block below the water.
Pete finds a neat way of recording this by drawing the blocks upside down like
this

so that it is easy to see the direct relation between the length of the submerged
part and the weight of the block.

The group showed what appeared to be a considerable progression in the
way they approached the task. Starting from rather gross qualitative
observations, of both the weight and the floating, they proceeded to use
measurement to refine their observations. It appeared that this early period of
rough observation was one of working out for themselves what the problem
was. Once they defined it in their own minds they tackled it in a more
systematic and precise manner. This may have taken some time (about 30
minutes) in this particular case because the task had been presented to them
on a sheet; it was not of their finding. But evidently they did become
interested in it and made it 'their own'. When children work on problems
they have found for themselves there is no need for this period of 'coming to
terms' with it. When they take on problems given to them, and they are
generally very willing to do this, time may be needed for rough exploration
before they begin to apply mental skills and ideas at the more advanced level
of their capabilities. This is not unlike the scientist who takes rough
measurements to 'get a feel' for the problem before setting up conditions for
more precise measurement.

The observations, and later measurements, of this group were very strongly focused by their idea that the floating was related to the weight of the blocks. This idea was introduced early on, it was not something they 'discovered' by induction from their observations. It was, in fact, stated before enough evidence had been collected to support it and became the framework for the observations and measurements they made later. It seemed that there was an immediate attempt to find a relation that might explain initial observations and that later observations were focused by the desire to test this relation. In the process another relation might be suggested which was then tested. Thus all the observations were made for a purpose and not just to gather any information which later would be put together to find patterns and relations. It is entirely reasonable that this should be so, for without a purpose it would not be possible to decide what information to gather. Here we see the close interplay of inductive and deductive thinking in action.

To see if this applies to others than just this one group, here is another group working on the blocks activity and apparently making much more open-ended observations. There are five girls, Kay, Lisa, Mena, Nicola and Ann (who is the recorder).

We join them after about 20 minutes of exploratory activity with the blocks, when Ann has just summarized what they have so far done and is rereading the activity sheet to make sure nothing has been omitted.

Ann	:	(reading) What do you notice about the way they float?
		(answering herself) Well, we've found out that they all ...
Nicola	:	... don't sink
		(brief laughter at this jokey statement of the obvious)
Mena	:	I know what it is, none of them float lopsided
Nicola	:	(who has taken two blocks out of the water and is holding them touching each other) They're magnetic!
Kay and		
Mena	:	(repeating what N has done) Yes, they're magnetic
Mena	:	And if you put them in like that, they go flat, look
		(she puts the blocks in with the largest face vertical and they settle with this face horizontal)
Kay	:	And D goes flat
Mena	:	Test with D and B
Lisa	:	They're getting water-logged now, aren't they?
Mena	:	This one goes flat last I think
Nicola	:	Hang on, let's put them all in and see which goes flat last
		(they do this)
Mena	:	C
Lisa	:	C
Kay	:	No, it may have been B

Mena   : I think it shouldn't be that, it should be D
Lisa   : That one's the heaviest, so it should go over first because it's heaviest
            (four pairs of hands go into the bowl, placing the blocks in vertically)
Mena   : I think B should go over first and D should go over last
Nicola   : Why?
Lisa   : (to Ann) And they're magnetic
Mena   : Yes, they're magnetic when they're wet
            (to Ann, who has been writing all this down) Write that down. They're
            really magnetic
Lisa   : (reading from the worksheet) What other things are different?
Mena   : Yes, look, the colour. The lightest in colour is the lightest in weight
            (Mena and Nicola take up the blocks and 'weigh' them in their hands)
Nicola   : ... and the darkest in colour is the heaviest in weight
Kay   : Yes, the darkest in colour is the heaviest
Nicola   : Yes, you know it's like white is very cool and dark is very hot ...
Mena   : Yes, you see this is the lightest and it floats the best and this is the darkest
            so it doesn't float so well
Nicola   : The lightest is ...
Ann   : (leaving the report writing) Let's put it against the side
            (she picks up the two blocks in question, the heaviest and the lightest and
            directly compares their dimensions)
            You see, they're all the same size
Lisa   : (pointing to the heavier one) It hasn't got so much light in it
Nicola   : They're magnetic as well
Mena   : That's probably only chance
Lisa   : If you get them really wet and then put the sides together
Mena   : (puts two blocks side by side)
            No, hang on — no, they are — even though they're shorter, this one's
            wider
Nicola   : They're all the same size, then
Ann   : The darkest is the heaviest and the lightest is the lightest
Lisa   : Look, get them all wet ...
            (dips two blocks in the water and holds them with the largest surfaces
            together)
Nicola   : (does the same as Lisa, holding up one block with another clinging
            beneath it) Yes, they do, look. They're definitely magnetic
Mena   : You've got to get them really wet
Kay   : Try C and D
Nicola   : Try the heaviest and the lightest
            (they try various combinations and find that the heavier block falls off
            when hanging beneath a lighter one)
Mena   : The heaviest ones don't work very well
Kay   : A heavy and a light work, but not two heavies

(A moment or two later they start weighing and measuring each block; Kay holds the
spring balance)
Nicola   : Put D on first

Ann : We can see that they're the same length
Nicola : Put D on, then we'll measure them all with the ruler
   (Kay puts D on the pan)
Nicola : That is ...
Lisa : (interrupting) But we should dry them all off first because the water may affect them
Mena : But they're water-logged already ...
Kay : Here you are, here's some dry towels
Lisa : The water may affect them. The water will affect to — er — thing
Kay : (pointing to the wet balance pan) This is wet — better dry that
Lisa : But that's going to be the same in all of them — so it won't matter
Ann : (still measuring with the ruler) They're about 12 cm

(Some time is spent taking measurements of the blocks. They decide to find the average dimensions, for some reason, and Lisa sits aside from the rest of the group doing this. The others are stood round the bowl apparently doing nothing in particular, but they are in fact watching the movement of blocks 'stuck' to the side of the bowl. The movement is very slow ...)

Mena : They'll never come off
Kay : I know, I'll give it a little jog and see which comes down first
   (both bang the sides of the bowl)
   They're not going to come down
Ann : This one should come down first
Kay : Yes, that one came down when I pushed (on the sides) but that one was harder to push down
Ann : So D came down, then A
   (Goes to record this. Nicola takes her place and continues to experiment in the same way, with Kay)
Nicola : We got to find patterns, what patterns have we got?
Kay : Well, we've got 2 dark ones and 2 light ones
Nicola : That's not a pattern
Kay : I know but ...
Mena : We've got to find out what sort of pattern the weight goes in — there may be a pattern in the weight
Nicola : Start with D, then A, then C, then B (weight order)
Ann : Press them all down to the bottom and see which comes up to the surface
Kay : ... I should say D should come up first
Ann : One, two, three, let go!
Nicola : D, A, C, B, so that went in the heaviest order, because we found that B was the heaviest and D is the lightest
Kay : ... and D came up first
Ann : ... so it came out right, so we know our facts are right

There are more widely ranging observations made by this group than the earlier one and some attempt to explain each one. Not all the ideas are put to the test, sometimes because other observations divert their attention, and the validity of many of the tests could be questioned. At the start of the extract the girls are following up their observation that if the blocks are placed in the water with the largest face vertical they do not float that way but turn over and 'go flat'. They have noticed a difference in the time taken for the blocks to 'go flat' and, at least in Mena's view, this is connected with the weight of the blocks. They decide to test all the blocks together rather than in pairs. The result does not satisfy Mena who says 'I think B should go over first and D should go over last', even though she saw that C was last. Nicola begins to question the assumption Mena is making and this might have led Mena to reconsider it, either by the force of argument or evidence or both.

They are interrupted, however, by the excitement over the discovery of the 'magnetism' of the blocks. It is interesting that none of the group members questions the use of the term 'magnetic' in relation to the blocks. They may indeed consider the effect to be exactly the same as found with a magnet or they may be using the word metaphorically. In either case the influence of previous knowledge in this interpretation of their observations is clear. The magnetic power of the blocks is tested by seeing if one block will support another hanging beneath it. They find the blocks differ in their ability to do this. Neither the test nor the conclusion from it is very soundly based but there is no challenge, from the teacher or the group, to make them reconsider it. Thus the idea that the blocks were 'magnetic' remained with them and was later reported as a finding from their group work.

The magnetism sequence is briefly interrupted when Lisa reminds the others that they are to look for other things that were different about the blocks. The colour of the wood is an obvious difference and Mena leaps immediately from the observation of difference to a relation which is more of an inspired guess than a pattern based on evidence ('the lightest in colour is the lightest in weight'). Indeed it is *after* this statement that the weights of the blocks are estimated by 'feel'. Nicola goes a stage further to try to explain the relation, 'you know it's like white is very cool and dark is very hot', again using previous knowledge, in this case of differences relating to colour.

In the final part of the extract the group of girls repeat in a more systematic way something that they had already done earlier (not covered by the transcript). They had held the blocks at the bottom of the bowl and noticed a difference in the rate at which they came up when released. These earlier qualitative observations were then being replaced by quantitative ones when they looked, not just for differences, but for whether these differences fitted their prediction. The pattern based on their ideas was indeed confirmed.

The only special thing about the discussions and activities of these children was that they were recorded. Such exchanges go on among children whenever they are truly co-operating and collaborating on a shared problem. Daily events in any classroom where opportunities exist for genuine group interaction and investigation would provide similar examples. The children's actions and thinking are interconnected. Their thinking, and therefore their actions, are influenced by previous experience and ideas drawn from it.

There is a complex interaction between existing ideas and the ways in which new evidence is gathered and used. It is this complexity which determines the outcome of children's encounters with school activities. We shall discuss some of the implications for teaching of the interaction of ideas and process skills in Chapter 3. First, we pause to clarify, in Chapter 2, the meaning of the skills, ideas and attitudes with which primary-science education is concerned.

CHAPTER 2

AREAS OF SCIENTIFIC DEVELOPMENT

It is now time to identify the main process skills, concepts and attitudes that can be developed in science activities and to describe the course of their development during children's first 7 or 8 years of school. There have been countless attempts in the past to produce lists of processes or skills and hierarchies and maps of concepts; attitudes have frequently been implied in lists of goals though not always well defined. The authors of every set of curriculum materials must, either explicitly or implicitly, define the outcomes which the activities they propose are intended to bring about or at least contribute toward.

No attempt is made here to review existing lists; this has been done by Thier (1973), Martin (1983), Harlen (1985a). Each list is consistent with a particular philosophy of science and of education and, just as ideas and values about these things vary, so will their expression as intended outcomes. The list proposed here should be considered in this context. It is one selection from many possibilities, one of which is consistent with a view of learning in which the learner is active both mentally and physically and with a view of science as a combination of inductive and deductive processes.

In this chapter the process skills, attitudes and concepts are discussed individually, but this does not deny the points made in the last chapter about their interaction in learning and use. All that is assumed by this treatment is that there are generalized bits of behaviour which can be recognized as expressions of particular skills, concepts or attitudes even though their expression will vary from one situation to another. Their interaction in learning and application is not denied by discussing them separately.

A considerable problem in proposing lists of these things and discussing the items in them is that one can become enmeshed in semantic argument. What, for instance, is the distinction between a conclusion, an inference and a prediction? If there is a distinction, is it important in the present context? A great deal of confusion has been caused by introducing terms which have a specific meaning in some contexts but a broader one in others. The hope here is to reduce confusion as far as possible by describing in some detail, and with the help of examples, the meaning of the terms used and how they may be expressed in children's activities. Each section begins with an overview of the selected group of process skills, attitudes or concepts.

There is also a problem of how specific the items in a list should be. It could be argued that many so-called process skills and concepts are collections of subskills and subconcepts. While this may be true, it may be unhelpful to proliferate subdivisions. The items listed in this chapter probably err on the side of being too global rather than too detailed and they might best be described as groups of skills, attitudes and concepts. Each of the following sections begins with an overview of the selected groups and is followed by a more detailed look at the items in the lists. The intention is to limit the present discussion to the nature and expression of the items. The important issues of how to encourage development are the theme of the second part of the book.

Process skills

Overview

The main titles in capitals are the ones which will be used subsequently. Also included are some of the terms commonly used as alternative titles or as titles of component subskills.

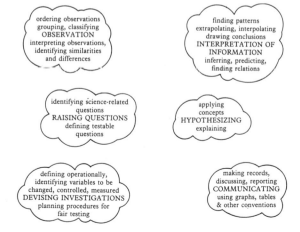

The layout of this 'list' is deliberately chosen to avoid suggesting a sequence or order of priority among the items. Sometimes observation leads to hypothesizing but sometimes a hypothesis leads to observation. Defining testable questions normally precedes the devising of investigations but further questions may also follow from it. Communication in its many different forms is clearly a skill which can be combined with or related to other skills in a variety of ways. In other words the list itself implies no theory of how a scientific investigation would or should be conducted. All the items are, however, seen as parts of the total process of investigation, which explains why neither 'performing investigations' nor 'experimenting' appears in the list. The process skills listed combine to define 'investigation' though they may also be part of more restricted activities that could hardly be called investigations or experiments.

Observation

Although observation involves the use of the senses to gather information, it is essentially concerned with more than merely 'taking in'. It is a mental activity, not just the response of sense organs to stimuli. The previous chapter has already mentioned the part that existing ideas and expectations play in this mental activity and the role of these ideas in observation is important in discussing its development.

The purpose of developing children's skill of observation is so that they will be able to use all their senses (appropriately and safely) to gather relevant information for their investigations of things around them. The significant part of this statement is the gradual development toward distinguishing the relevant from the irrelevant in the context of a particular investigation or problem. Children will not be able to make this distinction, and they may miss significant information, if they narrow the focus of their observations too soon. Thus in their early development children should be encouraged to make as many observations as they can, giving attention to detail and not just gross features.

Many young children are well able to do this in relation to objects which interest and intrigue them. For instance in one infants class two goldfish were named and recognized by the children, though they were apparently indistinguishable to a visiting adult. The children were clearly capable of noticing small details of difference and their ability to do so in other situations could be encouraged until it develops into a generalized skill. 'What is different about these things?' can be the start of a game with young children or of more serious enquiries for older ones. But it is important that the question 'What is the same about them?' should also be asked. There are many differences between these two objects but it is the things that are the

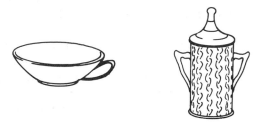

same which help to identify them. Thus it is important for children to make wide-ranging observations of similarities and differences and to pay attention to details as well as gross features.

Observations are, however, usually made for a purpose. Looking for similarities and differences for no particular reason except to see how many one can find soon palls. It is best pursued when the similarities or differences are needed for some reason. A contrived reason can be to group or classify. Children's classifying activities often start with their collections of objects. The collection itself is a set of objects with something in common and the children should be encouraged to identify the common features before subdividing them. Various alternative criteria to be used in subdividing should also be developed and discussed so that the children's attention is focused separately on different observable features of the objects.

Ordering objects or events is also a way of focusing attention on to particular features of difference between one and another. Encouraging children to make observations of events and objects which change in sequence, in the sky and seasonal changes for example, helps them to pick out from all the features that can be observed those which relate things in a sequence. This can also encourage them to observe a process carefully during its course and not just at its beginning and end. For example, if children can watch bubbles rising when they put water into a jar half full of soil, or see worms burrowing and making casts, their observations will help them not just to know what happens but something about how it happens.

Relating one observation to another and finding patterns or sequences in them is part of interpreting observations. This has to be included in the skill of observation, mainly because it cannot be left out. What is observed is selected by expectations and hence interpretation is built in from the start. Patterns are not found by first making all possible observations and then seeing what relation can be found. Rather there is a to-ing and fro-ing between observations and possible patterns while the observations are being made. This is why we often see or hear something more clearly a second time, not because we take in more information, but because we focus on selected parts and cut out the 'noise'.

The ability to interpret observations and select relevant information is indeed an important and advanced feature of observation. But at the same time as encouraging it in children it is essential to help them to be conscious of the selection they are making and to be aware that there is   other information to be used. If this is not done there is a danger of present ideas and ways of looking at things acting as blinkers which prevent us from ever seeing beyond what we expect. The level of development at which a person can reflect on the process of his observation and can consciously and spontaneously go beyond the limits of the framework of existing ideas is something to be aimed for throughout education. Although it will probably not be reached by many by the age of 13 years, the foundation has to be laid in the development of the other component process skills which have been mentioned.

Interpretation of information

This process skill comes into play when data are given or have been collected. It may lead to revisiting the source of information to collect more but it is essentially concerned with making sense and use of what is known or given at a particular time.

A term often used for this process is drawing conclusions (sometimes the last in the sequence of headings for writing up an experiment: apparatus, method, results...). When carried out logically and carefully this means putting various pieces of information or observations together and deducing something from them. For example, that if the level of water in a jar with a plant in it goes down more quickly than the level in a jar without a plant, then the plant has something to do with the disappearance of the water. Putting this together with a further observation that stems placed in a soluble red dye become red enables the conclusion to be drawn that the missing water passes up the stems. This is different, however, from 'concluding' from this evidence alone that water passes up into all plants and all parts of plants. Premature generalization has to be avoided.

Children all too readily jump to conclusions on limited evidence. For instance, one of the boys in the last chapter confidently affirmed 'all wood floats' (presumably he had never tried ebony or lignum vitae). To prevent this and make children more critical about the justification for their conclusions it is useful to distinguish conclusions which keep to the evidence available and those which draw inferences going beyond it.

It is often implied that a scientific way of working, reflected in children's activities, is to start by collecting data and then to look for patterns in them. In reality, this way of working comes naturally neither to scientists nor to children. Instead there is some hypothesis in mind that determines what data are to be collected and only a limited range of possible patterns can therefore be found, or not found, relating to the hypothesis. There is an important process skill, however, in deciding to what extent the data reveal one of the patterns which are considered likely.

Generally, the purpose of collecting the information itself suggests that it should be arranged in a particular order and having done this it will be possible to see whether other data also fall in the same order. For instance, some children measuring each other's lung capacity, by displacing water from a large jar, were interested in what might be the reason for some people having larger lung capacities than others. They took various other measurements of each other: height, chest circumference and weight. Their collected data were a confusing mass of measurements, none arranged in any order. They could begin to look for patterns, however, once the numbers had been rearranged to be in order of increasing lung capacity. It was then possible to see whether any of the other results were also in a sequence, ascending or descending. In this case none was exactly in order, but chest measurement was the nearest. By using a graph, of course, this sorting out is done automatically but it is useful to do it 'by hand', as it were, many times before introducing the idea of graphing. The concern with the conventions and mechanics of plotting a graph can too easily submerge thought about what is really being done to the data in the process.

As a start it is helpful to encourage the process skill of looking for patterns in cases where a clear pattern is there to be found. The distance a toy car rolls before it stops when started on a ramp of different heights, the pitch of a stretched string changed in length, the pitch of the notes made by striking bottles with different amounts of water in them, the lengths of shadows at different times of the day, all these will give patterns of clear regularity. Opportunities should be taken to use such patterns to help children make predictions which they can then check. How long a string is needed to give a certain note? How high should the ramp be to make the car reach a particular spot? Predictions that stay within the range of the original information are interpolations, whereas those that go beyond it are extrapolations. By using the patterns they find, children will realize the purpose and value of finding them. They will also have ways of systematically summing up their findings which are more reliable than jumping to conclusions.

Not all patterns are regular, of course. What should be done about the lung-capacity problem; is there a pattern or not if some of the numbers don't quite fit? Handling this kind of problem implies further development of the skill of interpretation, on from finding exact patterns to finding relations. A great deal of scientists' work is concerned with distinguishing trends or relations in numbers from total randomness (e.g. is the number of deaths among people given a certain drug greater than those not given it?). Young children cannot be expected to make precise tests of trends but they should be introduced to the idea that many patterns are not exact, for any of a variety of reasons. What is important in this elaboration of the process skill is that they do not just ignore data which do not fit an exact pattern. They can query it, repeat a measurement if possible, but if it still does not fit they must accept the pattern as an approximation. They should also be helped to realize that even when all their data do fit a pattern the relation is still a tentative one since they can never be sure that, if they found more information, some of it might not fit the pattern.

Ensuring that all the data are taken into account in a pattern is part of the skill of interpreting which becomes increasingly important as more complex data are encountered. In simple cases it is possible to 'get away' with taking note of only the extreme cases. This is what the girls did with the wooden blocks (see p. 19). 'The lightest floats the best and the darkest doesn't float so well' was to them a pattern, though they had not checked whether the colour and floating of the other pieces of wood fitted in with it. If in these simple cases children are helped to check that a pattern fits all the information then they will be in a better position later to deal with more complex patterns.

The process of inference takes the interpretation further than looking for patterns in numbers or other data to suggesting relations which account for the existence of the patterns. Generally, this is not something children need encouragement to do, they suggest reasons very readily, sometimes before a pattern has been thoroughly checked. In the chest-expansion example (p. 29) the explanation immediately offered was 'Yes it will be, because the bigger their chest the more room there is for air.' An inference goes well beyond the data in a different way than a prediction, for it would require not more of the same kind of evidence to check it but rather quite different information or a separate enquiry.

In a simple case, suppose a young child is rolling two tins, one half full of sand and one with a heavy weight attached to one side inside the tin. She finds that one tin will roll evenly and then stop whereas one moves in jerks and will oscillate before it stops. After playing with these for a while she may well be able to predict something about their movement: where they will come to rest or which side of the tin will be uppermost at rest. This can be tested by rolling them again. She may also infer that one has a solid lump stuck on the side and the other has not. This inference will not be checked by more rolling; it can only be checked by doing something different: looking inside.

It is useful to help children to distinguish between finding relations in observations, which can be checked by going back to the observations, and making inferences, which cannot be checked without more information. Inferences are always being made in science, as in everyday life, but it is important to know when a statement is an inference and when it keeps more closely to the available information. The distinction can usefully be introduced to children of 10 or 11 years and beyond.

Hypothesizing

It is a pity that this word is avoided by many teachers and pupils, probably because it sounds 'too scientific' or, perhaps, in the case of children, because it is difficult to pronounce and spell. It describes concisely an important process in children's scientific activity which otherwise needs a clumsy phrase such as 'suggesting tentative explanations'. To use the word 'explaining' implies a certainty which is rarely justified. If we want children to realize that scientific knowledge is tentative and always subject to disproof or change in the light of further evidence then it is useful to introduce the word 'hypothesis' more frequently.

The process of hypothesizing is attempting to explain observations or relations, or making predictions in terms of a principle or concept. Sometimes the principle or concept is one that has been established from previous experience, in which case the process is one of applying something learned in one situation to a new situation. (If the situation is the same as a previous one, it is a matter of recall rather than application.) In other cases the process may be closer to generating a new principle or trying out a hunch. The word 'new' should be qualified though, since it is new to the individual concerned and not necessarily new in any absolute sense. However, the distinction between generating and applying is less clear than it is sometimes thought to be. The process of applying a principle or concept is part of its development in a child (or an adult). It will be better understood, and so have a slightly different meaning, as a result of being applied. Thus applying it is part of the generation of a concept. Similarly, a 'new' idea is seldom created out of nothing, it may be an inspired guess that some relation exists but there are usually clues relating past and present experience to spark off this creativity.

To apply concepts or knowledge from one situation to another the child has to recognize some similarity between these two situations or events. The clues may be fruitful and lead to suggested explanations which stand up well to checking. For instance, the children's explanation that the floating of the same-sized wooden blocks depended on their mass was tested by 'weighing' the blocks in their hands as well as by using the spring balance, but the idea came to them before weighing of any kind was done and was presumably based on earlier ideas and experience about floating objects.

Sometimes less fruitful clues are used and the 'explanation' is soon found to be faulty. The explanation of the sticking of the wet wooden blocks to each other by the girls who said 'They're magnetic' is an example. It would not be long before someone challenged them to show that the wood was magnetic using some of the usual tests of magnetism, which would inevitably have failed. However, the girls did not fail in respect of attempting to apply knowledge to explain what they saw, but they may have needed more experience to distinguish useful clues from false clues.

Children's explanations can often be grouped as being at different levels. The levels bear a relation both to the children's general experience and to their experience of the situation involved in a particular case. These levels are best explained with the help of an example. A group of children were using a 'fast wheels' car track, making measurements of how far the cars went along a horizontal piece of track after starting at various points on a sloping part. One of the girls asked 'What makes it go further when you start it from here?'. The explanation given by one of the group was 'because it starts higher'. For him, this statement of the circumstances was explanation enough. He did not appear to understand that there was need to enquire further. Another child said, 'It's energy. It's got more energy.' She appeared to be satisfied to put a label on the problem. She may have been able to work out in her own mind why 'energy' explained the observations, but she certainly did not attempt to convey it to others. Eventually, the girl who posed the question in the beginning answered it herself. 'I know,' she said, 'it's my hand that gives it more energy when I lift it higher up to start with.' Here was a principle not just stated, but applied.

It is not difficult to agree that the child who stated only 'energy' is unlikely to have developed her understanding of the concept in this example, while the one who described how it applied may well have added to her grasp of the meaning and usefulness of the concept of energy. The interplay of concepts and process is very clear here; it is obviously to the advantage of children's understanding that they develop the ability to apply ideas beyond the levels of identifying circumstances or naming concepts toward describing how a general principle applies to a certain problem. Some ways of providing opportunities for this development and the teacher's role in it are discussed in the wider context of providing learning opportunities in Chapters 6 and 7.

Raising questions

It is not difficult to encourage children to raise questions, unless, that is, their natural inclinations to do so have been discouraged by thoughtless treatment from adults. In school, children who ask questions are sometimes made to feel foolish; at home, they may have been told directly by a busy parent to 'stop asking so many questions'. But a little encouragement on a teacher's part can usually revive children's questioning, especially if all questions are accepted as worth answering and not just those the teacher feels to be important.

It is particularly relevant to begin by reaffirming the value of children raising questions of all kinds when discussing one particular kind of question, the investigable kind, for it is not intended to give the impression that these are the only kind of question worth asking. Raising a variety of questions, including poorly expressed and vague ones, is important to children's learning, for questioning is the means by which a child can fill in some links between one experience and another and can make his own sense of the world. Such learning is helped, however, if teachers, and eventually pupils, recognize the distinction between the kinds of question that science is concerned with and questions which cannot be settled by scientific activity. Science addresses questions about what there is in the world and how it behaves. In answer to such questions assertions can be made which can be tested; for instance, 'Does wood float?' and 'Do you find trees on top of mountains?'. The answers 'Yes, wood floats' and 'There are no trees on the top of mountains' can be tested by investigation or by consulting someone who has found out. These are science-related questions.

The situation is very different, though, for questions such as 'Is happiness the only real aim in life?' or 'What is knowledge?'. These are philosophical questions and are not answered from observation or logical argument. Neither can science address questions of value or aesthetic judgement. It can tackle 'Which watch keeps better time?' but not 'Which watch is more attractive?' or 'Which is worth more money?'.

Within the range of questions which science attempts to answer we are particularly concerned in education at the primary and lower secondary levels with a small subset of questions. These are the questions to which children can find answers through their own activity. So they have to be not only empirical questions but questions to which the children can find answers or about which they can make and test assertions.

Questions that children ask range over all kinds and the children themselves are not aware that they are asking quite different sorts of questions and that some cannot be answered by science. To develop this awareness is a significant part of their education, but it will come only very slowly and through realizing the kinds of questions that can be answered by their own investigations.

The first step is to encourage children to raise questions of any sort. Putting collections of new things in the classroom, taking children out for walks or visits, ensuring variety in the materials they handle, are useful for this. The following list contains some of the questions that children asked after handling a range of different pieces of rock (Osborne *et al.* 1982):

> What are rocks made of?
> How do they get their colour?
> Why are they hard?
> How do rocks get their shape?
> Why do rocks have holes in them?
> Why are some rocks different weights than others?
> Why are rocks sometimes smooth and flat?
> Is gold a rock?
> Why is diamond the most valuable rock?

Similar sorts of lists of questions were reported by the same researchers on a variety of other topics. Not many of the questions seem capable of leading to investigations by the children. Faced with such a mixture of questions which have few straightforward answers, a teacher might well prefer not to encourage children to raise questions!

But a more positive response can be made after studying the questions carefully and trying to understand the children's reasons for asking them. Often the exact words used are not carefully chosen and so we should not read too much into them. 'How do rocks get their shape?' could easily be expressed as 'Why are rocks different shapes?'. Indeed, the researchers who reported this list collected questions from separate classes of children and found 'Why are they different colours?' sometimes and 'How do they get their colours?' in other cases. Questions such as these do not seem to ask for specific information but rather are an expression of interest, a way of saying 'Look at all the different shapes' or 'I've just realized that rocks are not all the same colour'. An appropriate response to such questions is therefore to share the children's interest and perhaps take it further: 'Let's see how many different shapes/colours there are'. A teacher will be able to judge from the children's reaction whether there is particular interest in the shapes and colours or whether these were passing comments expressed as questions.

Children's questions always include a number asking for straight information: 'Is gold a rock?', 'Why is diamond the most valuable rock?' or perhaps one that well might have been in the list 'Where did all these rocks come from?'. The answers to these can be given directly, if the teacher knows, or the children can be referred to a source of the information. They are facts, some a matter of definition; they add to children's knowledge, which is important to their understanding of the world but is by no means all of it.

Questions of a third type are more likely to lead to investigations. They are the ones that often give teachers most difficulty because they require complex, not mere factual, answers. Many teachers may not know the answers and those who do will realize that the children's existing concepts are not sufficient to enable them to understand the answer. 'Why are they hard?', 'Why do they have holes in them?', 'Why are rocks sometimes smooth and flat?' are examples of these. They ask for an explanation, but in fact if the children were to be given the explanation they would probably not understand it, and might well be deterred from asking such questions in future. So teachers should *not* feel inadequate at not answering such questions from their own knowledge; in most cases it would be the worst thing to attempt.

Instead of presenting a problem to the teacher these questions actually present the opportunity to help children define testable questions, that is questions which they can answer from investigations. 'Why are rocks sometimes smooth and flat?' could be used to lead to an investigable question by asking:

Where do you find rocks that are smooth and flat?
What is the same about places where smooth flat rocks are found?
What is different about places where rocks are not smooth and flat?
Could these differences account for the shapes of the rocks?
Could we make a rough rock into a smooth one?

So the end point may be a series of questions such as 'Does rubbing one rock against another make them smooth?', 'Does putting them in water make any difference?', 'Do you need a harder rock to rub against a softer one to make it smooth?'. Once children embark on answering any of these questions, inevitably others will occur. And since the further questions are generated in the context of activity, it is likely that many of them will be framed by the children in terms of things they can do themselves. Thus once begun the process of defining testable questions is self-generating.

Children soon realize from experience what kinds of questions they can and cannot answer from investigation and what kinds require a different approach. Ten-year-old Stephen, looking at a giant African land snail, wanted to know why it grew bigger than other snails he had seen, how long it was and what it could eat. He set about answering the last two questions for himself and when asked how he thought he could find out the answer to the first said 'I suppose I'd have to read a lot of books'. Knowing how to answer different kinds of questions is more important to children than knowing the answers, but it comes only through experience of raising questions and discussing the process of answering them. While not suggesting that we should never answer children's questions, if we do this all the time we prevent them from learning how to set about answering them for themselves.

Devising investigations

Since there are no widely agreed boundaries to the meaning of devising investigations it may be as well to begin by defining the limits of what is included here. The raising of questions has already been discussed and, though it could quite reasonably be regarded as part of the proces of devising investigations, is not included for the present purposes. Here we are concerned with what happens after a testable question has been raised or an investigable problem posed; we are not concerned with devising something to investigate but devising the way to investigate something already decided.

Although devising can be considered a theoretical process, different from carrying out whatever plan is devised, it need not precede or take place separately from the investigation. It is a characteristic of young children that they think out what to do in the course of doing it; they do not anticipate in thought the result of actions, unless the actions are already very familiar to them. For young children devising and performing an investigation are interwoven; they may plan no further than the first step and from the result of this think what to do next.

More extended planning becomes possible with maturity and experience. For instance, 9 and 10 year-olds who are used to devising fair tests can plan beforehand how to compare the hardness of tap water and spring water using soapflakes. Others of the same age with little experience of fair testing would be less likely to produce effective plans and would have to find out what is involved by trying something and probably making mistakes. At all ages, including adulthood, the process of devising an investigation will be more difficult with unfamiliar types of problem, but the more experience and understanding we have of the general principles of devising investigations the more widely we are likely to be able to apply them.

So what are the general principles? They can be readily listed, though the apparently simple logic in the order of items is not always reflected in practice:

- define the problem in operational terms
- identify what is to be changed in the investigation (the independent variable)
- identify what should be kept the same so that the effect of the independent variable can be observed or measured (the variables to be controlled)
- identify what is to be measured or compared or what circumstances are to be observed when the independent variable is changed (the dependent variable)
- consider how the measurements, comparisons or observations are to be used to solve the original problem.

The steps to be taken in a particular investigation vary according to the subject matter but the same principles apply. This can be illustrated by considering two apparently quite different types of question; ones which concern the effect of making some changes and seeing what happens and ones which concern the effect of things not under our control. Examples of the first type are 'What happens if we put soap flakes into the tap water and the spring water?', 'What happens if we use different strengths of liquid fertilizer on our plants?', 'Does salt dissolve in other liquids as well as it does in water?'.

These questions can be investigated experimentally because the things which can vary (the variables) can be changed at will. This is not possible in the other main types of investigation which concern relations between variables which are not susceptible to experimental control in classroom activities. Questions such as 'Does the moon's phase affect the weather?', 'Are the trees whose leaves open early in the spring the first ones to drop their leaves in the autumn?'. In these cases there is no control over the independent variable (the moon or the opening of leaves on the trees) and the investigation has to be devised so that the information is gathered from situations which arise naturally rather than those which are created experimentally.

Although other parts of planning may be carried out as the action proceeds, the first step has to be to define the question under investigation operationally. This means making clear what effects are to be measured or compared. For instance, 'Does salt dissolve better in cold or hot water?' is not investigable until 'better' is defined. It could mean: 'Can more salt be dissolved?' or 'Does the salt dissolve more quickly?'. Again, 'Which is the best wood for making a bow for shooting an arrow?' can be defined operationally as which wood is lightest, strongest, most bendy, stiffest, shoots the arrow furthest for the same effort or, even, cheapest.

Once the problem has been defined operationally there are two levels at which the planning of an investigation may take place, the general and the specific. The general level involves identifying the variables to be changed, controlled and measured, but their values are not decided. For example, to investigate whether salt dissolves in other liquids as well as in water, the planning at the general level would be:

What to change (independent variable)?	The kind of liquid
What to keep the same for a fair test (the variables to be controlled)?	The mass and temperature of the liquids
What to measure or compare (the dependent variable)?	How much salt will dissolve in each one
How will the result be found?	By comparing the amount of salt for each liquid

To take the planning to the specific level it is necessary to decide which liquids to use, how much of each, how the amount of salt dissolving will be measured. Before becoming enmeshed in detail, however, it is worth completing the plan at the general level as it helps children to keep their problem in mind and to see how the separate parts of what they are doing relate to the whole investigation. If planning starts with the details not only is this more difficult but it is almost impossible for children to realize the similarities in the approach to devising different investigations.

When the plan proceeds from the general to the specific level of planning procedures for fair testing, matters of practicality have to be considered. 'Can we obtain all the different liquids?' 'Are they all safe to handle?' 'Is there enough salt?' 'Do we have a balance on which to weigh the liquids before and after adding the salt?' If the answer to any of these questions is 'No' then the specific planning may have to be reconsidered. By taking a small mass of each liquid we can reduce the amount of salt needed but it may introduce a problem of accurate measurement. If there is no appropriate balance available it will be necessary to reconsider how the 'amount' of salt needed in each case can be compared. Instead of weighing, a measure of volume could be used: the number of spoonfuls added, for instance.

It can be seen that throughout these steps between the general and the specific planning the original problem has to be kept clearly in mind. Otherwise it is easy to end up answering a different question than the one posed. This is all part of the thinking which is essential to science education. Activity (doing things) is important but if children only do, without thinking about why they are doing certain things, the value of the activity is likely to be much reduced.

The planning of procedures in some investigations has also to take into account the order of events. Children quite often learn this through making mistakes. For example, they often fail to record initial conditions before making changes, seeing whether baking changes the weight of the dough by weighing only after the bread has been baked or looking at the effect on the fish in the aquarium of changing the water by changing the water first and then observing how the fish behave. A certain amount of learning by mistakes is a good thing but development is probably slower than need be if children keep repeating mistakes which could be avoided by some thinking and planning.

The importance of planning procedures carefully is greater for those investigations where the independent variable is not under experimental control. For example, to find out if the bulbs that are planted first also flower first, it is too late at flowering time to remember that the time of planting for each one was not recorded: the growth cannot be rerun. The same applies to other procedures for making fair comparisons or tests about subjects which cannot, or should not, be experimentally manipulated. One might investigate the effect on the populations of wild flowers in an area where a wood is cut down, but not cut down a wood to do this. Therefore, such an investigation would need very careful planning so that a fair comparison could be made before and afterwards. The planning skills which children can develop in other investigations, where mistakes can be made and put right more easily, have particular value in the investigation of natural events. When they are not applied there is little opportunity for investigation in such contexts and the activity is confined to making observations.

Communication

Communication is an outward extension of thought. It helps in the process of rearranging thought, linking one idea to another and so filling in some of the gaps in a person's network of ideas. Often communication gives access to information or alternative ideas which help understanding, as in a discussion, in listening to someone else or in reading a book. At other times the act of communication helps one over a difficulty of understanding without any apparent input as a result of communicating. The enlightenment that can come from writing is an example; a more striking one, commonly experienced by teachers, is of the child who comes to them with a problem and while explaining it, finds the way out of the difficulty with no help except a receptive ear on their part.

As thought is such an important part of learning science and communication essential to thought, both as a process and as a means to an end, so development of skill in communication is central to education in science. This same claim could, of course, be made for education in any area of the curriculum and we shall have to restrict discussion here to communication particularly relevant to science. It includes both verbal communication, that is, language in written and spoken form, and non-verbal communication, by using conventional symbols and ways of representation through drawings and diagrams, tables and graphs. There is also a formal and an informal side to communication, both of which have to be considered in developing the related skills.

The formal side of discussion is the class discussion involving all the children and the teacher. The aim may be to share ideas, stimulate interest, put forward possible explanations, decide how to test them or check them out in other ways: from books, for example. Such an exchange needs a structure or it may become a free-for-all with little achieved. In discussions people have to speak one at a time, listen to each other and keep to the topic. It is for the teacher to provide this guidance on structure, but without dominating the content of the discussion. 'Keeping to the subject' must not be used as an excuse to censor the discussion; if a comment is made which cannot be followed up in the context of the subject in hand, the teacher must remember to return to it later. The aim is to ensure that everyone who wishes to has a say and each is given a chance to rearrange his or her ideas through expressing them or asking questions.

Informal discussion, by its nature, is quite different. It is characterized by the exchanges children have in groups at playtime and out of school. They interrupt each other, sentences rarely get finished, they challenge and contradict others' views. In the context of group work in the classroom the exchanges are toned down, rather more formal, but still unstructured. Through these discussions the children learn that others' ideas are different from their own, have access to a wider range of ideas and can try out their own at an early stage in their formation. (There is more about the value of group discussion in Chapter 3, p. 71 and Chapter 7, p. 148) The children's discussions recorded in Chapter 1 provide some examples, the difference in the floating of the blocks is explained in terms of the air in them, bubbles of air, their weight, their being made of wood, all from one group in about 30 seconds. Later, several alternative reasons for one block floating lopsided are put forward and this leads to some of these being checked. It is not always the person who first voices the suggestion who follows it up. Thus the discussion advances the ideas and the activity of all the members of the group. Again, the teacher's role is largely one of ensuring that this happens. When it does happen the teacher can join in as an equal and unobtrusively inject ideas which the children may not have considered.

The formal side of making records of work is dreaded by children if it involves them in an apparently meaningless drudgery. Science work 'written up' only for the teacher (who already knows all about it anyway) hardly comes under the heading of communication. The purpose of writing should be clear to everyone involved so that it can be undertaken with this purpose in mind. It is easiest to begin by considering the purpose of recording informal notes, for it is often forgotten that children need help in how to do this to appreciate its value from experience.

Informal notes are a personal record of jottings and drawings which act as an extension of memory. They are put down in an individual manner for they are meant only for the individual, no other audience. If children are allowed and encouraged to do this they will realize the value of making records for themselves and this will lead them to understand the value of making more formal records as well. 'Being allowed' to keep personal notes means just this, that they are what the child, not the teacher, wants to record. The teacher can, however, make suggestions about what should go into the informal notes: observations and particularly measurements which may be quickly forgotten. Informal notes should never be 'marked' by a teacher, but it is useful to discuss them with the child for they are an important source of information about his progress. If the teacher can pick up points where the child can be helped (perhaps just in supplying a new word) then the notebook becomes a valuable means of communication between child and teacher as well as a personal record for the child himself.

More formal records of work can also become a medium for genuine communication between teacher and pupil. For example, Andrea's account of dropping balls of Plasticine of different weights (in Figure 1) seemed to leave some ambiguity in the mind of her teacher. The question 'How were you convinced?' was written to remind both of them to clear this up.

Falling Plasticine

We dropped four different weights of plasticine two at a time. The weights
weighed 50g, 100g, 150g, 200g.
First we dropped the 50g and 100g from a height of 1m 64cm. Then we did
the same with the 150g and 200g balls.

Results

We found that the balls
dropped at the same
time.

What I Decided

At first I thought that the heaviest would hit
the ground first but after a while Mrs
Griffithes convinced Robert and I that they
hit the ground at the same time.

How were you convinced

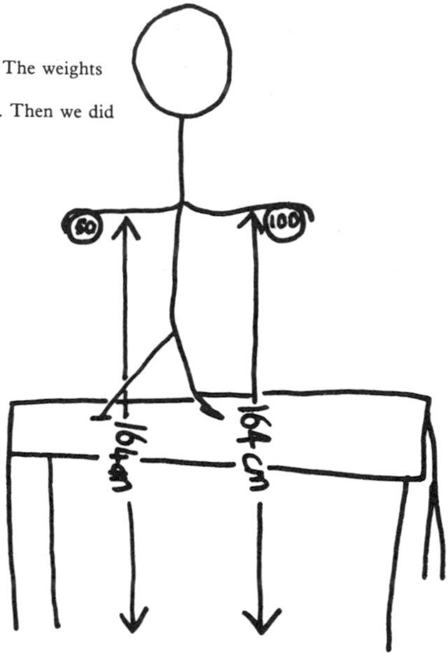

Figure 1

In other parts of Andrea's work there are several examples of the teacher's
question being answered in writing. At the end of the piece about the switch
in Figure 2 the teacher wrote 'Connected it to what?'. Before writing anything
else in her notebook, Andrea answered this question.

Alarms
For our first experiment we made an ordinary switch. We needed a thin
piece of balsa wood, six crocodile clips with plastic covered wire, a bulb,
a bulb holder and a battery.
We nailed two paper fasteners through the copper strips and through the
wood.

Then we connected the wire

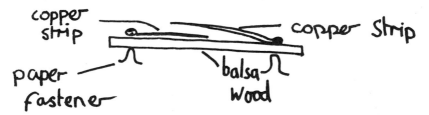

Figure 2

Later Andrea tested several materials in a simple circuit. The final section of her report is shown in Figure 3, including the teacher's question and Andrea's answer.

We found that all the metal like things allowed electricity to pass through to the bulb and all the things that didn't have any metal in didn't allow electricity to pass thou through to the bulb. What general names do we give these two groups of things? Conductors and insulators

Figure 3

As children grow in experience the information which they have to record becomes more complex and they need to use graphs, tables and other conventions to help them communicate. These should be introduced as appropriate as opportunities arise. Bar charts are a popular method of recording since they can be used while gathering simple information where the range and organization can be anticipated, forming a cumulative record (e.g. the number of children of different heights). For more complex data it is necessary to collect and tabulate it before deciding on the best graphical form to use to reveal the patterns, or whether a graph is needed at all. Tabulation is a skill not widely taught, rather suprisingly, but one of considerable value to children in organizing their observations and any measurements they may have taken.

Other means of arranging findings and displaying them should be introduced as and when they can be used. Making a plan of an area with symbols showing where various types of plant or building are found, drawing a cross-section, keeping a weather chart, creating a flow diagram to show changes in sequence, showing directions on a map: all these are activities in which children can be introduced to a range of ways of representing and communicating information. At first they will be used only when suggested by the teacher, but the children will gradually be able to take over the decision as to the most appropriate form to use in a particular case. This change will be helped by examples, from information displayed in different ways in the classroom and from seeing the teacher use appropriate representational forms during class discussions.

When there is a range of ways of communicating available to the children, formal reporting becomes more of a challenge and less of a dull routine. The purpose, whether it be a formal reporting from groups to the whole class or a display for the class, or an exhibition for a wider audience in the school, will be part of the decision as to appropriate forms of communication. With the audience in mind and the tools (the knowledge of different ways of presenting information) available, formal reporting can then have value both as a process and as a product.

Scientific attitudes

Overview

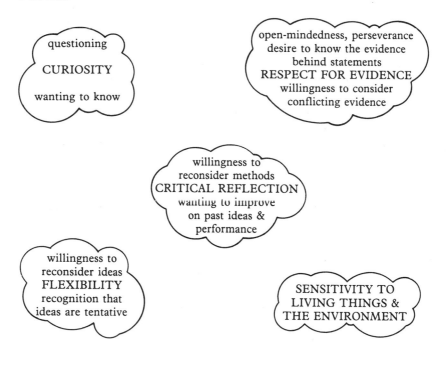

Attitudes have been defined in different ways. Here we take them to describe the state of being prepared or predisposed to react in a certain way to particular objects, persons or situations. The term 'scientific attitude' is sometimes used to describe children's reactions to science as a subject and the activities of scientists. It would seem, however, better to describe these as 'attitudes to science', reserving the term 'scientific attitudes' for the attitudes *of* science, the ones with which we are concerned here. These are predispositions toward the activities involved in science, such as the use of evidence, creating ideas and treating the natural and man-made environment in certain ways.

Describing a person as having a certain attitude is a generalization about his or her behaviour. An attitude can only be said to exist if certain behaviour is displayed in a range of similar situations. It cannot be assumed from an isolated instance of behaviour that this is part of a general pattern, but once a pattern has been established, and an attitude can be said to exist, it predicts to some extent the likely reactions in a related situation. A person who listens with interest to others' ideas on one occasion may or may not do so as a regular thing. If such behaviour is known to be a regular feature then this justifies the generalization that he or she is open-minded. Describing someone as open-minded is a succinct way of making a general statement about how he or she has reacted in the past and is likely to react in the future in certain situations.

Attitudes limit or facilitate the application of skills and ideas. If a child, or an adult for that matter, is not willing to try to understand an argument or an explanation, it is immaterial that he is capable of understanding. Attitudes therefore have an important influence on learning, as they do on the rest of people's lives: in their reactions to people, to objects and events. However, there is no reason to regard them as inborn and immutable, but rather every reason to consider attitudes as learned from experience. They develop in children gradually as a result of encouragement and example to act and react in certain ways. By their nature, as generalized aspects of behaviour, they cannot be taught in the way that specific facts and skills can be; they are transferred in subtle and often unsuspected ways. (The teacher's role in this is discussed later in Chapter 7, pages 158–162.)

There are many attitudes of value to all kinds of learning, but we have picked out for consideration here five that are of particular relevance to science. As with the process skills, various titles could be given and some of the subsumed attitudes are included as well as the main title in the list. We will leave discussion of teaching to encourage these until later and confine the next sections to brief descriptions of the nature of each one.

Curiosity

A child with curiosity wants to know, to try new experience, to explore, to find out about things around him. It is obvious that this is an attitude that will help learning of all kinds and especially learning by enquiry. Curiosity often shows in the form of questioning, but asking questions is not the only sign of curiosity nor the only symptom to be encouraged. Inviting children to ask questions is indeed one way of showing that curiosity is valued and the attitude can be fostered this way *if* the result is satisfying and interesting to the child. There is a danger, however, of asking children to verbalize their questions too early. Something new, on first encounter, may elicit questions which are no more than expressions of interest. Time has to be allowed for a child to take in what is there and relate it in his or her mind to what is already known. Then will come the questions that help him make sense of it.

On first seeing black swans in a bird park a group of 8 and 9-year-olds were full of questions such as 'Why are they black?', 'Why do they have red eyes?', 'Are they the same as white swans?'. If their teacher had tried to answer these questions, the children would not have listened to the answers. It was as if they had said 'Look, they're black', 'Look, they've got red eyes' and so on. Only later, when they had watched them for a while and answered some of their own questions by observation, did they put the questions that they really wanted to have answered, such as 'Do they mate with white swans?', 'Are there other colours of swans besides black and white?'.

Young children and those with a limited attention span may get no further than asking the superficial question that expresses interest before they turn to another topic. Questioning brings satisfaction if it helps them to share their pleasure and excitement with others. This is part of a natural course of development and to discourage it by disapproval will risk a decline in curiosity. On the other hand, the satisfaction that comes from expressing curiosity will help children reach a more mature stage where interest is sustained for longer and questions are more thoughtful. There may be fewer questions, indeed curiosity can be expressed in other ways, but there will be more interest in finding the answers, for the questions will be designed to help relate what is already known to the new experience.

Then curiosity appears not so much as a flow of questions but as a wanting to know. This desire to find out stimulates effort to find out, perhaps by investigation, perhaps by using a library or making a special visit. The questions need not have been asked of anyone else, the motivation comes of having asked them of oneself. When children have reached this stage, putting new experiences in their way is more likely to lead to learning through their own effort.

Respect for evidence

Science concerns both the process of describing how things behave and the product of this endeavour. The process is essentially one of gathering and using evidence to test or develop ideas. Although a theory may have its beginning in an imaginative guess, it has no status until it has been shown to fit evidence or make sense of what is known. Thus the use of evidence is central to scientific activity; this is true at school level as much as at the level of the work of scientists, so attitudes toward it are of great importance in science education.

Children talking among themselves have a keen sense that an unsupported statement is not necessarily to be believed. 'How do you know that's true?', 'Prove it' feature in their private arguments in one form or another. (There is an example in Chapter 1, p. 13, where Cheryl challenges with: 'How do you know it's the varnish when we haven't even looked at it?'.) It is when they are in the company of adults who expect children to accept statements because of the force of the authority behind them that the desire to ask for evidence often has to be suppressed. If an adult appears to accept statements without evidence, or at least offers none in passing on the statements, the attitude transmitted can be the opposite of what is educationally desired. Thus the part of respect for evidence which appears as a desire to know the evidence behind statements is something which has to be preserved and developed by presenting evidence whenever possible or at least indicating that supporting evidence does exist.

To obtain really convincing evidence may well take some perseverance and it is sometimes this quality which determines whether or not an initial idea leads to a useful concept. There are splendid examples of perseverance in the work of famous scientists, such as Charles Darwin and Marie Curie, who persisted against difficulties of various kinds to gather the information required to give their ideas a thorough test before feeling sure enough of them in their own minds to advance them in public.

In their own way children can extend their ideas further with a little perseverance; what may at first appear beyond their grasp may come within it if their tendency is to continue rather than give up when faced with difficulties. Perseverance is not merely persistence; this may be part of it, but persistence in an unrewarding line of action or argument is not rewarding. The willingness to try again has to be accompanied by learning from the earlier failure so that later attempts or ideas are modified by experience.

Even young children can respect evidence in the sense so far discussed but it takes rather more maturity to extend this respect to situations where other evidence or other ideas may conflict with the evidence and ideas so far taken into consideration. A prerequisite here is open-mindedness or a readiness to listen to, or attend to, different points of view. In the activity with the blocks of wood the girls quoted in Chapter 1 were not the only group to discover what they called the 'magnetic' attraction between the blocks. Another group did so as well but they considered an alternative idea that the air and water caused the force rather as in a suction pad. They argued the pros and cons for some time and showed open-mindedness in changing their original view. One might say that the girls quoted showed less open-mindedness since they were ignoring the evidence that pointed against the force being magnetic.

The willingness to consider conflicting evidence is another facet of this attitude. Take the example of three children timing the bobbing of a weight on a spring. John wanted to time only one bob, up and down once, while Gary said it was better to see how many times it went up and down in a minute and Maria wanted to time 20 bobs. John argued that it would gradually slow down after the first bob, so his idea was best; Gary's point was that it would be easier to compare with different weights if you kept the time the same; Maria's reason was that you should time complete bobs but more than one. They all listened to each other, and to that extent showed open-mindedness, but they each decided to do it in their own way and did not use the result to consider the pros and cons of each approach.

In these cases, however, there is not enough in one example to make a judgement. In any single instance many other circumstances may affect the outcome; it is only when a pattern of similar response is noted across several instances that comment on the attitudes of the children could be worthwhile.

Flexibility

Flexibility of mind bears a similar relation to the product of scientific activity as respect for evidence does to the process. The concepts that we form to help our understanding of the world around change as experience adds more evidence to develop or contradict them. Sometimes it is a gradual refinement, as when the idea of energy develops from being related to what people can do, to being associated with moving things, to being possessed by things which can move other things and existing in a variety of forms. In other cases there has to be a sudden change, as in conceiving of light as behaving both as wave motion and as particles. The changes are most rapid in children's early years since their limited experience means that their first ideas are often quite different from what they need to understand wider experience later. Unless there is flexibility, each experience that conflicts with existing ideas would cause confusion and create a rival idea instead of modification and a growth of an existing one. Flexibility is needed to adapt existing frameworks to fit increased experience.

Since even young children manage this adaptation quite readily they show willingness to reconsider ideas though they may not realize how much their ideas have changed. For instance, 5- or 6-year-olds tend to have views about whether things sink or float which relate to size. Soon size is found not to be important and weight takes over: 'heavy things sink, light ones float'. Then children find light coins sinking and heavy logs of wood floating and their ideas have to change again, and so on it goes.

As children become older and their ideas closer to those of adults they change less often. There is a danger that flexibility of mind may decrease and the idea creep in that at last they now have the 'right' ideas. This is disastrous to continued scientific development. Instead the aim should be for flexibility to mature and extend to the recognition that ideas are tentative. An understanding of scientific activity can be reached, eventually, only through realizing that all its products (concepts, knowledge, principles and theories) are valid as long as they fit the evidence we have, but as we never have all the evidence there is no certainty about their validity. Although children of the age we are considering may be some way from this realization, their path toward it can be kept clear, and not blocked off, by the attitudes they develop at this earlier stage. It is worthwhile developing the habit of prefacing conclusions with 'As far as we can see...', 'On the basis of this investigation...' or words to the same effect. It also helps to discuss with children at times just how their ideas have changed, how they used to think that all wood floated (until they tried ebony and lignum vitae) and that metal sank (until they tried hollow metal objects). Fostering this attitude also helps children to feel that they can participate in developing ideas rather than receiving 'the right ideas' from others.

Critical reflection

In the context of science activities this means looking back over what has been done, deliberately to see if procedures could have been improved or ideas better applied. It is an attitude that is related to respect for evidence and flexibility but relates to making a more conscious effort to consider alternatives to what has been done. In practice it may be manifest in self-critical comments, in repeating part of an investigation or even starting again in another way. On the other hand, there may be no critical comment to make; the recognition of having taken a useful course of action is also evidence of having reviewed what has been done. In any event the attitude shows in reflecting on what has been done, using it as something to learn from; pausing instead of dashing off without a second thought to another activity.

Such indications of critical reflection are not often part of young children's spontaneous behaviour. The encouragement of this attitude demands positive action and good examples. Action is best begun in small groups, where the group activity is reviewed and there is no danger of an individual child being put in a defensive position. A teacher might well ask the group at the end of an investigation to consider what changes might have improved their work and leave them to do it alone. Their experience of trying in the way they did is then likely to help them learn the pitfalls to be avoided in future activities. Once they embark on their own critical review and find some benefit from it they are more likely to do this for themselves more generally and so to develop willingness to reconsider methods and ideas.

The value of developing this attitude is clearly that it increases the potential learning, of the processes and ideas of science, from each activity. But if children are to indulge willingly in a critical review which may indicate flaws in methods and thinking there must be some perceived benefit.

Part of this can be the satisfaction of finding better ways of investigating and more powerful ideas, but this intrinsic reward may not be enough; support and approval from the teacher is also needed. It may not be easy in many cases to respond positively when children find that they could have improved what they have done without giving the impression that they should have done better to begin with. But encouragement to reflect critically can be so effective that it is worth the effort to praise and to show an example by ensuring that suggestions made by the teacher, too, are reviewed. Eventually, children will not only be willing to join in but will take the initiative in wanting to improve on past ideas and performance. This commitment represents a higher level of maturity in developing the attitude, which may become evident in reviewing previous experience and possibilities before embarking on an investigation as well as afterwards. Not many children do this by the age of 13 years, but it is an aim worth keeping in mind.

Sensitivity to living things and the environment

In science education children are encouraged to investigate and explore their environment to understand it and to develop skills for further understanding. Unless investigation and exploration are governed by an attitude of respect for the environment and a willingness to care appropriately for the living things in it, such activities could result in unnecessary interference or even unpleasant harm. So it is important that growth in skills of enquiry and concepts should be accompanied by a development of sensitivity toward living things and responsibility toward the environment.

These attitudes are ones that are more obviously linked to particular concepts and understanding than those we have considered so far, though one of our main themes is that all attitudes, concepts and skills are interrelated to some degree. It is more likely that someone with an understanding of, say, the effect on wild flowers of over-picking, will look and not pick than someone without such understanding who may pick the flowers innocently. There is no certainty about this; the knowledge helps but it is not enough to create the attitude. The converse is also true, fortunately, that lack of understanding is not an inevitable barrier to forming these attitudes. Thus, although many of the concepts relating to care of the environment are too complex for very young children to grasp (air pollution and interdependence, for instance), and some are controversial (the need to preserve endangered species, seal-culling, even fox-hunting), it is still possible to begin the development of attitudes toward the environment by example and rules of conduct.

Young children soon pick up the signs that certain living things have to be treated differently from non-living things. The analogy is with themselves and their own need for food, rest, etc. As their understanding of 'living things' extends from being confined in the early primary years to furry mammals to a wider range, including things such as spiders, worms and plants (see p. 82) it is worth making an effort to ensure that their caring attitude is also extended to these things. Keeping ants, snails, a wormery, etc., in the classroom is certain to help children appreciate these as interesting creatures with fascinating and complex behaviour patterns. Such animals can be brought into the classroom for a while to be studied and then carefully replaced in their natural environment. Helping their teacher do this is a significant step toward adopting such caring behaviour themselves.

The mature form of this attitude shows in responsible behaviour to the street as much as to the countryside environment, to animals of all kinds as much as to pets. This requires commitment, and a degree of understanding, not reached by many children in the primary years. In the meantime it is necessary to ensure that children are willing to obey simple rules designed to prevent thoughtless harm to the environment. At first rules will have to be imposed by the teacher and discussed with the children so that they appreciate that there are reasons behind them. But an aim should be to involve children in deciding on rules and procedures as soon as possible; the preparation for a trip, nature walk or starting a school garden patch gives opportunity for this experience. It is useful to introduce and discuss the appropriate codes of conduct issued by various organizations concerned with the countryside [listed in Environmental Education: Sources of Information, (DES, 1981b)].

Rules help to establish a pattern of response toward the environment, but it is only when children begin to *act* responsibly (not dropping litter, defacing buildings or tearing branches from trees), when unsupervised as well as when controlled by agreed rules, that the attitude can be said to be developing. It is important not to mistake compliance for commitment and the way of avoiding this is to gradually hand over to the children the responsibility for making decisions about how they should behave.

Concept areas

Overview

The title of each group should be read as being preceded by the words:
CONCEPTS WHICH HELP THE UNDERSTANDING OF ...

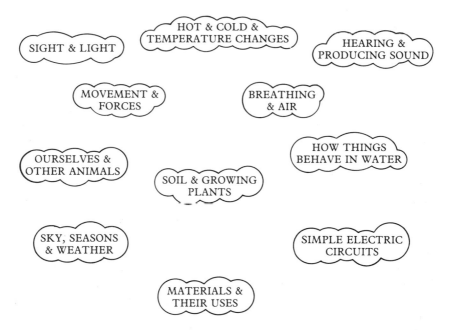

The items here could be seen on the one hand as comprising a small section of science or, on the other, as the whole of human knowledge, depending on how they are interpreted. Clearly, it is necessary to be more specific about the extent of the concepts intended and the meaning of 'understanding'. A very useful first step toward this is to identify the criteria to be used in defining appropriate concept statements.

One criterion already evident in the titles of the groups above is that they concern children's immediate everyday experience. Several deal with children's own senses and the types of information they bring, some with everyday phenomena involving air, water and common materials around, others with what can be seen if children look up to the sky or down to the ground. None deals with things too small to see (e.g. atoms and molecules) or properties which are generalizations about other properties (e.g. acids, bases and salts). This criterion is regarded as a central one for two related reasons. The first is that it means that children are developing concepts about the things around them; the growth of understanding of these things is a large part of the reason for learning science. The second is that it is to these ideas that children can most readily relate their own experience and first-hand knowledge. It is through applying and using ideas that they develop and become part of children's own ways of understanding. Ideas that do not link in with experience are unlikely to remain long in children's minds, however simple they may be.

A second criterion indicative of the level of ideas that children can be expected to develop relates to their ways of thinking. There is no doubt that these are limited for primary children and whether the reason for this is argued in terms of their experience or mental maturity is to some extent irrelevant. The point is that experience indicates that the understanding of many of the abstract concepts of science is reached later in the secondary school and only then by some pupils. It can be argued, as it is here, that such understanding is helped by earlier exposure to concrete examples of the phenomena to which the abstract concepts will later be related. It is likely, too, that with this experience many more children than at present would achieve a better scientific understanding. But this is not an argument for introducing abstract ideas and generalizations at the primary level. Rather the reverse, for a sound foundation of ideas tested and tried in a variety of practical contexts is far more useful to later learning than a superficial knowledge of theoretical ideas.

A closely related criterion, but one that is distinct because it acknowledges that the concepts being identified are scientific ones, concerns their accessibility to children through the use of process skills. Children should be able to collect evidence and see that it is consistent with the ideas being generated; they should be able to use the ideas to make predictions which can be put to the test; they should be able to see for themselves whether or not the ideas 'work' in a range of cases. This does *not* mean that the ideas are only those which can be 'discovered'. It is the usefulness of an idea that gives it meaning for children, not the source. Useful ideas can and do come from other pupils, from teachers, books, television and radio. Neither does the condition that children should be able to 'make the idea their own' by the use of process skills mean that we are only concerned with ideas about things children can physically touch and manipulate. Many of them will be, and should be, of this kind but it is important not to exclude ideas about events in children's experience which cannot be manipulated, such as ideas about the sun, moon and stars and about the weather. Children can develop these ideas by the use of process skills. Careful observation and recording reveal patterns and give rise to hypotheses and predictions which can be checked by further observation.

A fourth criterion links concepts at the primary level to those required for further learning in science. Such a relation has already been proposed as part of the rationale for including science in primary education and it will be mentioned again in the next chapter.

In summary, then, ideas relating to the concept areas listed on p. 52 should be selected according to these four criteria:

- They should help children's understanding of everyday events and the world around them and be applicable to their experience.
- They should be within the grasp of primary-school children, taking into account their limited experience and mental maturity.
- They should be accessible and testable through the use by children of science process skills.
- They should provide a sound basis for further science education.

Since the selection of content is closely connected with the concept goals, further discussion of the ideas emerging from applying these criteria will be included in Chapter 4.

Having looked in this chapter at the meaning of the process skill, attitude and concept goals separately it is important to bring them together again as they are in children's learning. It is the purpose of the next chapter to do this and to show how the development of processes, attitudes and concepts is interrelated and interdependent in learning.

CHAPTER 3

CHANGING CHILDREN'S IDEAS AND WAYS OF THINKING

The only man who is educated is the man who has learned how to learn, the man who has learned how to adapt and change, the man who has realized no knowledge is secure ... a reliance on process rather than static knowledge is the only thing that makes sense as a goal for education in the modern world.
(Carl Rogers, 1983)

The interconnectedness of children's ideas with their ways of gathering and processing information was described in Chapter 1. The interdependence of skills, concepts and attitudes has also been evident in Chapter 2, even though the meaning of each one was considered separately. In this chapter attention is turned to the possible mechanism by which skills and ideas develop hand in hand, and to the implications of this for primary-science activities.

It has to be admitted from the start that what can be said about how children learn amounts to no more than hypotheses. There is no certain knowledge of how children's ideas are formed or how change in them can be brought about. All that anyone can do is to study the evidence in children's behaviour, put forward possible explanations for it and then see which of these hypotheses seems to be contradicted the least. This is what Piaget (1929) and Bruner et al. (1966) and their associates have done; they looked in detail at children sorting pebbles, swinging pendulums, solving problems involving physical principles, and so on, and hypothesized about what might be going on in children's minds to explain the outward behaviour they observed. Evidence of this kind is always open to various interpretations and sometimes the evidence itself is disputed. What a child does with some pebbles or a pendulum depends on so many other things than the concepts and skills he has; it depends on whether he has seen the same or similar things before, on how interested he is in them or in other things instead, on how they are presented to him and by whom, on whether he is in company or alone, on what he did immediately before, how tired or alert he feels. Any generalization about children's learning must be interpreted as being an account of what is likely to be happening but not one which necessarily will hold in all incidents of learning and for all children.

Development of ideas

The starting point in this discussion is the premise that children will have some ideas about the objects and events around them; development is interpreted as change in some ideas which already exist, not creating ideas from scratch. Children's ideas about objects or events they have encountered often previously or investigated may already have passed through various changes. When new phenomena are encountered there is an immediate attempt to understand them in terms of existing ideas. So, for example, the girls with the wooden blocks in Chapter 1 explained to themselves the way in which the blocks stuck together in terms of the force they already knew to be responsible for apparently similar events: magnetism. With more exploration of the blocks they may well have changed their ideas about how the observation could be explained.

Development generally happens through the use of the suggested explanation to predict that something will occur and then to see whether or not it does. There were several examples in the group discussions in Chapter 1 of children leaping ahead of their observations to say what will or might happen. After the girls tested to see which block 'went flat' last, Mena said 'I think it shouldn't be that, it should be D'. Later, they pressed the wet blocks against the side of the bowl, above the water level and waited to see which would slip down first. Ann said 'This one should come down first' based on some idea she had that the force holding them varied among the blocks.

Whether or not the children's ideas change as a result of seeing if what they predicted does or does not happen depends on more than just what happens; it depends, too, on the way they reason about it, on the nature of their own idea and their readiness to change their idea for a better one. This is a crucial matter for teaching since it just is not enough to show children something that is in conflict with their ideas and expect this to bring about change. The children not only have to see for themselves that there is a conflict but to develop, again for themselves, an alternative explanation that is more effective in that it leads to a prediction that does fit the evidence. The lack of an alternative explanation for the order in which the blocks 'went flat' may be the reason why Mena was reluctant to give up her idea and insisted, in the face of the evidence, that something else should have happened.

Another example illustrates how different existing ideas and experience determine the outcome of children's attempts to understand phenomena. A group of children of a wide age range were discussing the common experience that expanded polystyrene feels warm to the touch. They had a big block of the plastic which was going to form part of the props for a school play. There was general agreement at first that 'there is something hot inside'. The younger children apparently found this quite a reasonable explanation. Their experience, after all, of large warm objects such as hot-water bottles and radiators, was that there was something inside that was hot and stayed hot for a considerable time. So their prediction was that the polystyrene block would stay warm, and it did.

The older children, however, brought to this problem the more complex idea that hot things generally cooled down if there was nothing to keep them hot. They knew that there was nothing but polystyrene right through the block and so predicted that if it was warm at one time then it should get cooler as time went on, and it didn't. They even tried to make a piece cool down by putting it in a 'fridge and it obstinately refused to feel cold. It was quite a puzzle to them and they had to think of some altogether other way of explaining the warmth they felt. In the event they came to it through playing with some other pieces of polystyrene in the form of very small pellets. They ran their hands through the pellets and one said 'It's like putting on warm gloves'. 'But gloves aren't warm, they just keep you warm' said another. 'That's what's happening with the blocks, it just keeps your hand warm, it isn't warm itself.' Here was a possible explanation (though expressed with a great deal of certainty, it was still a hypothesis) and an associated prediction. If the idea was right then the block would not be any warmer than anything else around. This could be checked with a thermometer, and it was.

Note that the 'new' idea was not new in the sense of being discovered from the observations, it was only new in that it had not been brought to bear on the problem before. In itself it was well known to the children that gloves and clothes keep them warm without having any heat source to do this. What they had to do to use this existing idea was, first, to recognize the possible connection, secondly, create a possible explanation (hypothesis) based on it, thirdly, to use it in making a prediction and, fourthly, to test the prediction.

In reality the thinking often happens in a flash and it is in no way being suggested that children consciously think through from one step to another. It is the analysis of the event that proposes the existence of these four steps; they represent a convenient way of looking at what happens. In the polystyrene example it shows how the same processes led to different emerging ideas for the younger and older children: the younger finding their ideas confirmed and therefore not needing to change them and the older finding a conflict because their existing ideas were different and did not fit the evidence.

Similar developments take place in other ideas and the influence of the mental processes of applying, hypothesizing, predicting and checking predictions can be traced. Take ideas about dissolving, for instance. Younger children accept that sugar stirred into water 'disappears' in the sense that it is no longer there. The ideas they bring do not conflict with the observation for they do not include the concept that matter such as sugar does not just disappear in this sense. The experience of older children will probably have led to the idea that matter usually turns up again when you think it might have disappeared and it makes more sense to them to consider the disappearance as only apparent. They may find a way of checking this hypothesis readily: for example, if the sugar is still there you should be able to taste it. If it works, then the idea might be accepted or confirmed that substances like sugar are able to change in some way so that they cannot be seen in water but are still there. This is an advance on the earlier 'disappearance' idea but may itself not last for long. Other problems may require a more sophisticated idea, one which suggests an explanation of what happens to the sugar when it becomes invisible in the water. Generally, children will have wider experience and will probably have reached the secondary school, when the need for a more advanced explanation occurs and they can then call on a greater range of ideas that can be tried in searching for the explanation.

Four steps in the metamorphosis of an idea

The process of developing ideas can be thought of as a network in which existing ideas and new experiences are brought together and a 'new' or modified idea emerges from the operation of the four steps which have been suggested. One part of this network might be as represented in Figure 4.

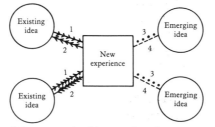

Figure 4   Part of the network of interactions between experiences and ideas

To understand the new experience a connection is made with one or more of the existing ideas; this is step 1. An idea thought to be possibly connected then creates a hypothesis, step 2 (e.g. 'the sugar is still there'). The hypothesis is used to make a prediction, step 3 ('if the sugar is still there we'll be able to taste it') and is tested, step 4 ('let's see if the water tastes of sugar'). There are various possible outcomes of this process represented in Figure 5. One is that the existing idea appears to give a good explanation and so emerges in much the same form as before, as with the younger children's idea that the sugar disappeared. The evidence of the taste may not affect the children's ideas because they focus on only the confirming observation. Their idea predicts that the sugar disappears and so the experience confirms it. Another outcome may be change from an existing idea (the sugar can disappear in water) to a 'new' one (it's still there). This may happen because the evidence of the taste was taken into account or because an alternative existing idea (things don't just disappear) was competing with the idea of disappearance. A further possible outcome is that a 'new' idea is tried and rejected if the evidence does not fit the prediction (perhaps that the sugar divides into very small, but still solid, particles and all attempts to detect these fail).

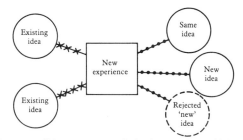

Figure 5   Various possible outcomes of the interaction of ideas and experiences

What this argument suggests is that change of ideas takes place when:
● alternative ideas are applied, not just one
● all the available evidence is taken into account in applying possibly connected ideas
● the possible ideas are used to make predictions of a kind different from the original evidence and require some investigation of the experience
● predictions are checked against all the available evidence.
All these points imply the use of process skills. Note also that when ideas are not changed into more valid ones similar things *appear* to be happening (observation, application, prediction and testing), but *the way* in which these

processes are carried out is inadequate. Only one idea appears to be considered and the evidence used is partial and selected to confirm it. The supposed prediction involves a circular argument for it does not go beyond the already available information. It follows from this line of thinking that as ideas are used they are more likely to be changed and developed into ones which more closely fit the evidence and help to explain experience if process skills are used with effect.

A network of ideas

So far only one part of what was described as a network of ideas and experiences has been considered. The whole network can be thought of as being made up of a series of such parts as in Figure 6.

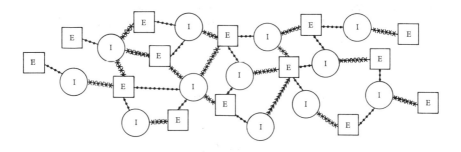

Figure 6   Network of ideas and experiences

The diagram is intended to represent the development of ideas (I) relating to different experiences (E) through a time scale from left to right. Each idea is the product of both experiences and earlier ideas; it is at some time the 'existing idea' brought to bear in attempting to understand a new experience. The connecting lines with arrow heads pointing both ways indicate the processes of application of an idea and its use in suggesting an explanation of the experience. The dotted lines indicate the processes of prediction and the testing of the prediction by further observation or exploration of the experience. Both the connections from I to E and from E to I represent interactions. Things happen in both directions along them; they are not lines of one-way transmission.

Before considering how this model may help in understanding the effect of teaching and school-science experiences, there are some other points to make about it. It is proposed as a description of how ideas may be used and changed by all kinds of experience in daily life. It goes on all the time and has gone on all the time. This raises the questions of how it all started and whether all ideas fit the model.

Origin of ideas: old wives' tales or products of thinking?

The interaction of children with things around them, part of the 'experiences' in the model, are central to learning. Children learn through their activity; what the model makes explicit is that existing ideas play a part in determining this activity and its outcome. But is this always the case? What happens at the very beginning of the process? The ideas must start somewhere.

Where does it all start?

Although this is an intriguing problem it is one that we should perhaps not dwell on too long. To do so might raise the model to a level of reality far beyond that intended. It is only a hypothesis, a suggested way of looking at learning which, like any hypothesis, is useful as long as it fits evidence and helps understanding. Nevertheless, a brief attempt at an answer may help credibility at this point.

The clearest guide seems to come from the work of Piaget, who did more than anyone else to show that children have their own ideas which make sense to them in terms of their own logic. Piaget also studied the behaviour of very young children. His ideas suggest that for young children (in what he called the sensorimotor period) actions take the place of thought. Children at this stage appear to 'know' the world through patterns of their own action. Gradually, these patterns of action are internalized and the child's world is no longer essentially centred on himself. These internalized actions later become the thoughts and thought processes. External experience can then be considered separately from internal ideas but before this they are as one.

It seems likely then that the answer to whether it is ideas or experience which comes first is that it is neither. The young child's actions are all that exist and these gradually separate into what later are described as 'ideas' and 'experience'. Once distinguishable the interaction of these may, according to the suggested model, bring about the development of ideas in the course of which they pass through a range of stages such as Piaget's work described.

The question we now turn to is whether all ideas are formed by the processing of experience and existing ideas or whether ideas can be received or generated in other ways. It is sometimes hard to believe that some of the more strange ideas of children (and of adults) come about through experience. An adult interpretation of experience often suggests something totally different from what children appear to believe. If, as suggested, though, children's ideas are a product of the way they process the experience as well as their existing ideas, then it is easy to see that these may not always lead to what an adult would view as a logical outcome. Either the existing ideas or the way of thinking about them, or both, may differ considerably from their counterparts in adult thought.

The notion of ideas being formed from experience is not therefore contradicted by the fact that children's ideas seem very strange and illogical to adults. Piaget's later work provides an example of apparently strange ideas having a basis in children's earlier experience. Joan Bliss, who worked with Piaget at that time, tells of how children were shown a smooth board across which balls could be 'fired' by a spring-loaded device. They were asked to predict the direction in which the ball should be fired to bounce off the edge at a given angle. Their drawings of the expected paths of the balls across the board were not straight. When asked about this they explained it in terms of how they knew balls to behave. In their experience, of rolling balls across bumpy paths or grass, it was quite natural for balls to move erratically. Their ideas were not fanciful but based on experience.

Response to 'ready-made' ideas

A different problem is posed by the ideas current in everyday life, some amounting to 'old wives' tales' and some forced on us by advertisements or political activists. 'Nothing tastes better than butter' is not usually an idea developed from experience. So does it have the same status in making sense of experience as an idea which has been developed, as it were, from within? There are plenty of ideas around that would have a confusing influence on children's scientific understanding if they were taken seriously. For example my Mother 'taught' me that if the sun shone through the window onto the fire it would put the fire out, that maggots were made of cheese and developed spontaneously from it, that placing a loose-fitting lid on a pan of boiling water made it boil at a low temperature, that electricity travelled more easily if the wires are straightened out. In my science education I found that these ideas did not stand up to the test of experience (but my Mother still believes them).

Many similar examples can be found every day, where people (and some of them science teachers!) are explaining things in terms of ideas which can very easily be shown not to fit experience.

These everyday examples are only some of the 'ready-made' ideas to which children are exposed. The expression 'ready-made' is used to denote generalizations or facts which have been created by someone else and not generated through the processes of applying, testing out and modifying existing ideas. Many more and more potentially useful ideas are deliberately presented to them in lessons at school. The model can be adapted to take them into account by regarding these as injected ideas which do not emerge from experience and so are free-floating (F−F I) and not part of the web, as represented in Figure 7.

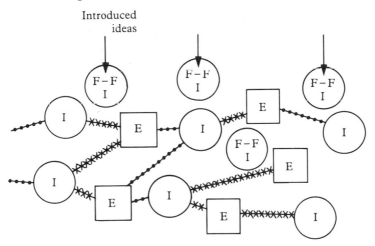

Figure 7 Ready-made ideas introduced into the network

When ready-made ideas are encountered they do not simply join the stock of a person's existing ideas. They may be tried as alternative ideas to existing ones in making sense of experience and as a result become tied into the web. But unless, or until, they are fitted into the web of existing ideas, they are not a person's own ideas and will not be used in making sense of the world around. Whether or not they are fitted in will depend on the result of trying them out against experience and how much sense they make compared with competing existing ideas.

A ready-made idea can be tested to see if it is a useful explanation for an experience by the steps suggested on p. 59 for the development of ideas. Does the idea lead to a prediction which fits the evidence? The answer may depend on how the 'prediction' is made and tested. Consider, for example, the 'old wives' tale' that the sun shining on the fire will put it out. Here is how it might be incorporated into a person's own ideas:

Ready-made idea	The sun puts the fire out
Prediction	If this is true, when the sun shines on the fire it will burn less brightly
Test of prediction	When the sun shines on the fire the flames cannot be seen and it glows less brightly
Result	The evidence is consistent with the idea; it works

Here is another way in which this idea might be tested:

Ready-made idea	The sun puts the fire out
Prediction	If this is true, a fire on which the sun has shone will go out more quickly than one on which no sun has shone
Test of prediction	The sun makes no difference to how quickly the fire goes out
Result	The evidence is not consistent with the idea; it doesn't work

Probably the same observation which led to the rejection of the idea created a link with another idea that was the basis of an alternative hypothesis; perhaps the sunshine only appears to make the fire die down:

Prediction	If the effect is only apparent, then the fire will not be permanently affected by the sunlight on it
Test of prediction	Shade a fire that seems to have been 'put out' by the sun and see if it remains less bright (or apply a more elaborate test, depending on equipment available)
Result	The evidence is consistent with there being no detectable effect; the new idea has not been rejected

The difference between the prediction and the test in the case where the 'everyday' idea, or old wives' tale, is accepted and in the case where it is rejected is central to the distinction between a scientific and an 'everyday' approach. A scientific approach involves a prediction which is a logical result of applying the idea and the test of it involves doing something to obtain relevant evidence, in this case perhaps timing how long a fire burns with and without the sun shining on it. The 'everyday' approach does not extend the prediction beyond what is already known; a circular argument replaces a logical prediction. The test is therefore bound to be confirmatory, for no new evidence is sought. The process of relating the idea to experience is once again shown to be as important as the nature of the idea. 'Everyday' ideas can be accepted because whether or not they 'work' is judged in an 'everyday' way.

These arguments can account for the acceptance by my Mother and others of her generation that cheese maggots are spontaneously created from cheese, whereas I and others of my generation regard such an idea as strange and would not accept it as our own. My Mother, having had no science education, would seek and notice only confirmatory evidence. I and my generation would not only find this evidence unconvincing but would also have alternative ideas which are more convincing (that is, give predictions which fit the evidence better).

Before going further I must apologise to my Mother if I overstate the position to make a point. She is not, of course, the only one to have strange ideas. Thurber's mother apparently thought herself surrounded by devices which had to be treated in particular and peculiar ways to prevent all kinds of disaster:

> The telephone she was comparatively at ease with, except, of course, during storms, when for some reason or other she always took the receiver off the hook and let it hang. She came naturally by her confused and groundless fears, for her own mother lived the latter years of her life in the horrible suspicion that the electricity was dripping invisibly all over the house. It leaked, she contended, out of empty sockets if the wall switch had been left on. She would go around screwing in bulbs, and if they lighted up she would hastily and fearfully turn off the wall switch and go back to her *Pearson's* or *Everybody's*, happy in the satisfaction that she had stopped not only a costly but dangerous leakage. Nothing could ever clear this up for her.
> (Copyright © 1933, 1961 James Thurber. From *My Life and Hard Times*, published by Harper & Row)

In more serious vein the chance of acceptance of ready-made ideas handed to children at school must now be considered. There is no doubt that some scientific ideas seem as strange to pupils as 'old wives' tales' seem to teachers. 'What we're taught in science is often difficult to believe' is a remark from a thoughtful 12-year-old, really trying to make sense of some ready-made ideas handed out by her teacher. She found the teacher's ideas difficult to believe because she tested them out in an 'everyday' way, not in a scientific way, and they did not fit experience as well as 'everyday' ideas. Take the idea that air has water vapour in it. This was used by the teacher to 'explain' the formation of dew on the grass. But the girl already had an explanation for this in her own idea that the coldness of the grass created the water. Her own idea also fitted other experience: the coldness of a 'fridge created water drops on bottles and cans taken out of it. What she was unable to do was to test either her own or the ready-made idea in an adequate way. Although the teacher's idea did not make sense to her, she was not free to reject it; it remained as an idea which she knew about, and could recall if asked, but it was not her own idea.

Children are exposed all the time to ideas of others (their teachers, other children, parents) and those which come through the media. There is no way in which children can be cut off from these other ideas and be allowed to form their own, nor would this be desirable. They must have access to a range of ideas which may be different from their own and challenge their existing ideas. If they are to consider these alternatives rationally, and not simply recite the ones which are forced hardest on them, they must have the mental skills and other skills needed to test them adequately against experience.

Role of process skills in developing of ideas

Many people have recognized the difference between rote learning and popularly called 'meaningful' learning. Some, like Douglas Barnes, have attempted to account for the difference in terms of a mental process which determines whether the potential learner can forge a link between existing knowledge and new ideas. As Barnes puts it 'Wherever school learning has gone beyond meaningless rote, we can take it that a child has made some kind of relationship between what he knows already and what the school has presented' (Barnes, 1976; p.22).

Evidence in support of this statement can be found at any time in any classroom. The children's conversation in Chapter 1 is full of examples of children interpreting what they find using what they already know. The same is true when new information is encountered as verbal statements instead of the input coming from the children's actions and investigations. Ideas are offered by teachers, peers and books and the process of learning is one of modifying one's ideas successively until they make sense of more and more experience and provide more links with the ideas of others. It follows, then, that learning can be helped by encouraging the forging of these links between existing ideas, other ideas and experiences so that more adequate ideas emerge. The big question for education in general is how to do this; for science education in particular it is how to do it when the ideas concern the behaviour of things in the natural and physical world around.

Some of the more persuasive ideas for education in general have been proposed by Barnes and his views on the role of communication in changing ideas will be considered later (p. 71). For the moment, however, we return to how the model of developing of ideas suggested earlier can be extended to take into account ready-made ideas which are encountered. These ideas were described earlier as free-floating, because they are not part of the web. If they remain free-floating they are 'learned' only in so far as they are rote-memorized. Indeed perhaps more can be said for certain about how ideas do not become linked into the web than about how they do become linked. It is worth considering this negative case first, for we know from experience and research quite a lot about how learning fails to happen!

Ways of not learning ready-made ideas

Figures 8 **a, b, c** propose some ways in which the new ideas do not become incorporated into the web of ideas.

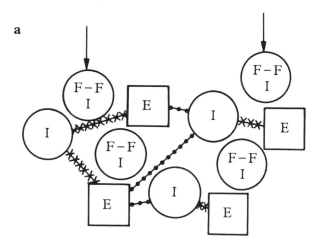

Figure 8(a)

In (**a**) they are not applied to experience and do not impinge on existing ideas. Hopefully, teaching of the kind that presents ideas in such a way is not common these days. (An example would be being asked to learn that 'air exerts a pressure in all directions' when you have no idea of 'pressure'.)

In (b) there is an attempt to relate the introduced ideas to experience, but only to carefully engineered school experience. These children may well agree that the new experience fits the introduced idea but still use their own ideas to explain their everyday experiences. (For instance, when a teacher uses a 'collapsing can' to demonstrate that air exerts a pressure in all directions, but children still explain drinking through a straw in terms of a 'sucking' force.) The idea remains linked, if at all, to an isolated experience and is not applied to others.

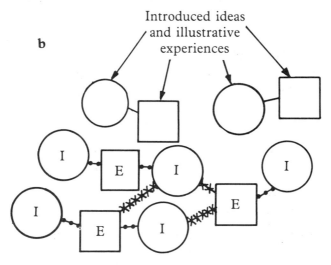

Figure 8(b)

In (c) there is a more thorough attempt to link the new idea to experience but the only way to do this is to let the children think out the connection for themselves. The failure in this case results from rejecting the idea, not because it is not a potentially relevant and useful one but because the way in which the children apply it and test it is at fault.

In this third case we have the reverse of the situation in which an old wives' tale is accepted; in this case a potentially acceptable idea is found unacceptable because of inadequate application and testing. If we pursue the air pressure example, the situation might be that the prediction the child makes from this idea is that all cans should collapse under the presure of air. As this obviously does not happen the new idea seems to have failed its test. What is at fault here is the process of hypothesizing, predicting and testing.

c

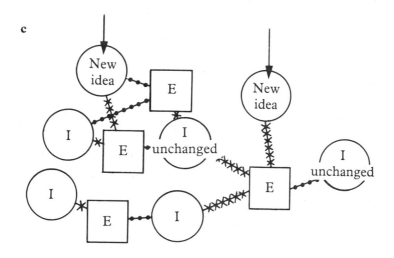

Figure 8(c)

Avoiding rejection of school inputs

Most probably these are only some of the many ways in which learning can fail to take place but they give some clues as to how to avoid failure. Such negative statements are perhaps as positive as we can be, for success can never be assured but known ways of being unsuccessful can be eschewed.

High on the list of ways of avoiding failure to develop or accept ideas which help understanding of the world around must be the development of the ways of thinking that we have called science process skills. The arguments presented in this chapter point to the conclusion that it is not enough to introduce new ideas and new experiences to children. These are quite inadequate to bring about learning unless the children are able to relate ideas to experiences and test the resulting predictions in a logical way.

In terms of the model this means that inputs from school must be concerned with *ways of thinking about experience and with gathering and using evidence as well as with introducing new ideas and experiences.* Figure 9 shows these essential features added to the model.

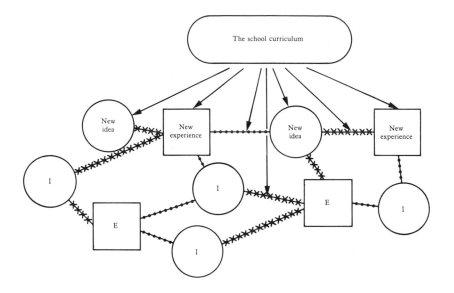

Figure 9 Linking ideas introduced in school into the network

It is important to interpret the arrows as opportunities to be provided, not as something being conveyed from school to pupil. The purpose of science activities as part of the school curriculum should be to provide for all the opportunities indicated by the arrows. How this can be done cannot be conveyed in a few sentences; indeed it is the purpose of this book, particularly the second part, to spell out the pedagogical implications. A first step, in the form of some very general guidelines, is made at the end of this chapter.

Role of language

The importance for learning of children's activity, mental and physical, has been stressed in what has been said so far. Physical activity is essential since much learning in science comes from rearranging the world around. It is in this respect that scientific enquiry differs from enquiry in other areas of the curriculum. In history and social studies, for example, children can learn to seek and use evidence and to suggest hypotheses, but they must use what they find to test their hypotheses, they cannot rearrange history to see what would have happened if, for instance, a battle had been won by the opposite side. Thus the active investigatory part of scientific enquiry is what distinguishes it from other types of enquiry.

The point has already been made, however, that physical activity without adequate mental activity can be non-scientific. Part of the context that binds mental and physical activity together is language. Douglas Barnes has provided some telling evidence and arguments to support his contention that 'The more a learner controls his own language strategies, and the more he is enabled to think aloud, the more he can take responsibility for formulating explanatory hypotheses and evaluating them' (Barnes, 1976; p.29).

By studying children's speech when involved in group tasks, Barnes showed how individuals contribute to an understanding of an event (or process, or situation). An idea of one child is taken up and elaborated by another, perhaps challenged by someone else's idea and leads them back to check with the evidence or to predict and see which idea stands up best to a test. With several minds at work there is less chance of ideas being tested in a superficial 'everyday' manner than there is if one child uses an 'everyday' approach with no-one to challenge it. The challenge can only be made if the thinking is made open and public through the use of language. Thus Barnes argues that talking is essential to learning. By 'talking' he does not, however, mean the formal reporting or answering of teachers' questions which in some classrooms is the only speech officially sanctioned. Barnes lays particular emphasis on the value of talk among children with no adult authority present. In such situations children with a problem to solve use non-formal speech: they interrupt each other, hesitate, rephrase and repeat themselves. Barnes sees this hesitant or 'exploratory' talk as signifying the openness of the situation and constituting an invitation to all involved to throw in ideas.

The opportunity for exploratory talk of this kind comes only when the children are in charge of the situation. Generally, this does not happen when the teacher is present, for his or her presence provides an authority which children expect to be greater than their own views. As Barnes (1976) says:

> the teacher's absence removes from their work the usual source of authority; they cannot turn to him to solve dilemmas. Thus ... the children not only formulate hypotheses, but are compelled to evaluate them for themselves. This they can do in only two ways: by testing them against their existing view of 'how things go in the world', and by going back to 'the evidence'.
> (Barnes, 1976; p. 29)

It is not difficult to see that learning through talking is exposing children not only to different ideas from others but compelling them to think about how those ideas relate to previous and new experiences. In other words they are finding better ways of dealing with ideas and checking them against evidence; they are developing the mental process skills. Hence what Barnes has to say, while relevant to all learning, is particularly significant for science. In making this point, he goes further in proposing a role for language in helping children to reflect on the way in which they have processed the ideas and information available to them:

> Much learning may go on while children manipulate science apparatus, or during a visit, or while they are struggling to persuade someone else to do what they want. But learning of this kind may never progress beyond manual skills accompanied by slippery intuitions, unless the learners themselves have an opportunity to go back over such experience and represent it to themselves. There seems every reason for group practical work in science, for example, normally to be followed by discussion of the implications of what has been done and observed, since without this what has been half understood may soon slip away. Talk and writing provide means by which children are able to reflect upon the bases upon which they are interpreting reality, and thereby change them.
> (Barnes, 1976; pp.30–31)

Some implications for changing children's ideas

In trying to draw together the threads of the argument in this chapter it seems best to proceed from the more general to the more particular points. If children are to achieve the aims of science education of developing understanding of the world around them, then we must cater for change in both their ideas and their process skills. If process skills are not gradually made more scientific and logical then 'everyday' ideas will not be challenged and potentially more useful ideas will be rejected. If initial 'everyday' ideas are not gradually transformed into more useful ones then process skills will be limited in their effect and so in their contribution to understanding.

From this it follows that the aims of science teaching must include the following:

● to help children become aware of their own ideas and to have access to those of others (peers, teacher and other sources) to set against them

● to help children apply ideas (their own and others) to a problem or situation, and to test the usefulness of the ideas in particular cases

● to help children reflect critically on how ideas have been used and tested and to find more effective ways of doing these things.

In working toward these aims experience shows that it is worthwhile avoiding certain situations and trying to supply others. Some of the ones for teaching to avoid include:

● ignoring children's own ideas or assuming that children do not have ideas about an experience or problem which is new

● introducing ready-made ideas without opportunities for children to try them out and compare them with their own ideas

● expecting children to accept the wider usefulness of ideas introduced to explain a contrived classroom experience which has little obvious parallel in their experience of everyday life

● accepting from children judgements about whether or not ideas work without asking them to explain their reasoning and show how evidence has been used

● confining children to tasks so circumscribed that they are not free to discuss and share thinking with others.

Some of the more positive things that are suggested about teaching are that it should provide the following:

● opportunities for children to investigate problems and events from which useful ideas can be developed

● opportunities for children to think of alternative explanations or solutions and test them fairly

● the introduction of ready-made ideas in such a manner that they are regarded as alternatives worth considering, not as right answers

● opportunities for children to share in groups a task or problem where they are responsible for the ideas and ways of testing them

● invitations for children to explain the thinking which led to a solution or idea being put forward in terms of how the idea came to their mind, how it led them to make a prediction and how the prediction was tested.

● acceptance of the ideas and explanations of children which are consistent with their limited experience and ways of processing evidence even though these may require refinement later in the light of wider experience and knowledge.

CHAPTER 4

THE QUESTION OF CONTENT

The content or subject matter of a topic is its most visible feature, what it seems to be about, its justification. This may lead, or rather mislead, us into regarding content as the most important consideration in choosing or devising science activities. While content *is* important, since it provides the situation in which learning can take place, it should not be the first thing to be considered. We should start by being clear about what learning we want to take place and using this as a guide in selecting content. If things are the other way round, and content is chosen before consideration has been given to the nature and continuity of the opportunities for learning that we wish to provide, then the learning is almost certain to be fragmented and lack coherence.

While it is important to have content that is of interest and relevance to children there have to be other criteria for deciding what to study. There is so much around children that is interesting and relevant to them and all of it cannot be included. Take a group of children out into a busy street and they will soon be asking enough questions to keep them productively absorbed for a whole year's science: the structures, the materials, the lights, the movement, the colours; these are just some of the topics that could be investigated. Take them to a wood and an equally long list of topics comes readily flooding in: a river, a park, the sea-shore, an airfield, mine or factory; the possibilities are endless. Thus one argument for establishing a basis for selection is expediency, but this is less important than the need to provide opportunities for the development of the range of process skills, attitudes and concepts that were discussed in Chapter 2.

Concepts and content

There is an apparently simple distinction between concepts or ideas and the content or the subject matter in which the ideas are encountered. The content of an activity can be described in terms of the objects or materials or events that it concerns: putting bricks in water and watching the air bubbles rise, watching snails to see what food they eat, seeing how long an ice-cube can be kept from melting. These activities could also be described as concerning porosity of materials, food preferences of animals, insulation, descriptions which refer to the underlying ideas, or some of them, that the activities could help to build up or to illustrate. The ideas do not uniquely define the activities as the content does: other materials than bricks could be used, other animals than snails and so on, to contribute to the same ideas. Care has to be taken to avoid confusing one kind of description with the other, for while we can with some certainty say that a group of children have kept an ice-cube from melting for a long time we can be much less sure that they have grasped ideas about preventing heat transfer. They would very likely need experiences of activities with other subject matter to consolidate, or possibly to revise and modify, their ideas.

A basic concept or important idea can be envisaged as being built from contributions from a variety of activities, each of different content. The relation might be envisaged as in Figure 10.

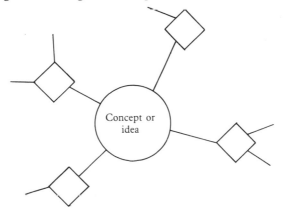

Figure 10 A concept or idea built from various activities □ represents activities each of different content but involving the same concept

The figure suggests that the content of an activity may well involve more than one concept and so could be linked to other concepts outside the figure, forming a network. The concepts or ideas in this network will be similar for all children, although the particular activities can vary as long as they bear a relation with the same concepts or ideas. The involvement of a concept is not the only criterion for selecting content of activities and we shall discuss other criteria later. But it is a central one, for if we wish children to come to understand the world around they must have opportunity for constructing ideas necessary for this understanding. So the content must provide this opportunity; it is no use hoping to develop children's ideas of the porosity of materials if they only study the food that snails will eat. So content selection depends on the concepts that are important for children's understanding and before taking further the question of content it is necessary to examine further the nature of the concepts. At the end of Chapter 2 11 'concept areas' were proposed and criteria were defined for identifying ideas in these areas. The discussion is now taken on from that point.

Identifying basic concepts

The words 'concept' and 'idea' are being used interchangeably (possibly at the risk of causing irritation to the reader) since there is little common agreement as to any useful distinction between them. There is some philosophical controversy about the meaning of 'concept'. Some, like Lovell (1962) define it as 'a generalization about data which are related'. His view is that concepts 'arise out of perceptions', by putting together various experiences and drawing out what is common to them. The examples he cites are the single-word concepts: substance, number, area, transport. Others have argued that such concepts are merely labels and that learning them involves learning the conventions of using these words. Thus, for instance, children have problems understanding the concept of 'animal' because they do not know that this label is used for all objects sharing certain properties and this includes human beings as well as worms and spiders.

One view of a concept proposed as an alternative is that it is not a label but a relation between things which take part in a process. Ohm's law would be an example of a relational concept, as would the generalization that the hotter an object is compared with its surroundings the more quickly it cools.

A useful approach is to define a concept in terms of its function rather than what it is. It enables a person to use past experience in going beyond the observed features of objects or events to make inferences when further objects or events are encountered. These inferences may be based on common properties or they may be based on relations. This leads to the working definition of a concept as 'the network of inferences that are or may be set into play by an act of categorization' (Bruner et al., 1966). Concepts in this view have a dual function, first, of categorizing new experience so that related ideas are called into play from earlier experience and, secondly, in providing an inferred link with all the features which are brought together in the existing concept. Through these links new phenomena can not only be labelled but invested with implied mechanisms through which they begin to be understood.

Taking this functional view of concepts, we are concerned both with common-feature (sometimes one-word) ones and with relational concepts and it is to be expected that both will appear in any list of basic ideas that children should be constructing through their science activities.

In whatever form the concepts are expressed, however, it is important to interpret them developmentally. No idea is constructed all at once; it develops along a path that is idiosyncratic, varying according to the experience, both inside and out of school, of each child. As Chapter 3 has attempted to show, children's ideas develop through a process of constant modification as earlier versions are tried out against experience and modified to form the later versions. The statements below indicate the point in this series of changes that most children might have reached at the *end* of their primary schooling. Before this their ideas may be different, even in conflict with what they will come to think at a later stage. There is some danger in attempting to plot the way this development takes place for it may be interpreted as the way things *should* happen rather than the way things *sometimes* happen. However, so that teachers may have some ideas of what to expect during the course of the development, a few examples will be given later.

The list below should be considered with the following points in mind:

● they should be interpreted at a level that meets all the criteria proposed on p. 54 appropriately for children at the end of primary education

● they are 'basic' ideas in the sense of being a necessary foundation for later learning and they will continue to be refined and further developed by later learning

● they may seem simple and 'low level' but their value for children will be in the extent to which the ideas are used where relevant in the whole of their experience, so a superficial grasp is not enough

● other more complex ideas may well be constructed by primary children but this should not be at the expense of these basic ones

● each statement is a point of development of an idea; it will have been reached via a succession of relevant activities over a period of years when at any point the existing idea is challenged and revised

● each idea can be arrived at through a host of different activities

● there are both key words (italicised) to understand and relations to grasp.

Sight and light

Seeing things involves *light* coming from the objects seen into our eyes. Light passes from one place to another in straight lines but can be made to change direction if things are put in the way.

Hot and cold and temperature changes

When *hot* things cool down or *cold* things warm up there is a change of *temperature* which can be felt and measured by a *thermometer*. Things hotter than their surroundings cool down as they lose *heat* and things colder than their surroundings warm up as they gain heat. These changes can be slowed down by various devices and materials. Gaining or losing heat can change things (*melting, freezing, evaporating, condensing*).

Hearing and producing sound

Hearing things involves *sound* coming from them reaching our ears. Sound is created by objects moving rapidly (*vibrating*).

Movement and forces

Moving from one place to another takes a certain time; the shorter the time for the same distance the *faster* the movement. *Speed* is a measure of how fast something moves, usually how far it goes in a certain time, a second, minute or hour. *Force* is what tries to start or stop something moving or change its motion. When there is any change in motion there must be a force acting.

Air and breathing

There is air in the 'empty' spaces around us. We feel it only when it moves, as a *wind*. Air is a substance, called a *gas*; like all substances it has mass. Water, a *liquid*, can go into the air in the form of a vapour (*evaporation*) and comes out under certain conditions (*condensation*). Other things can mix with air; some can be detected by *smell* when they reach our noses. Living things need and use air.

How things behave in water

Some, but not all, things *dissolve* in water. Some, but not all, things *float* in water. Whether a thing floats or not depends on how heavy it is for its size.

Ourselves and other animals

There is a wide variety of different living things called *animals*; different kinds feed, grow, move, protect themselves and reproduce in different ways.

They usually do these things in ways which suit them for living in particular environments. Animals of the same kind go through the same *life cycles*.

Soil and growth of plants

There is a wide variety of different living things called *plants*; different kinds feed, grow and reproduce in different ways. Many are green and produce the food they need through a process which needs light. Soil is a mixture of different things some of which are needed by plants to grow.

Sky, seasons and weather

The sun, moon and stars move relative to the earth in regular repeated patterns. Changes in the apparent positions of the sun in the sky are connected with night and day, and seasonal changes in the weather. Water condensing from the air under certain conditions gives rain, cloud, frost and snow.

Materials and their properties and uses

Materials are grouped according to their properties, such as whether they are *hard, bendy, transparent, strong*; different types are used for different purposes on account of their properties. The *strength* of structures made from a particular material depends on their form.

Simple electric circuits

Some materials allow an *electric current* to pass through them (*conductors*); others effectively prevent a current from flowing (*insulators*). There always is a continuous path of a conducting material when electricity flows from one terminal of a battery to the other.

Children's construction of basic ideas: three examples

The force of some of the points made earlier about the developmental nature of children's ideas is realized best through some examples from recent research. They show that it takes time and reflection on a wide range of experience for these ideas to be transformed into the ideas that we as adults recognize to be their meaning. They confirm, too, the suspicion that just because children use a word with confidence, sometimes appropriately, it does not mean that it evokes for them the same whole range of experiences and properties that it does for their teachers.

Floating

Take 'floating' for a start. Some research in New Zealand (Biddulph & Osborne, 1984) explored what children understood floating to mean by using cards showing pictures of various objects in water, some floating and some not. The children ranged in age from 7 to 14 years and over 100 were interviewed individually. The results from the interviews were backed up by a survey of a larger number of children which served to confirm the main findings and establish where there appeared to be a trend with age in the children's ideas.

When discussing the pictures showing objects floating with part above the water surface and part below (a person floating in a life-jacket for instance) the children's decision as to whether or not it was floating appeared to be influenced by how much of the object was above the water and how much below the surface. If a large proportion was above the surface there was general agreement that it was floating, but if only a small part was above the surface (as in the case of a bottle floating with only the neck above water) there were many (42% in the survey) who said it was partly floating and partly sinking. A 9 year-old was reported as saying in an interview that 'It's floating and not floating. The top is floating and the bottom's not.'

The inferred movement of an object also affected judgement as to whether or not it was floating. Half of the pupils thought that the yacht in Figure 11(a) was not floating, and several of the younger children also claimed that the speed boat in Figure 11(b) was not floating because it was moving. An 8 year-old said 'It's going fast, and floating is staying still and floating around.' With objects totally submerged (such as a person snorkelling) just under a half described them as not floating.

(Figure 14; from Biddulph & Osborne, 1984)

(Figure 10; from Biddulph & Osborne, 1984)

Figure 11   Floating: **a**, yacht in trouble
                        b, speed boat going fast

The children were also asked about a range of possible variables that might affect floating, such as the size of the object or the depth of water. The results show a definite trend with age. Only 10% of the 8-year-olds thought that a whole candle would float at the same level as a short piece of the candle. This proportion was 30% for 10-year-olds and 65% for 12-year-olds. Even at the age of 12 years, however, a quarter of the children thought the full-length candle would float lower than the short piece. To investigate the effect of changing the depth of water the children were shown the picture in Figure 12 and asked to compare the level of floating of the launch in the deep and shallow water. Half of the 8-year-olds said it would float lower in the deeper water, but only about a fifth of 10 and 12 year-olds gave this answer. About two-thirds of the 10 and 12 year-olds said the level of floating was unaffected by the depth but only 40% of the 8 year-olds said this was so.

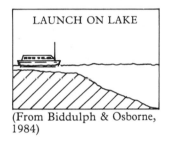

LAUNCH ON LAKE

(From Biddulph & Osborne, 1984)

Figure 12   Floating launch on lake

The results of this research could be readily tested by teachers by discussing examples of floating with their own pupils in an informal way. Those who have done this have been surprised at how similar their findings are to the ones of the New Zealand researchers. They realize, too, how easy it is not to notice the children's different interpretation of what floating means.

Some implications are:
● the use of the word does not indicate a grasp of its meaning
● one example to illustrate the meaning of floating would not be sufficient; the initial idea will have to be tried out in other situations and broadened as found necessary
● children's understanding of what floating means and what affects floating changes as they become older
● there is a range of possible meanings that children may have in mind when they describe something as floating

- the existence of different meanings may not come to light unless a wide range of floating objects and activities is provided and discussed
- this wide range of objects and activities relating to floating is necessary for children's ideas to be challenged and modified.

Animal

The influences on children's ideas are not totally under the control of the teacher, however, as was mentioned in Chapter 3. The everyday usage of words has a considerable effect, which is particularly strong in the case of the next example, the concept of 'animal'. An investigation of children's ideas about what things are animals and how children decide whether or not a given thing is an animal, was carried out by Bell & Barker (1982) involving interviews and a survey of children from age 5 to 17 years. The results showed that children's initial idea of what is an animal is restricted to large land mammals. For instance a high proportion of their sample of 5-year-olds recognized a cow as an animal and the proportion rose to 100% by the age of 7 years. However, creatures such as worms and spiders were not considered to be animals by three-quarters of the 9-year-olds and only a slightly higher proportion of 12-year-olds. Only a fifth of the sample of 5-year-olds considered a human being to be an animal and this proportion rose to just over a half for 9- and 12-year-olds.

Commenting on these findings Osborne (1985) makes the point that signs in shops such as 'No animals allowed' would reinforce a narrow view of the notion of animal. So would the label 'animal house' in a zoo and the distinction between animals and fish that tends to be part of the common usage of the words. These everyday ways of using the word conflict with the 'correct' use, based on the common features shared by all animals. The conflict can have serious consequences in children's misunderstanding if there is any uncertainty as to which meaning of the word is being used in a particular instance. A teacher can do nothing to prevent the word being used loosely in everyday situations but can do something to find out what meaning the word conveys to the children. Bell (1981) suggests that the teacher should help children to form the scientific idea of 'animal' and at the same time make them aware that this is different from the everyday meaning.

Seeing

As a third example, take the idea that seeing something involves light coming from it into our eyes. Children who are past the stage of believing that objects no longer exist if they are hidden from view or if they close their eyes, nevertheless describe the process of seeing as if it is their eyes that produce the light that makes the objects appear. Figure 13 shows a 10-year-old's drawing of how you see a bottle standing on a table when the light is switched on.

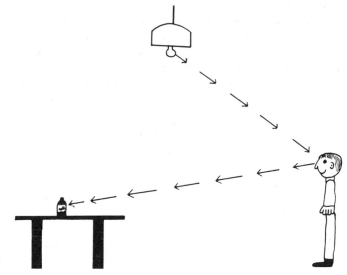

Figure 13

In a class of 26 9–11-year-olds, eight showed arrows from the eye to the bottle, four showed the light rays with arrows from the bottle to the eye and two had them going both ways, as in Figure 14.

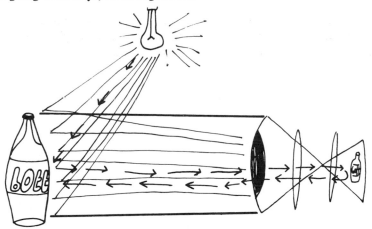

Figure 14

The remainder (12) showed no connection between the eye and the bottle. Their responses, however, leave one in no doubt that they have worked out their own explanation of experience, which is not the same as the explanation given by physics.

It is perhaps understandable that the eye is seen as an active agent rather than a receiver, for this fits the subjective experience of 'looking'. When we choose to look at something we do feel our eyes turn as if we are the active agent in the process, and indeed the arrow from receiver to object does represent the line of sight. A variation on this idea is to regard the presence of light as somehow activating the eye, as described in Figure 15.

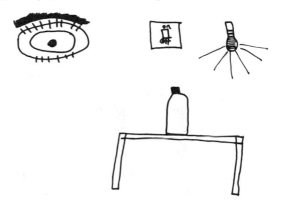

'With no light your eyes cannot see anything as soon as you turn the light on your eyes can see again your eyes sort of work like a light when there's no light you can't see but when there is light you can see'

Figure 15

Figure 16 is typical of the responses from a class of younger children (7–9-year-olds). All but four of the 27 in the class showed light spreading to the eye and the bottle but nothing between bottle and eye.

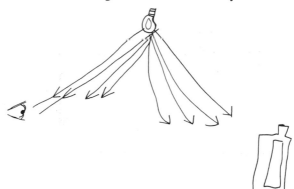

Figure 16

The children's interpretation of the situation does not take into account the need for light to fall on the object and to be reflected by it, or to be given out by it, for it to be seen. Piaget showed in his early work that 9 and 10 year-olds did not connect the onset of darkness at night with the lack of sunlight, they 'explained' darkness by describing it *as* night, something that comes because people get tired and need to sleep (Piaget, 1929). Thus the children's grasp of the relation between what is seen and the person seeing it depends on their linking up various ideas about daily experiences and noticing the patterns in them: that the sky goes dark when the sun disappears, that the more light that falls on an object the brighter it appears, that if you want to see something in a dark room you shine a light on it not into your eyes and so on.

These examples serve as a reminder of some points made in the last chapter about the role of process skills in the formation of children's ideas. The experiences needed to grasp the relation between an object and the conditions in which it can be seen can be based on common everyday occurrences. The development of the idea depends on the way the children process these experiences. If they are selective in the evidence they choose to take into account they may find their ideas reinforced. For instance, if they consider only what happens when they look from one object to another and when they close their eyes they may confirm the notion that something must come out of the eyes to see the object. But if they are made to challenge this idea by trying to make sense of the inability of the eyes to see in the dark or the changes that appear in an object if different coloured lights are shone on it, then they may have to consider alternative ideas that fit this evidence better.

The more an apparently simple idea is explored, the less simple it becomes. The first thought might have been that the idea that 'seeing things involves light coming from them into our eyes' is rather trivial and can be taught in a sentence, or even assumed. On further thought this appears to be far from the case. When we try to understand the origin of children's ideas we find a certain 'logic' in them, but only if we accept their selection of the evidence they use and, like them, ignore other possible reasons and reasoning. The appreciation of their 'logic', however, brings a realization of the difficulty of changing children's ideas. It is not just a matter of broadening their range of experience; they have to be willing and prepared to give attention to evidence which does not fit their view, to reflect on it and to relate one piece of experience to another (for instance that the effect of the sun going down and a torch being switched off in a dark room are both connected with being able to see things).

Quite a number of different activities can be suggested as relevant to this one relational concept. Children can explore the conditions in which objects can be seen, try to explain what is happening in each case, try to predict the effect of changes in the surrounding light, of the object's position, of putting a screen in various positions. They can turn attention to the eyes that see; how they move when a person looks in different directions, what happens when they are covered with different materials: opaque, translucent and transparent but coloured. Once they begin to realize that the eye is a receiver it might be appropriate for them to find out about its structure in human beings and other animals, but the purpose being to consolidate and refine the idea that seeing involves light coming into the eye not to learn the names of the parts: lens, retina, cornea, etc.

It turns out, then, that far from teaching children a simple statement the development of a basic idea such as this one about light requires quite an extensive list of experiences. These would probably be best not tackled all at one time but taken in two or three sets spread over a year or two or perhaps incorporated into other topics, for evidently there are many other ideas embraced by the kinds of activities that have just been outlined. Revisiting ideas and progressively developing them is often preferable to trying to focus on them for a single prolonged period of time. The interconnections between one idea and another mean it is better to make small advances in several and return to each later than to try to press one forward at a time. It is rather like trying to raise a heavy platform on a number of supporting jacks: each one must be raised by a small amount at a time to maintain stability. This analogy is quite apt, for it reminds us that we should not be in too much of a hurry to force the development of children's ideas and skills. It is a slow process and important that there is a reasonable equilibrium between a child's ideas and his experience; this provides the confidence that he can make sense of the world around and the motivation to do so. Then as experience expands, as it must do, he will strive to relate his ideas to new challenges and change them as found necessary.

Selection of content

The criteria for selecting concepts, summarized at the end of Chapter 2, took into account the aims of primary science as expressed in the kinds of learning intended and the role it should take as the basis of later science education. These are things that teachers have to have in mind, although the pupils may be unaware of them. Children are not likely to be conscious of learning 'basic concepts'. The ideas described above are ones that form gradually. Children will be aware of 'finding what you can see if you look through a long narrow tube' but not of 'finding that light from one object has to reach the eye to be seen'. If the latter *is* the case then it could well be that they are learning a form of words and not a concept. The point is that the concepts are embedded in the content of the activity. It is the content of which the children are conscious; the teacher has to be conscious of both.

The criteria for selecting content are therefore somewhat different from, though connected with, the criteria for selecting concepts. One criterion must be that there is opportunity for developing the basic concepts. Another is that the content must provide the interest and motivation for children to become involved in an activity that is going to challenge and so develop the ideas that it embodies and the skills required to carry it out.

Children's interests

Interest for children is an important consideration but it is not the only one. Much valuable time has been used less productively for learning than it might have been by following too slavishly the dogma of 'following children's interests'. The effect has often been to narrow children's range of experiences by seizing too early on things in which they have already shown interest instead of attempting to expand their interests. The readiness with which children are intrigued by new things, or new ways of looking at familiar things, shows that interest can be created. It is perfectly possible for children to become completely absorbed in activities that they did not themselves suggest, but this does not mean that their interest can be captured by *any* activity. The criterion of interest should be applied after there has been chance for children to encounter new phenomena. This makes the question of starting points for topics particularly important.

What makes an activity interesting? It is generally because there is something puzzling about it, something that we have an urge to settle in our own minds. If I've always wondered how they make plastic bottles without a seam showing then I am interested to visit the factory where they are made. If someone shows me a new material that I've never seen before ('Potty putty', for instance) then I am interested to touch it, play with it and perhaps investigate its properties in a more ordered way. Each person's puzzles are slightly different, of course, and so what interests me will not necessarily interest another. It will depend on their previous experience and whether the links between this and new experiences raise problems to be solved. To some extent the outcome of this process is unpredictable for any individual. It is more predictable for children than for adults, however, for their experience is more limited and the possibility of puzzle raising consequently greater. But it is not just the new and unexpected that can puzzle children. The familiar has puzzles in it and these are often the most intriguing to them. Who would have thought that four blocks of wood floating in a tank of water would keep children busily investigating literally for hours? This is what happened to the children quoted in Chapter 1, and not just those; the same activity invariably creates similar intense interest in children. There was nothing apparently new except that the materials were selected to make them puzzle about floating in a way that they may not have done before and offered the chance of working on this puzzle. So in seeking to create interest we should have in mind links with previous experience when presenting either novel phenomena or familiar ones in a new light.

Relevance to things around

The potential interest in activities concerning familiar things leads to another criterion for choice, that the content should be related to things around children. At one level this means using the environment as the source of content; the idea of the variety of different living things can be developed on the shore, at the zoo, in the park, in the wood, according to the location of the school. At another level, however, it means ensuring a link between real phenomena and the activities in the classroom. Fine, if the study of a swinging pendulum really does have some function in helping to understand things in the world around, but not if the link is theoretical and obvious only to the scientist.

The degree to which problems should be simplified for children is a complex issue. One approach is to suggest that children should tackle the problems they find in their exploration of the world around. These problems are inevitably complex, for reality is not simple. The complexity can indeed be so confusing that the underlying basic ideas may not be apparent. The understanding of what makes winds blow in certain directions at a particular speed is a case in point. An alternative approach is to simplify the real situation and take it apart to study its component ideas separately. So we look at one time at how air moves upwards over a source of heat, at other times at how it moves toward places where the pressure is reduced and so on. The danger here is of creating activities which may not seem to have much relevance, in the eyes of a child, to what is happening in the world around and which they cannot combine in puzzling over the real problem. Science activities then become things that the children do in science lessons rather than means of increasing their understanding of things around them.

There is no easy solution to this dilemma; in some cases the better course of action may be to accept the complexity of the problem and in others to break it down into simpler component problems. It may help in deciding which is better in a particular case to recall two points: first, that the children's ideas at any time need not be the ones that remain with them for ever; secondly, that they will form some ideas about the things around them even if we, as educators, consider them too complex. If we want children eventually to understand that wind is moving air and how its movement is created we can discuss and investigate the children's ideas about the wind so that they realize their ideas don't fit all the evidence and they will keep puzzling about it. Or, we can ignore the children's ideas and attempt to create the 'right' ones about how air is made to move through activities designed to illustrate relations, such as heat causing air to rise, and which 'work'. Experience at the secondary level, where the latter approach has been tried for years (and with children who might be more able to abstract the relevant ideas), suggests that it is not very successful. Many pupils do not see the point of the activities they do and are far from making a connection with the world around. (Much evidence of this is summarized in Osborne & Freyberg, 1985.)

It seems, then, that there is a strong case for interpreting the criterion of relevance of content to things around as 'relevance perceived by children', not as relevance perceived by teachers, scientists or other adults. Once the children are investigating a relevant problem it may well be possible to separate out one aspect for study, to test out an idea or hypothesis. This does no harm, as the connection with the real problem is already established. For example, some of the children working on the problem of how to keep an ice-cube from melting (without putting it in the freezer) wondered whether the materials they used to surround the ice to stop the 'cold' getting out would or would not keep heat getting out of a warm object. They ended up using food cans filled with hot water and covered by jackets of various materials. This is a fairly common activity, suggested in books both at primary and secondary levels, and can mean little to those undertaking it if it comes 'out of the blue'. For the children who came to it via the ice-cube problem, however, it had a great deal of meaning and marked a considerable advance in their ideas about heat and changes of temperature.

Chance to use process skills

Although the link between concepts and content is particularly important, since the content of activities largely determines the opportunities for concepts and ideas to be developed, the interrelation of concepts and process skills means that opportunities for using and developing process skills have also to be considered in the selection of content. This opportunity is mainly a matter for the *way* in which the content is encountered in the activity, something discussed in the next section, but it may also influence the range of content selected. Stirring of sugar, salt and other things into water is particularly 'rich' for the development of the meaning of 'dissolving'; similarly, other examples of content could be found that would be included in most lists aiming to cover the basic ideas on pages 78 and 79. But some content can be chosen because it is 'rich' in opportunities for process-skill development rather than for concept development. Examples are content that helps patterns to be detected (adding marbles to a pan on the end of a spring), that helps children to separate variables and test their effect separately (the simple pendulum, for instance), that requires the devising of fair tests (finding which paper is best for backing a book). The content of these activities is linked, tenuously, to the basic ideas (movement and properties of materials) but they are justified not by these links but by the process skills they involve. In some programmes of science activities (e.g. Science, a Process Approach, 1966–1976) the content has deliberately been chosen to have no link with science concepts to focus more sharply on the process skills being used. So, for instance, children make inferences about the contents of black boxes and seek for patterns in the colour changes that occur when unknown liquids are mixed.

The issue of the process dimension in relation to content is somewhat parallel with the issue discussed in relation to the concepts. Should the content be simplified, made trivial, so that it does not interfere with the smooth application of a scientific approach to gathering and processing information, or should the content be 'real', but messy, and not necessarily easy to handle with a scientific approach? The danger of the former is that the process skills may be developed but not seen to be relevant when real problems are encountered. The danger of the latter is that scientific processes are carried out only superficially and children fall back on everyday ways of thinking.

Again we have to admit that there is no clear cut rule to be followed and the only viable approach is to weigh the pros and cons in particular cases. It can be wasteful on two counts to select content that is trivial. In the first place, learning the skill has then to be followed by learning to apply it. Secondly, the chance to develop concepts while learning the skill has been missed. Against these criticisms it has been claimed that teachers who worry about not knowing enough science themselves to deal with real problems are more confident in handling 'set pieces' that focus on the processes. The arguments based on children's learning, however, lead to the conclusion that if we wish children to come to understand the world around by their own reasoning and trying out their own and others' ideas then they must be using this reasoning and testing it out in their investigation of real things and problems. The ideal is that while solving a problem or checking an idea they also become aware of better ways of solving problems and testing ideas. If this awareness does not come about, for one reason or another, there may be a case for introducing some special activities with simplified content, but these should not become the only or even the main content encountered.

To sum up, the main criteria that have been considered for the selection of content are:

- that it gives opportunity for the basic concepts or ideas to be developed
- that it is interesting and intriguing to children
- that it should help children understand the world around them by investigation and interaction with the objects and events they find in it
- that it gives opportunity for the development of science process skills.

We have seen that not all these criteria may be met by all the content. But most of them should be met most of the time and it should never be the case that none of them is ever met.

Activities and content

The devising and selecting of activities is the subject of a later chapter, but it is relevant to anticipate some of it briefly here, for an activity is more than its content. Content as it has been discussed here is the subject matter the children are aware of: what food caterpillars will eat, what colours show up best on road signs, what happens when ink drops spread across filter paper. The activity in which they take part includes what they do with the subject matter and how they do it. The teacher's role and the organization of the class have important parts in determining the activity and it is not difficult to imagine rather different outcomes from contrasting ways of dealing with the same content.

Take, for instance, an activity commonly included in a topic on 'Ourselves', whether taller people generally have larger feet than shorter people. (The concepts to which this can contribute concern the variation among individual living things and any patterns in these variations.) The children could be set to plan for themselves how to carry out this investigation, deciding on what information they will need and how they will gather it, bring it together and interpret it. They might also be asked to report to others what they find out.

They would be involved in using skills of planning, in thinking about variables to be controlled and variables to be measured and in coming to their conclusions they would check their findings against the evidence to present a convincing case. Alternatively, the same children could be given a set of instructions:

- take 20 people and measure their height
- measure the length of their feet
- make sure you do all the measuring in the same way (all without shoes on)
- put your results in this table (given)
- etc. ... ...

The subject matter as far as content is concerned is the same, but in the second case the amount of thinking that the children do is much less and indeed they could complete the activity and do very little working out for themselves about the reasons for what they were doing. Clearly, the opportunities for process skill and attitude development are much less in this second activity than in the first. It could be speculated also that the information and relation (if any) that the children obtain would mean more in the first activity since they would have a much clearer idea of the reasons for taking and interpreting the measurements.

In designing or selecting an activity, there is, then, more to be taken into account than the content. The presentation and management of the content determine the learning opportunities to a large extent. The more the children have to think things out for themselves and take responsibility for decisions about the evidence to be sought and how it will be used, the more they are likely to gain both in terms of advancing ideas as well as process skills.

Decisions about the nature of the activity, as opposed to only its content, also determine the extent to which scientific attitudes can be developed. Opportunities for fostering attitudes depend only marginally on content but heavily on the way the content is handled. The situation is the reverse for concept development and somewhere between the two for process skills (see p. 123). With almost any content children can develop the habits of not accepting the first idea to be suggested, of listening to others' ideas, of checking all possibilities against evidence, of suspending judgement if there is insufficient evidence, of critically reviewing their approach to solving a particular problem. So criteria for devising or selecting activities must include opportunities for development of such attitudes.

A further consideration that comes at this level is that of equipment. Much more will be said in later chapters about equipment but certain general principles are pertinent here. In most primary schools the problem is not usually one of choice (should we use jam jars or laboratory flasks?, saucers or Petri dishes?) because there are usually only jam jars and saucers available anyway, but rather of feeling that the lack of specialized equipment is a disadvantage to primary science. If, instead of modelling what is done in the primary school on the image of secondary science, we consider the learning we want to bring about, then the use of everyday equipment has strong positive advantages.

Use of things that are familiar to children to help them explore and understand their surroundings emphasizes that they can do it through their own actions and thinking. They are not prevented from observing the diffusion of colour from a coloured dissolving crystal by lack of a glass beaker, a bunsen burner or the right chemicals; they can use things very readily available in the classroom or at home. The directness of the use of simple equipment emphasizes the point that answers can be found in the objects or situations themselves. The use of specialized equipment too early interrupts this message, makes science something distant and mysterious. When more precision is appropriate, later in the secondary school, then the equipment used has to allow this. If by then the pupils have formed the basic ideas and are building on them there may be no disadvantage in separating problems from their context. When these basic ideas are still being formed, however, they must be seen to be relevant to the understanding of phenomena in everyday life. Unfamiliar equipment can present a barrier to this relevance.

To bring these points together, when creating or selecting activities the criteria to be applied are:
● that the content meets the criteria listed on p. 91
● that there are opportunities for scientific attitudes to be developed
● that the equipment is simple and familiar and does not constitute an obstacle to studying, or draw attention away from, the phenomenon or event being investigated.

The three sets of criteria that have been proposed, for selection of concepts (p. 54) content (p. 91) and activities nest one within another as follows:

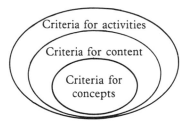

It is salutary to remember, however, that this relation has been based on theoretical arguments. There is no necessity in practice for activities to be chosen by using criteria which subsume those relating to content and concepts. Indeed the choices are often made for quite other reasons. But if we wish to bring about learning of the kind discussed in earlier chapters and help children's understanding of the world around, then there is no escaping the implications of carrying the argument into classroom decisions. The criteria that emerge from this process can be used in evaluating the activities that children actually experience, the subject of the next chapter.

CHAPTER 5

EVALUATING OPPORTUNITIES FOR LEARNING SCIENCE

It is useful to have in mind some examples of children's science activities for the purposes of the discussion in this chapter. The following are the typical experiences of children resulting from different approaches to organizing science. They are not meant to be 'good' or 'poor' examples, just illustrative of the activities children experience. Judgements may follow later when the nature of evaluation and the basis for carrying it out have been discussed.

The 8/9 year-old children in the first example are in the class of Mr Carter. Science takes place regularly on Tuesday afternoons for 1 hour. Mr Carter uses a scheme of work cards, for each of which he has collected a box of equipment. The 36 boxes are stored neatly on shelves in a corner of the room, clearly labelled so that when a child or group has selected a card the appropriate box can be readily identified. As the 35 children in the class work in two's or three's the number of cards used at any one time is less than half of those available, so choice is not usually a problem. There are some paired cards where one has to be done before another, but otherwise the order in which the activities are carried out depends on the pupils' choice.

Mr Carter has concentrated on physical science in his cards, being aware that previously the children's experience was heavily biased toward nature study. The main topics covered are weather recording, simple circuits, magnets, making sounds, comparing the hardness of materials, finding the volume and mass of large and small objects, making and separating mixtures, reflection of light and chromatography. The work for each card is designed to occupy about one lesson but it can be more or less than this. The children help to keep the record of what they have done by ticking a list next to the box of cards.

The large amount of work put into setting up this system, that the children quickly learn to operate, has its rewards for Mr Carter in relieving him of major planning and decisions with regard to science throughout the school year. During the science lessons he sees that the routine runs smoothly, helps with faulty apparatus and explains the cards to any children having difficulty in understanding what they have to do. The children are always busy, but their enthusiasm wanes as the year progresses.

The sorts of things the children are doing can be judged from some examples of the work cards:

HARDNESS TESTS

Different substances have different hardnesses. A hard substance is not easily scratched.

Do these tests to see how hard certain substances are.

Materials: in the box you will find labelled pieces of
Perspex
copper
aluminium
flint
limestone
wood

What to do:
Take each substance in turn and try to scratch the others with it.
Be careful to see whether the result is a scratch or a mark on the surface.
A scratch cuts a ridge into the substance.

How to record your results:
Draw a table like this

	Perspex	copper	aluminium	flint	limestone	wood
Perspex						
copper						
aluminium						
flint						
limestone						
wood						

Use Perspex to try to scratch all the others. Fill in the first row of the table, putting a tick if Perspex scratched it. Then do the same for the other substances.

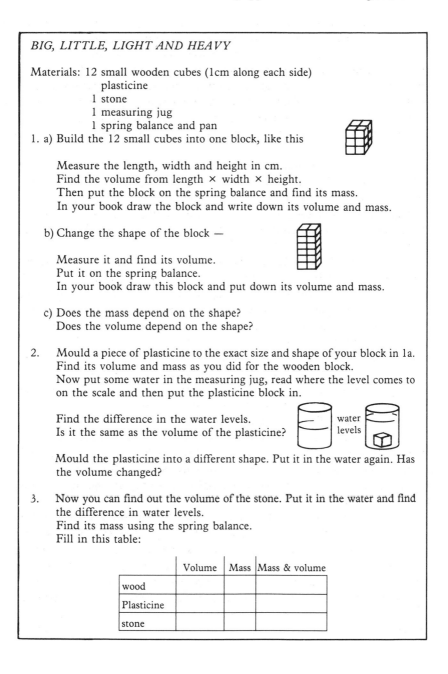

BIG, LITTLE, LIGHT AND HEAVY

Materials: 12 small wooden cubes (1cm along each side)
plasticine
1 stone
1 measuring jug
1 spring balance and pan

1. a) Build the 12 small cubes into one block, like this

Measure the length, width and height in cm.
Find the volume from length × width × height.
Then put the block on the spring balance and find its mass.
In your book draw the block and write down its volume and mass.

b) Change the shape of the block —

Measure it and find its volume.
Put it on the spring balance.
In your book draw this block and put down its volume and mass.

c) Does the mass depend on the shape?
Does the volume depend on the shape?

2. Mould a piece of plasticine to the exact size and shape of your block in 1a.
Find its volume and mass as you did for the wooden block.
Now put some water in the measuring jug, read where the level comes to
on the scale and then put the plasticine block in.

Find the difference in the water levels.   water
Is it the same as the volume of the plasticine?   levels

Mould the plasticine into a different shape. Put it in the water again. Has
the volume changed?

3. Now you can find out the volume of the stone. Put it in the water and find
the difference in water levels.
Find its mass using the spring balance.
Fill in this table:

	Volume	Mass	Mass & volume
wood			
Plasticine			
stone			

As a second example we take the children in Miss Evans' class. In her second-year junior class science is not a separate subject but included in 'topic work'. There is a topic for each term, chosen to emphasize different parts of the curriculum so in 1 year the topics were 'communication', 'Red Indians' and 'our town a 100 years ago'. Communication was the topic where most science was expected to feature and it was brought in at various points where it appeared to be appropriate. Sometimes 2 weeks passed without any recognizable science and then several half-days on end would be spent on science.

One week the teacher initiated a class discussion on ways of communicating across a distance. The children made and tried out string telephones to see if this helped the sound to travel further. They investigated sound travelling through other substances (including water during their visit to the swimming baths). Later some children had the chance to use a buzzer and find out about Morse code.

In other parts of the topic they discussed communication with people who were blind or deaf or both. A visit from a blind person created interest in Braille and they devised ways of testing how good they were at identifying Braille signs when blindfolded. The topic of hearing led to the investigation of the ranges of hearing of themselves, other people and other animals. Miss Evans secured the help of another teacher to program the school's microcomputer to produce sounds of different pitch, which they used to test all the teachers and a number of children. A visit to a museum gave them access to information about the range of hearing of various animals and they began speculating about reasons for these differences.

The instructions for carrying out these activities were given in discussion by Miss Evans; there were no work cards. Usually, the children would all start out on a science activity together, but later on those finishing first would continue with some other work in progress. Miss Evans expected some written work at the end and this was usually a joint report from the children working together.

The third example is the class of a fictitious Miss Dean described by Len Ennever in an article describing good practice in primary science [in Rogers (Ed.), 1970]. Miss Dean is pictured in a class where 10 year-old children are working in groups of two or three, some on science and some on the activities. She discusses with one group how to count the number of buttercups in a field, skilfully leading them to make the suggestion of sampling the field in different places. She then talks to two boys at a workbench in the classroom. They tell her that they are making a model of a bowstring bridge, having completed one of the Severn Bridge. She agrees that it is a good idea and suggests a book that would help them. Two children trying to make an electric bell work then ask for her help. Next she passes to a table where some children have been using a work card on pendulums and want to take up the challenge on the card to find a way of making the pendulum draw the path of its own swing on paper. She pauses to listen to a child who has been writing some poetry and to encourage another who is writing about using a camera and developing a picture. Then some more critical comments are offered to a group who have been making weather recordings.

As Ennever admitted:

> This composite scene was made from actual incidents that happened as described and as near as memory serves. They did not all happen in the same classroom, nor all on the same day, with the same teacher—indeed, if they had, it would have been a very good day for that teacher. Nevertheless, the scene is none the less authentic for being intensified...

In the subsequent analysis of Miss Dean's work it becomes clear that she has a class of 40 children. Her classroom is in an old building and is fairly small, but often children work out in the corridor or in the school grounds. She moves the furniture around often to suit the activities in progress at any time. Children are not usually doing science work all at one time but sometimes a topic arises that is treated as a whole-class discussion or lesson. She has a set of work cards at hand and uses them judiciously, often when it is necessary to get several groups started at one time or to give suggestions to a group that is stuck for ideas.

Many of the ideas for the content of activities come from the children themselves, one thing leading to another, as in the case of the boys building the bridges. Miss Dean ensures by her guidance and discussions that they work 'in a scientific way' and feels this is best assured when they work on problems arising from their own questions or observations.

Questions of evaluation

Is it possible to decide if the children in the classes of Mr Carter, Miss Evans and Miss Dean are being provided with the right kinds of opportunities for learning science? Can we say that the provision for science is 'better' in one class than another? In what ways might any one of these teachers improve their children's opportunities for learning science?

To try to answer these questions there has to be some evaluation of the children's learning experiences. Evaluation is the process of gathering and using information to help in making decisions or judgements. It involves value judgements about what is relevant information for the decision in hand and what criteria are to be used in gathering and judging the information. It is by no means the objective value-free process that some might have supposed and others would wish it to be. Indeed it might well be said that understanding the nature and limitations of evaluation is essential to its usefulness. Naive assumptions as to what can be achieved by evaluation, what faith can be placed on its results, must be avoided. If this can be done then it has an important part to play in the many decisions that have to be made in teaching.

Evaluation is an essential aspect of a scientific approach to teaching science. We would do well to regard all our teaching, all the activities we provide for children as hypothesized solutions to the perpetual problem of how best to develop their process skills, ideas and attitudes. We should constantly be putting these hypotheses to the test, looking for alternatives and then testing them out. Evaluation is the means for testing our ideas about teaching.

Purposes of evaluation

The carrying out of evaluation involves collection of some information that is relevant to a decision to be made and judging it against appropriate criteria. Just what information is collected and criteria used depend partly on the nature of the problem and partly on the purpose of the evaluation. One can evaluate a new play, for example, by collecting information by going to the theatre to see it, asking opinions of others, reading reviews, etc.; this information could then be judged against different sets of criteria: Would it be suitable for a party of tourists after a hard day's sight-seeing? Would it be understood by/interest/frighten young children or very old people? Would you feel comfortable seeing it in the company of a sweet but narrow-minded older relative? Knowing the decisions to be taken and the criteria to be used would also influence the information gathered and reported about the play. For instance, one might particularly take note of verbal innuendo and jokes that play on words if suitability for foreign visitors or young children had to be judged.

The range of purposes of evaluation in education is extensive and even if we narrow down concern to evaluation within a school the list is still quite long, including some purposes which have direct effect on the school and some having little direct effect. For instance, the work in a school could be evaluated as part of a wider research into the use of certain curriculum materials or the effects of a certain kind of class organization. The findings would add to the information generally available about the materials or the organization but not necessarily have direct impact on the school. In contrast an evaluation can be carried out in a school solely for the purpose of informing decisions to be taken in that school, when the results would not necessarily have value to others unconnected with it.

Importance of criteria

As in the case of evaluation of the new play, so in the context of school evaluation, different criteria can lead to different judgements. Take the following example:

> Suppose that we apply two different sets of criteria, A and B, to the information about the class experiences of the pupils in this class. Set A is based on the notion that a satisfactory experience in learning science is that which gives pupils access to careful and correct explanations of major science concepts and their applications in scientific phenomena. Set B is based on the notion that a satisfactory experience in learning science is that which gives opportunities in developing and using the processes of science. The statements below put these two views into operational terms.

Set A	*Set B*
Pupils should have opportunity to:	Pupils should have opportunity to:
listen and pay attention to the teacher	manipulate equipment and materials at first hand
work in an orderly and quiet atmosphere	carry out investigations for themselves
be given correct information and explanations	discuss ideas with each other
see evidence of concepts in action	make and record their own observations
keep accurate records of demonstrations	interpret observations
be instructed about the interpretation of the results of demonstrations etc.	make predictions and suggest hypotheses
	devise investigations to test their predictions/hypotheses etc.

> It hardly needs to be said that the judgement, based on the same information, would be different according to whether criteria A or B were used. Similarly, another class's experiences, judged as good by criteria B, would almost certainly be seen as much less than good by criteria A.
> [quoted from Evaluating the Curriculum, A. Paisey (ed.) *The Effective Teacher*, 1983]

The choice of criteria also influences the information that is gathered. If the criterion to be applied in deciding between two reading schemes is whether the children learn to recognize more words more quickly then the information gathered might be scores on a Schonell reading test. If the children's enjoyment of reading were to be the criterion applied then quite other information would have to be gathered.

By bringing together some of the points so far made about the process of evaluation it is clear that one of the first questions to be answered is 'What is the purpose?'. When this has been answered, the next question is 'What information is required to serve this purpose?'. This question cannot be completely answered without anticipating the way in which the information will be used and identifying the criteria that will be used in judging it. It is not necessarily the case that only one set of criteria may be applied, for it may be that different people will want to be able to apply their own distinct sets of criteria (rather as in the example quoted above). Such a possibility adds to the importance of considering how the information may be used since information relevant to all criteria likely to be applied should be gathered.

Figure 17 shows the process schematically. The questions to be posed in planning the evaluation are shown in rectangles and the results of answering the questions in circles.

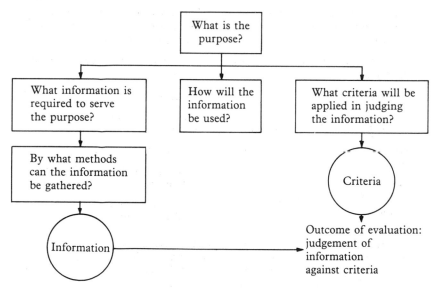

Figure 17   Process of evaluation

It is clear in this diagram that choosing methods for gathering information follows after the extent and kind of information required has been decided. The point may seem obvious, but it is often the case that instruments are chosen because they are at hand or can be easily obtained, rather than because they are really the most appropriate. This often happens where the decision is taken to administer tests to children as part of an evaluation without considering how such outcome measures will be used or whether they will provide relevant information.

Evaluation to improve opportunities for learning

Clarifying the purpose

Returning to the questions posed (p. 99) about the learning opportunities in Mr Carter's, Miss Evans' and Miss Dean's classes we will apply these ideas about evaluation in working toward some answers. The third question — in what ways might the teachers improve their children's opportunities for learning science? — is the most important and to some extent subsumes the first two questions, so we shall concentrate on this one. From it the purpose of the evaluation becomes clear: the teachers are the ones who will use the information; any action that is found to be necessary will be taken by those within the school; the information will help the teachers with decisions that have to be taken anyway (in that some activities have to be provided whether there is an evaluation or not).

Selection of criteria

Next come the three interconnected questions about the criteria and the kinds of information to be gathered. Suppose, for the purpose of illustration, we accept the criteria for selecting activities that were reached at the end of the last chapter. (This is an easy decision to take at this point since all the work of thinking through what ideals we have in the matter of children's learning opportunities has already been done.) Of course, there are many alternative sets of criteria that could be used; there is nothing absolute that recommends this set over any other. It is, however, a set that has been argued through at length so that it is consistent with a certain view of learning and any alternative set should be equally firmly based and internally coherent. The choice among different sets is then a matter of values. There is no way in which it can be proved, for instance, in the example on p. 101, that the criteria in set B 'ought' to be used in preference to those in set A. As we shall see, subjective judgements such as this are made at many points in an evaluation. (For a philosophical discussion of the concepts of values and evaluation see Straughan & Wrigley, 1980.)

The decision has been made, then, for present purposes, that the criteria to be applied are the ones discussed in Chapter 4. That is, that children's activities should:

● give opportunity for developing the science process skills of observation, interpretation of information, raising questions, hypothesizing, devising investigations, communicating

● give opportunity for developing the scientific attitudes of curiosity, respect for evidence, perseverance, flexibility, critical reflection and sensitivity to living things and the environment

● give opportunity for developing basic concepts about sight and light, hot and cold and temperature changes, hearing and producing sounds, movement and forces, breathing and air, how things behave in water, ourselves and other animals, soil and growing plants, sky, seasons and weather, materials and their uses, simple electric circuits

● be interesting and intriguing to children

● help them understand the world around them by investigation of and interaction with the objects and events they find in it

● involve the use of simple and familiar equipment that does not constitute an obstacle to studying, or draw attention away from, the phenomenon or event being investigated.

Selection of information

What information should be gathered to serve the purpose of improving opportunities to learn? Evaluators in the past have disagreed quite fundamentally on this issue. Some of the early evaluations, particularly those carried out in the United States, were based on a view of education where the outcomes of learning, that is, what children do or do not know, what they can or cannot do, are assumed to give the only rational basis for deciding the quality of classroom experiences:

> However, since educational objectives are essentially changes in human beings, that is, the objectives aimed at are to produce certain desirable changes in the behavior patterns of the student, then evaluation is the process for determining the degree to which these changes in behavior are actually taking place.
> This conception of evaluation has two important aspects. In the first place, it implies that evaluation must appraise the behavior of students since it is change in these behaviors which is sought in education. In the second place, it implies

that evaluation must involve more than a single appraisal at any one time since to see whether change has taken place, it is necessary to make an appraisal at an early point and other appraisals at later points to identify changes that may be occurring.
(Tyler, 1949; p. 106)

So Tyler advocated testing ('appraising behaviour of students') before and after children have experienced certain activities to see whether expected changes in their performance are found. Decisions have to be made about what the expected changes are and the level of change that would be considered acceptable. If the changes were found to be below that level then the learning activities would be judged to have been inadequate.

This may sound a reasonable approach to evaluation at first; it is attractively logical (we do wish to change children's skills, ideas and attitudes: all things which influence their behaviour); it is neatly scientific, too, using measurement of a dependent variable (knowledge) to test the effect of an independent variable (children's classroom experiences). What it ignores is that education concerns people, not objects that can be treated and tested under controlled conditions in a scientific laboratory. Learning does not depend only on what activities are provided, but on how the individual interacts with them and on what sense they make of them in the light of their previous experience and ideas. Furthermore some of the changes in behaviour that we hope to bring about are long term, difficult to assess and quantify, so the 'instruments' needed for measuring the dependent variable would be hard to find.

There is another serious set of objections to the Tyler approach to evaluation, which concerns the other question which has to be considered at this point in an evaluation: 'How will the information be used?'. Even supposing that appropriate and valid tests were available and were used, the results would indicate only that certain outcomes were or were not found; this information would have little value for the purpose of improving the learning activities. Tyler makes the assumption that there is consistency between the 'treatment' and the 'outcomes'. The link is provided by the learning objectives which are stated in terms of changes in children's behaviour and used for devising the activities being evaluated. In the context of curriculum materials development it could be argued, perhaps, that this assumption is justified, though many would disagree. In the context of evaluation of the existing curriculum, however, one of the main purposes is to question whether opportunities for certain kinds of learning are actually being provided, not to assume their existence. Evaluation thus has to be more diagnostic than is possible if it relies on information about outcomes alone.

Arguments such as these (and experience of applying the 'measurement of objectives' approach and finding it wanting, see e.g. Harlen, 1975) have led to a series of alternative approaches to evaluation being proposed. The most useful for the present purpose is an approach depending on information about the classroom processes rather than the outcomes, or products. To put it another way, the evaluation is investigating the extent to which the independent variable (the provision of intended learning experiences) is in operation and is not concerned with the dependent variable (outcomes or changes in children's behaviour). This is not to deny the value of finding out what knowledge and abilities children have, but to acknowledge that there is not really any point in doing this until there is some confidence that related learning opportunities are being provided. It would be as ridiculous as testing pupils to see if they had learned to swim regardless of whether they had ever had a chance to learn. We can still agree with Tyler that the purpose of education is to change children's behaviour but disagree that this means that useful information for evaluation of education has to concern these behavioural changes only.

At the same time it must be acknowledged that there are equally strong arguments against an approach to evaluation which depends wholly on information about classroom processes and ignores the products. For a start the whole notion of 'learning opportunity' implies an identification of the expected learning and it would seem ingenuous to make such judgements without establishing that 'opportunity to learn X' can lead to 'learning X'. Thus at some stage it is necessary to relate process and product. If we ignore one or the other then assumptions are being made that may not be justified.

A second point, is that obtaining the information about classroom processes is not easy, either for a teacher or for an outsider. The teacher is a central figure in the very transactions being examined and thus experiences both practical and psychological difficulty in gathering information that is not so biased by subjective judgement as to be useless, or even dangerous. An observer, who must be an 'outsider' to the classroom climate, experiences different but equally serious problems in attempting to gather information that is not distorted by his or her presence and provides an adequate sample of the variety of activities going on.

A third, related, point is the difficulty of deciding exactly what information about classroom processes is required and what would constitute an adequate sample of the events being evaluated. There is no well-established methodology for collecting this kind of information, as there is, for instance, for assessing children's learning. Moreover, it is not possible to know all about the activities going on and any selection is biased by the judgements and eye of the beholder.

So there are both advantages and disadvantages to the gathering of information about classroom processes and about learning products. If one is selected as a focus, then inevitably it turns out that information is needed about the other as well. In the first instance, though, the emphasis to be placed on one or the other should be decided by reference to the purpose of the evaluation. If the main purpose is to monitor the curriculum to see if progress is being maintained as expected, an emphasis on learning products (given that suitable instruments are available) may be appropriate, especially if there is no intention to make immediate curriculum changes based on the information. But if the purpose is to investigate the curriculum to improve it, however, the balance would be in favour of information about classroom processes. It then becomes appropriate to find out if the learning is taking place after we have taken steps to ensure that learning opportunity is there. Consistent with this order of priorities the subject of the assessment of children's learning is left until later in this book and this chapter focuses on the way evaluation can help to improve the provision for learning to take place. It is not being assumed that providing opportunity necessarily means that learning will follow, but it is assumed that if there is no opportunity then intended learning is unlikely and there is little point in looking for effects of non-existent causes.

For the purpose that we are considering here it seems most appropriate to gather information as directly as possible about children's experiences in the classroom. This means examining the content, the way children interact with it, the teacher's role, the class organization, the resources used, and considering to what extent all of these match the children's abilities and interests. The answer to the question of how the information will be used is that it will be compared against the criteria. This can be done both at the level of each activity, to see the extent to which it contributes opportunities for various kinds of learning, and over longer periods of time to see the effect of a combination of different experiences. Later we shall see, through examples, what this means in practice. But first there is the question of how the information can be gathered.

Methods of gathering information about classroom events

The aim is to describe the activities as fully as possible. This cannot be done in complete detail, for the record would then probably equal the actual events in length, multiplied by the number of children in the class. It is necessary to take a sample; to collect several different kinds of information during a series of short periods is preferable to an extended and perhaps repetitive record of a limited kind. The sampling depends on whether:

- the main interest is in the class as a whole or one group or one child
- various groups or individuals are working on similar or different activities at one time
- science activities are discrete and well defined or are integral parts of topic work.

The circumstances of particular cases will decide the convenient and useful sample of activities to be considered. For this sample of activities we need some record to be kept of what the children did, what they felt about it, what the teacher did, what the teacher felt about it, etc.

The methods that can be used to gather this information are clearly more limited if a teacher is trying to evaluate the events in the classroom single-handed. In such a case the methods that can be used include the following:

Making notes during lessons These can only be the briefest jottings made at the time and should be written up more fully immediately after the lesson. They can include factual details, such as what each observed group did, how many children the teacher spoke to, for how long, what difficulties arose, whether they were overcome satisfactorily, to what extent the teacher's intentions for the lesson were realized.

Collecting any worksheet, textbook or other written material used by pupils These would be analysed later to determine the kinds of mental and physical activity they encouraged or allowed. It is important to note at the time the extent to which children used them, how they followed or departed from the activities offered, etc.

Collecting any written notes, drawings or other products made by the children These provide some record of what the children did and may also indicate whether there has been any productive thinking or, in contrast, show where time has been spent in straight copying from books or cards. Analysing pupils' work in this way is quite different from 'marking' it and might well be supplemented by a discussion with the pupils.

Discussing their work with children A quiet moment after a lesson might be used to talk to two or three children about what they had been doing, when the equipment and notes are still at hand. The teacher has to try to turn into an interviewer, to listen and encourage the children to talk about their work, what they understood and did not understand of it, what they found interesting, what was easy, how they arrived at any result or solution. The teacher can either make notes immediately afterwards or tape record the conversation.

Tape recording A tape recorder is a most useful piece of equipment for the teacher attempting any self-evaluation. Its use should be carefully planned, however, for too much recorded tape will be a deterrent to the use of recorded information. It is better to record two or three samples of 5 minutes' conversation with a group than to be faced with 60 minutes of tape and no basis for sampling from it. However, when recording pupils' conversations without the teacher present there is a case for placing the tape recorder near a group and letting it run. The children soon forget its presence if attention is not drawn to it by continued switching on and off. In listening to the tape it is then necessary to listen consciously for 5 minute periods, running on 10 minutes or so between each section.

The methods just discussed are the main ones available to the teacher working single-handed. If help with gathering information can be given by a colleague or a visitor then these same methods can be used with less effort and other methods can be added. Often a pair of teachers in a school can arrange to help each other in this matter. Such a reciprocal situation has many advantages; each then knows from experience the problems of being the observer and the teacher and will interpret the information accordingly. More important, however, is that when the purpose, process and findings of the class observations are shared between observer and teacher the anxiety that usually accompanies being observed while teaching is dispelled.

The main additional methods of gathering information that can be used by an observer but not by the teacher are systematic and detailed observation of pupils and teacher. These can range from a simple record of the movements of the teacher or a few selected children (made on a plan of the classroom) to a structured observation schedule for recording previously defined behaviours or events.

An example of such co-operative evaluation took place in the context of an inservice course in primary science where teachers were organized in groups of four all from different schools. Each week the four met in one school and observed the lesson of the teacher in that school. The next week they visited another member's school, so each was observed in turn. The three observers

Class: ....   Topic: ....

No. in group: ....   Date: ....

Observation of group (group work)	1-2	3-4	5-6	7-8	9-10	11-12	13-14	15-16	17-18	19-20	21-22	23-24	25-26	27-28	29-30	31-32	33-34	35-36	37-38	39-40	41-42	43-44	45-46
Relating to task																							
Making observations																							
Using measuring instruments																							
Handling other materials/equipment																							
Interpreting observations (pattern finding)																							
Suggesting explanations (hypothesizing)																							
Posing question																							
Proposing investigation																							
Proposing procedure (variable control, measurement)																							
Recording																							
Reading worksheet																							
Relating to teacher																							
Asking about topic																							
Asking for help/about procedure																							
Answering teacher's questions (fact/recall)																							
Answering teacher's questions (ideas)																							
Reporting/explaining actions																							
Listening to teacher																							
Relating to each other																							
Organizing task (co-operatively)																							
Organizing task (argument)																							
Talk about topic/task																							
Talk about record/report																							
Non-topic/task talk																							
Listening/responding to others' ideas																							
Independent working																							
Number actively/purposefully working																							
Other (specify)																							

Figure 18   Schedule for observing a group of children involved in science activities

had well-defined tasks to carry out. One observed one group of children, using the schedule shown in Figure 18. Another made a plan of the classroom and recorded the movements of the teacher and at the same time made regular assessments of the proportion of children appearing to be working purposefully, noting the possible reasons for non-task activity. The third observed the teacher, recording on a schedule similar in design to the one used for the group of pupils, the verbal and non-verbal behaviour of the teacher.

The observation schedules asked for a record to be made for successive 2-minute intervals throughout the lesson. If any of the listed behaviours was observed during a 2-minute interval it was ticked, whether it occurred once or several times. At the end of the 2 minutes the observer moved to the next column. Observers were instructed constantly to scan the list to remind themselves of the behaviours to look for and to add any of significance which were not included. However, the schedules were not designed to record everything happening, only those behaviours which were of interest for the purpose of the evaluation.

Analysing the information; applying the criteria

The use of several of the methods just discussed can result in a mass of varied and apparently disparate information. Some of it will need further analysis before it can be used in making evaluative judgements. The collection of worksheets and pupils' records provides information in this unanalysed form, as do any tape recordings of conversations. By contrast, the observation schedules contain information that has already been 'filtered' since the criteria were used in deciding what behaviours to record and what to ignore.

To analyse the 'unfiltered' information it has to be reviewed to find out whether children did any of the things that are suggested by the criteria on page 104. Some of the items on that list are not sufficiently specific for this purpose. There may well be differences of opinion, for instance, about what in practice is meant by opportunity for 'interpretation of information' or 'critical reflection'. It is helpful therefore to expand some items and list observable actions or occupations that are agreed to be indicators of particular opportunities. For example, the following 'indicators' of the process skills have been found useful:

Observation

- Using the senses (as many as safe and appropriate) to gather information
- Identifying differences between similar objects or events
- Identifying similarities between different objects or events
- Noticing fine details that are relevant to an investigation
- Recognizing the order in which sequenced events take place
- Looking for patterns that may exist in observations

Interpretation of information

- Putting various pieces of information (from direct observations or secondary sources) together and inferring something from them
- Using patterns or relations in information, measurements or observations to make predictions
- Identifying trends or relations in information
- Realizing the difference between a conclusion that fits all the evidence and an inference that goes beyond it

Hypothesizing

- Attempting to explain observations or relations in terms of some principle or concept
- Applying concepts or knowledge gained in one situation to help understanding or solve a problem in another
- Recognizing that there can be more than one possible explanation of an event
- Realizing the need to test explanations by gathering more evidence

Raising questions

- Asking questions which lead to enquiry
- Asking questions for information
- Asking questions based on hypotheses
- Realizing that they can find out answers to some of their questions by their own investigation
- Putting questions into a testable form
- Recognizing that some questions cannot be answered by enquiry

Devising investigations

- Deciding what equipment, material, etc., are needed for an investigation
- Identifying what is to change or be changed when different observations or measurements are made

- Identifying what variables are to be kept the same for a fair test
- Identifying what is to be measured or compared
- Considering beforehand how the measurements, comparisons, etc., are to be used to solve the problem
- Deciding the order in which steps should be taken in the investigation

Communication

- Using writing or talking as a medium for sorting out ideas or linking one idea to another
- Listening to others' ideas and responding to them
- Keeping notes of actions or observations
- Displaying results appropriately using graphs, tables, charts, etc.
- Reporting events systematically and clearly
- Using sources of information

The precise content of each list of indicators would inevitably vary according to the group working on it (another area where subjective judgements are unavoidable in evaluation), but it is worth accepting this variation, for the value of taking part in the thinking required to generate the lists would be missed if lists written by others were adopted without such thought.

When detailed expansions of each item are available the review of the activities in a work card, for example, can be carried out and summarized by using a grid such as in Figure 19. The division of the activity into subsections is based on natural divisions relating to the type of activity rather than on the basis of time intervals. So, for instance, the subdivisions for the work cards shown on pages 96 and 97 might be as shown in Figure 19.

	Activities						
	Hardness tests			Big, little, light & heavy			
	Test	Recording	Conclusion	1	2	3	etc.
Observation	✓			✓	✓	✓	
Interpretation		✓			✓		
- - - -							
Curiosity							
Respect for evidence							
- - - -							
Concepts (write in)	Materials vary in hardness			Volume and mass	Volume and shape	Density	

Figure 19 Evaluation of Mr. Carter's Workcards.

A grid such as Figure 19 can be used to assess the potential of an activity before it has been carried out. If the activity has been carried out then additional information can be added from other sources to record what actually happened, rather than what was intended, and to add data about the children's reactions, the sense they made of the activities and the suitability of the equipment. This information may come from analysis of the children's notes, writing, drawings or other records of the activity, from talking to them and, if possible, from observing them while the activity was being carried out. out.

When all the information available about a sample of activities during a sample period of time has been brought together, applying the criteria is a matter of sifting through it systematically to see to what extent each one was met. This could be done by taking each subdivision of an activity and all information relating to it, including the teacher's interventions and relevant information about the class organization, and then ticking each criterion which is met. Some measure of the extent of meeting the criteria could then be provided by the number of ticks across all the activities. The disadvantage here is that the interaction of one activity with a subsequent one may be ignored. The alternative procedure, avoiding this disadvantage, is to take the criteria one at a time and to scan across all the activities, noting how often it is met.

These procedures may seem rather rough and subjective, as indeed they are, but in practice greater refinement is not needed for the purpose being considered. It is usually the case that the areas where there is a gap between what we would like to be happening (as represented by the criteria) and what is happening (evident in the information gathered) are large and obvious. This becomes clear as we now return to the classes of Mr Carter, Miss Evans and Miss Dean and apply the criteria to the information we have about the science activities of their pupils.

Diagnostic evaluation of learning opportunity

We have not given enough details in the earlier brief sketches of the three classes to provide a basis for an evaluation and it is necessary to add information at this point. We shall also have to make assumptions which may do less than justice to the teachers in question. Such assumptions would not be made if the evaluations were being carried out in reality instead of for the sake of illustration as is the case here, for it is the point of evaluation to make decisions on the basis of evidence and to withhold judgement if relevant evidence is not available.

Mr Carter's class

In this case let us assume that an analysis has been carried out of all 36 work cards used during the year and that the results echo the analysis of the two examples given on pages 96 and 97. For the results of this analysis we can conclude that as far as the content of activities is concerned most children will have had opportunity to develop some ideas relating to:

- sight and light
- hearing and producing sounds
- the weather
- properties of materials
- simple circuits.

Science is confined to the 1-hourly session per week and no noteworthy opportunities for science-concept development occurred outside these lessons. So we can conclude that during the year the children's experiences at school did not touch on ideas about:

- hot and cold and temperature changes
- movement and forces
- breathing and air
- how things behave in water
- ourselves and other animals
- soil and growing plants
- uses of materials
- sun and seasons.

By looking at the opportunities for process skill and attitude development the analysis of the cards show opportunities for:

- observation
- interpretation of information
- communication
- perseverance.

Before deciding that these were the only skills and attitudes involved we should look at other evidence. Perhaps the children were raising questions, hypothesizing, etc., in their group work; perhaps Mr Carter questioned them on the basis of their conclusions and encouraged them to reconsider evidence that did not fit; perhaps they went beyond the work on the cards and devised their own investigations. These matters could be decided by classroom observation, looking at the children's records and listening to any tape recordings of group discussions. As indicated briefly on p. 96 (and we will have to assume that the evidence woud bear this out) Mr Carter restricts his interventions in the work of the groups to helping them set up the apparatus properly, interpreting the instructions on the cards and general management of the activities. He never asks children to give their ideas about possible reasons for what they have found and discourages investigations 'on the side'. The children have accepted that the point of their activity is to complete the work on the card.

Having scanned all the evidence about the interactions between pupils, materials and teacher we therefore find little sign of opportunity to develop the following skills and attitudes:

● raising questions
● hypothesizing
● devising investigations
● curiosity
● respect for evidence
● flexibility
● critical reflection
● sensitivity to living things and the environment.

Were the activities interesting to the children? For this question we need information about the children's reactions and feelings that come from talking to them and watching them at work. At first they were intrigued by doing things, using equipment and getting results (all the activities usually 'worked'). The novelty did wear off, however, and there was no attempt on the part of Mr Carter to awaken interest in the activities on a card; he would have had difficulty organizing to do this, of course, when a dozen or so different activities might be involved at one time. He had to rely on the intrinsic interest in the activity and though this seemed to operate for some children some of the time it was clearly ineffective for others, particularly in the second half of the year.

Did the activities help the children understand the world around them through investigation and interaction with objects in it? Again the answer is mixed and depends on close observation of the children and discussion with them. Certainly, the children were all busy interacting with objects and materials, but for some the connection between the 'world in the box' and the real world was not clear. For example, two children who had completed the 'Hardness tests' card seemed to have no idea of whether or not the metal of a drill that made a hole in some concrete was harder than the concrete. It seemed that although the ideas were in theory relevant to the understanding of things around them the children had not made them part of their own thinking, to use in making sense of everyday happenings.

Was the equipment familiar and simple? For the most part this was the case. Mr Carter had used considerable ingenuity in selecting everyday objects. However, he was apologetic about having to improvise and was looking forward to the day when he could replace all the bits and pieces with 'proper' apparatus.

Miss Evans' class

Most of the science work of Miss Evans' class took place in the term when the class topic was 'communication'. Although in other topics children were handling materials (Red Indian feathers and head-dresses, for example), making models (of Victorian houses) and collecting information (about the occupations of people in the town a century before) the opportunities for scientific investigation in such activities were not developed. In the communication topic there were regular points where Miss Evans would bring the whole class together to talk about something new, suggested by herself or some of the children. The preparation for the visit of a blind person was a class discussion and work on the string telephones began this way. So all the children had some encounter with activities involving ideas about:

- sight and light
- hearing and sound
- movement and forces
- ourselves and other animals

but little of the kind of investigative work that could have developed ideas in the other concept areas (listed on p. 104).

The way of working that Miss Evans employed was to introduce a topic in a class discussion, invite lots of ideas about what could be done (about how to make a string telephone, for example, and how to improve it) and then leave the children to decide how to tackle the questions raised. Observation of the children in groups and discussion with them afterwards showed that they did listen to each others' ideas and were prepared to try out various suggestions. Each was keen to be sure that their own idea was given a fair trial and so, perhaps not altogether for scientific reasons, they showed a respect for evidence.

The process skills and attitudes being used were the following:
- observation
- interpretation of information
- raising questions
- devising investigations
- communication
- curiosity
- respect for evidence
- perseverance
- flexibility
- sensitivity to living things

The missing items were 'hypothesizing' and 'critical reflection'. The observations of Miss Evans' interventions in the group work showed that she accepted and praised descriptive answers from the children and rarely pressed them to speculate about reasons for what they found out. Also, there were few discussions, either with groups or the whole class, where the children were encouraged to review their work critically. When the active parts of the work had been finished the results were displayed but not discussed; instead another activity was begun.

As to the other criteria, there was evidence that the children were interested in what they were doing at all times. They saw their science activities as exciting and liked being able to decide about how to do things. In discussion they were prepared to suggest what hearing aids did and how fish and whales might use sound for communication. So they did seem to be taking something from their activities to use in making sense of other things around them. Most of the equipment they used was simple, apart from the computer and Morse code buzzer. The use of the computer was not a problem since they knew what it was being used for and indeed it was a solution to a problem that they had posed: how to make some sounds of different pitch in a way that would make a fair test of people's hearing. The Morse code buzzer was a different matter; it had not been the children's idea to use it and they were not clear about what it was for. Introduced in the way it was it appeared to be a solution to a problem that they really did not appreciate. Consequently, it was little more than a game for them and some useful opportunities for learning, for instance about making and breaking an electric circuit, were missed.

Miss Dean's class

The activities present in Miss Dean's class at the time the 'snapshot' was taken provided opportunities for some children to develop ideas about the variety of plants, forces and movement, materials and their uses and electric circuits. If we were to make a detailed analysis of the work of one group it is likely that this would be more limited. It is possible, for example, that the boys working on the bridge models had spent 6 or 7 weeks on these, so their opportunities for developing ideas would have been very different from those of children who probably spent a similar time investigating the numbers of different kinds of plants in the school field. We don't know the extent to which Miss Dean kept a record of the experiences of individual children and made sure that they encountered a wider range of content. This is clearly important if Miss Dean's way of working is not to end in individual children having a rather 'unbalanced diet' of science activities. It requires the co-operation of other teachers too, since 'balance' for any one child would have to be created over a number of years.

From the information we have about Miss Dean's work it seems likely that the children have opportunity for developing all the skills and attitudes indicated in the criteria. Indeed it appears to be that her teaching approach is designed to make children think about what they are doing, to use their past experience in working out how to tackle problems and to improve their methods of investigation by being self-critical. The opportunities for process skill and attitude development were therefore similar for all children regardless of the content of their activities.

How might the opportunities for learning in these classes be improved?

This is the main question that an evaluation of the kind described should be able to answer. Even with the limited and somewhat speculative information we have been able to use here, certain quite severe gaps in the provision for learning science in each of the classes have become clear.

In Mr Carter's class it is evident that despite the orderly busyness of children working through the cards, there is little hard thinking, puzzling and probing going on. There is no feeling of children wringing information out of the things around them by their own physical and mental effort. The spread of concepts involved in the activities was limited, but this was the result of a deliberate decision to compensate for earlier imbalance. It could easily be changed by a different selection of cards. This would not, however, have gone very far toward increasing the amount of learning in the science lessons. The children's opportunities to use and develop process skills and scientific attitudes were too limited; there was plenty of doing, but not enough thinking going on. It seems that this was partly because the activities were too constrained, self-contained, cut off from the rest of the children's experiences both in school and outside. Mr Carter's own role in their activities was as a provider of equipment and instructions. He may have fully expected that the written words would sufficiently stimulate the children's interest in the activities and provoke their thinking; so he may not have seen his role as touching on these things. The evidence of the evaluation shows that this expectation was not well founded. Improving opportunities for learning in this class might well involve some reorganization of the timetable, the less frequent use of the cards and boxes, the review of the cards to see if they could be rephrased to involve the children in using more process skills, the introduction of different activities and the reconsideration of the teacher's role.

In Miss Evans' class the range of concept areas encountered was also limited, but she had not chosen this deliberately as had Mr Carter; it just happened. There was in fact no overall policy in the school on this matter and little consideration was given to the ideas children had already begun to develop at a certain point and how further development might be ensured. It seems likely that development of process skills had been given little consideration either. Miss Evans tended to accept everything the children offered by way of observations and suggestions which meant she played a very limited part in developing their skills. The evidence of the evaluation might well help her to realize that she should be asking for more detailed observations where appropriate, helping children to check their ideas against all the available evidence, making them think of other explanations than the first one to occur to them, encouraging them to make suggestions of how an investigation might be improved.

There were messages from the evaluation for Miss Dean also. Her usual way of organizing the activities, with children working for much of the time on independent projects, not only made it very difficult for her to keep track of their progress but also made the sharing and exchange of ideas and experiences a rare event. She was not taking advantage of the value to children's thinking of discussion and exposure to others' ideas. Some improvement in the learning opportunities in her class might therefore be made by introducing variation in organization of activities aimed at pooling ideas about a shared problem and ways of tackling it.

Since perfection in teaching is unattainable there is always value for any teacher in evaluating the opportunities for learning in the classroom. Most teachers are constantly getting some feedback about their work and reflecting on changes that should be made; evaluation as described here is just a way of doing this more systematically. It can help a general feeling of dissatisfaction turn into a realization of particular aspects of provision which need attention. It does not, of course, give a prescription for what to do that will necessarily improve the situation. Something has to be tried; if the effect of the change is evaluated we learn more from the experience. But not all changes need rely on trial and error. There is a great deal to learn from others' experience and it is the purpose of the next part of this book to present and review ideas about classroom practice.

CHAPTER 6

PROVIDING OPPORTUNITIES FOR LEARNING SCIENCE

Introduction

The notion of 'opportunity to learn' is complex and its translation into practice difficult to confirm. The most carefully planned and potentially exciting activity can fail to engage the children it was designed to fascinate, whereas the unplanned or apparently peripheral event seizes their attention. Teachers who drain their energy taking children abroad know the feeling well; surrounded by the grandeur of Versailles the children appear more interested in their collections of metro tickets or whether they can take one of the paving stones in a single stride. In school it is often the same; our judgements about how to find the key into children's minds can never be certain. Even though, in the classroom, we narrow the range of tasks to focus on the ideas and skills we intend the children to develop, in the end the focus they adopt is their decision. Grouped round an aquarium to look at and discuss the way the fish, snails and other animals move, there will be some who take away more ideas about reflection at the water surface than about the living things beneath it.

Most activities that enable children to observe and investigate phenomena which are real and have relevance to understanding their world provide opportunities for learning many and various things. To focus closely on one selected aspect, and artificially reduce the distraction of others, the activity would have to be stripped of the features that make it relevant and real. As mentioned in Chapter 4, this is not a profitable route to take, for any ideas the children may develop from such 'cleaned up' content are unrelated to making sense of more messy reality. So it is better to accept, and take into account in planning, that the content of science activities provides multiple opportunities for learning; which ones are seized by children will depend on other circumstances relating to the children themselves and the teacher's role in bringing the children into contact with the objects and events to study.

What this means is that the provision of activities which meet the criteria discussed in Chapters 2 and 4, and brought together on p. 104 of Chapter 5, is a necessary but not sufficient condition for 'opportunity to learn'. In particular, whether the children are able to use scientific process skills and bring scientific attitudes to bear will determine what they learn. This depends both on the way the children interact with the subject matter (reading, listening, first-hand investigation or watching a demonstration) and on the teacher's role. The three main determinants of learning opportunity are, therefore:

● subject matter or content
● type of interaction with content
● teacher's role.

These make different proportional contributions to the development of ideas, process skills and attitudes, roughly estimated in Figure 20.

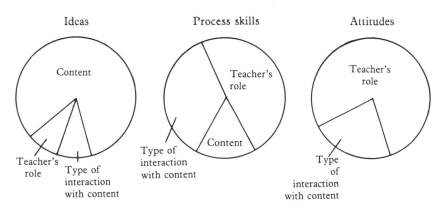

Figure 20

The development of attitudes can take place with almost any content and depends very strongly on the example and encouragement of the teacher. Content determines opportunity for process-skill development to some extent; some subject matter lends itself more to study by careful observation and recording, whereas other provides more possibility for experiment. Opportunity to develop ideas depends largely but not entirely on content. What is learned about, say, a simple circuit, will depend on whether a child is investigating one himself, watching others or reading about it in a book and on whether a teacher asks him to say what he thinks is happening and find evidence to support or change his views.

Opportunity to learn is implied in the concept of 'matching', which we will look at in the next section. The central section of this chapter is concerned with the general description of activities likely to provide opportunities for learning for children at different points in development. In the last section we return to the problem of matching for the individual child, which is rather a different matter from the general provision of activities at an appropriate level.

Matching

Although there have been some different views expressed about 'matching' and its likely effect on learning [for instance, Neville Bennett once suggested that learning takes place better when there is some mismatching (TES 3 November 1978)], it is now generally agreed that matching is a good thing and, by definition, a condition that promotes learning. Indeed Bennett and co-workers, endorsing this view, have since carried out a valuable study of matching in infants' classes from which they concluded that 'More than half of the observed tasks were mismatched... Mismatching appeared to have important immediate consequences in terms of lost opportunities and limiting experiences for high attainers and confusion for low attainer' (Bennett *et al.*, 1984).

The meaning of matching was made clear in the Plowden Report:

> The teacher's task is to provide an environment and opportunities which are sufficiently challenging for children and yet not so difficult as to be outside their reach. There has to be the right mixture of the familiar and the novel, the right match to the stage of learning the child has reached.
> (DES, 1967; para. 533)

Ten years later the HMI survey of primary schools presented the first attempt ever made to quantify the extent of matching for 7-, 9- and 11-year-olds. There were clear trends in their findings (DES, 1978) that were presented for different areas of the curriculum and for children in three broad ability bands (as judged by their teachers). The greatest degree of matching was found in reading, mathematics, writing and physical education; the least was found in art and craft, history, geography and science, the last taking the lowest position in every table. The less-able groups were better matched in all subjects than the children of average ability who in turn were better matched than the more-able groups.

If the results for 7 year-olds given by Bennett *et al.* (1984) for number and language are compared with those given by HMI for 7 year-olds, there is a considerable discrepancy. Bennett's team found a much lower level of matching, much of it arising from children being given tasks judged to be too easy. They also reported a difference between their own judgements and those of the teachers as to the degree of match. Half of the activities judged by teachers to be a match were thought too easy by the researchers. If indeed the HMI, like the teachers in Bennett's study, overestimated the matching (by as much as 50–60%), then the results for science begin to look even worse. In less than one in five classes would there have been science activities which matched the average and more able children, with only a slightly higher proportion for the less-able groups.

It is perhaps not necessary to dwell on the possible reasons for this state of affairs that have been proposed [e.g. by Harlen in Richards (ed.) 1980]. More important is to consider what can be done to alleviate it. First, it must be clear what is meant by matching. Then the practical implications of having matching as a desired aim have to be worked out.

Matching is not giving children more of what they can already do. Therefore it isn't valid to take success on an activity as an indication of matching. A child can have completed the activity successfully without having advanced his ideas or done more than used skills already practised. The reason why matching is more common with less-able children may well be that the mismatch is usually one of overestimation and so the signs of mismatch are visible in failure or inadequate performance. When performance is satisfactory it is not easy to distinguish a match from a mismatch due to underchallenging the child.

The essence of matching is progress; the child makes some advance in his ideas, skills, attitudes. This advance may only be made by experiencing some initial failure: a first idea that does not work and is replaced by another that fits better, some observations that have to be made more carefully, plans that have to be reconsidered and so on. If these initial difficulties are overcome, resulting in learning, then the activity did provide the opportunity for some advance in thinking. Matching means challenging children to take a step forward. But of course the step has to be of the right order; not too big so that they stumble and not too small so that they are marking time. Just what is the right size depends on many features particular to the individual child and to the activity; it can never be accurately predicted.

The fact that we cannot provide prescriptions for the succession of steps of the right size to ensure matching at all stages of learning is not a reason for abandoning the attempt altogether. We can do better, too, than to avoid the gross errors of expecting 8 year-olds to understand the particulate nature of matter and 11 year-olds the theory of relativity. By studying the children and using the findings of others who have studied their learning we can define the boundaries of the kinds of experiences that are likely to provide genuine opportunities for learning for children as they grow and develop. Within these broad boundaries the 'fine tuning' to match individual children requires a strategy for adjusting and adapting the demands of an activity to provide the steps that individuals may be able to take.

This strategy is something we shall return to later, after considering in more general terms the broad bounds of the experiences that provide opportunities to learn for children from 5 to 13 years. In taking four overlapping age ranges, 5–7, 7–9, 9–11 and 11–13 years, there is no implication that 'stage' is being equated with age for individual children. We are dealing for the moment at a general level, ignoring the individual differences among children that will be considered later.

Learning opportunities for infants (5–7 year-olds)

The mental characteristics of young children have been the subject of much study by Piaget and others. Whether one believes that these characteristics cluster into well-defined 'stages' between which there is a distinct qualitative change, or whether the change is regarded more as a continuous development, makes no difference to the accuracy of the description of children's thinking at various points. Both research and teachers' experience confirms the broad features of the thinking of 5, 6 and 7 year-olds. Those that are most relevant to scientific development can be summarized as follows:

● They cannot 'think through' actions (unless these are very familiar ones, often performed) but have to carry them out in practice. This makes for severe restrictions on reasoning. For example, if they pour water from one container to another of a different shape in which its quantity may appear to have changed they will affirm that it has changed. They cannot imagine the water being poured back and therefore realize that its quantity must have remained the same.

● They take but one point of view of events, their own. They do not take another's point of view or realize that a different view point can make things look different, unless they physically move to the other position. Even then they may not realize that it is a different view of the same thing.

● They focus on one aspect of an object or situation at a time. Thus their judgement of the amount of water in the container takes into account one dimension, probably the height the liquid reaches, not the height *and* the width of the container.

● They tend not to relate one event to another when they encounter an unfamiliar sequence of events. They are likely to remember the first and last stages in the sequence, but not the ones in between. For example, a 6 year-old, after watching sand run through a timer, was reported as being able to draw the timer and its contents at the beginning and end, but not in between. Given five drawings of the timer as the sand was running out he could not arrange them in sequence (Match & Mismatch, 1977).

● The results of actions not yet carried out cannot be anticipated. Whereas, older children could work out, for instance, that if they increase their size of step they will take fewer steps across the room, the 5 or 6 year-old will have to get up and do it.

There are clear consequences of these points for the sorts of activities the children will be able to learn from. The children's limitations are obvious. It will be no use expecting them to see patterns in events until they have begun to connect events in a sequence; the notion of a cause being related to an effect is still developing, so the idea of separating two or more variables to test the effect of each separately is still a long way off; their limited experience will mean that their ideas tend to be based on few very specific instances, selectively observed, having little explanatory power as far as new experience is concerned.

Equally clear are the indications for the kinds of experience that are appropriate at this age. Action and thinking are closely related to each other, reflecting their even closer identification at an earlier, preschool, stage. Thus infants need to be able to act on things, to explore, manipulate, describe, sort and group them. First-hand experience and exploration of objects in their immediate environment is the chief aim of teaching science to infants.

The content of the activities is therefore found in what is around the children and suitable topics start from observation of everyday events. For example, the Science 5/13 unit *Early Experiences* suggests a number of activities to do with:

Sunny-day things	Doing things	Cooking things
Rainy-day things	Listening to things	Looking after things
Writing things	Growing things	Looking at things

Similar groupings of activities are proposed by Romola Showell in her book *Teaching Science to Infants*. For each topic she provides a web which is admirably restrained (so much more helpful than those that show how a topic on food can include potato prints and land reclamation if you really stretch it!); for example, see Figure 21.

PLAYING WITH MIRRORS

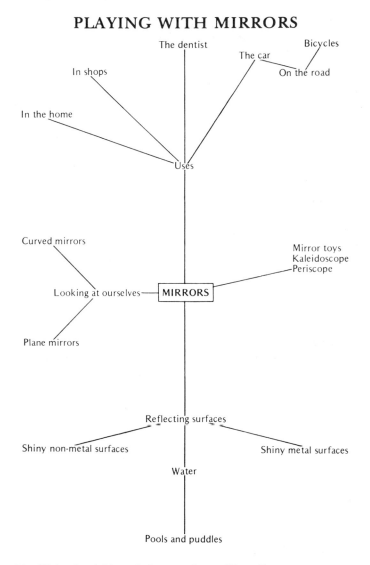

Figure 21   Web of activities relating to mirrors (Showell, 1979; p. 60)

All the items in this web are ones children will have encountered in their daily lives. The purpose of studying them in the classroom is to enable children to observe more carefully (when you look at yourself in the mirror do you see yourself how others see you?), link one observation with another (can you see a reflection in other surfaces besides mirrors?), try to make predictions (how many images will you see with two mirrors?), solve problems (how to write a word so that it can be read through a mirror) and develop ideas that help the understanding of events (why a dentist puts a mirror in your mouth). Romola Showell's book provides many ideas for children's activities and useful lists of books and equipment for each topic, though the teacher's role is not made explicit.

We shall deal with the teacher's role in the planning and execution of activities in the next chapter; our concern here is with the overall nature of activities and their goals. Starting from the familiar the content should gradually introduce new experiences to the children (making a periscope with mirrors, for example). Though the main emphasis in terms of process skills used will be on observation, raising questions and discussion, there should be a gradually increasing demand in the use of these and development of other skills. When the children have had plenty of experience of acting on things and using the skills they already have with success, they will become able to replace some action by thought and they are then on the way to rational thinking and the development of higher-level process skills.

The children's activities should therefore include plenty of:

● looking, handling, using other senses on material collected and displayed in the classroom
● watching, standing and staring at things in their natural state in the immediate neighbourhood
● collecting things and sorting them
● trying things out
● making things, particularly models, that in some way 'work'
● taking things apart and reconstructing them
● talking about what they have observed and sometimes recording it in pictures and models and in words when they can
● discussing their ideas and trying to think of explanations for things they have noticed.

During these activities the process skills they will be using and developing are the following.

● Observation: ordering observations, grouping, interpreting observations (simple predictions)

● Raising questions: asking all kinds of questions
● Communicating: discussing, making records (painting, modelling, etc., as well as using words)
The relevant attitudes to emerge are the following.
● Curiosity: questioning, wanting to know
● Flexibility: willingness to reconsider ideas
● Sensitivity to living things and the environment

Children's ideas about all the main concept areas will be developed through observation, discussion, checking observations. An important contribution to the formation of ideas at this early stage is the learning of new words to describe objects and properties of objects. Infants' teachers often have more confidence than teachers of older children in their ability to introduce new words at the 'right' moment and have less difficulty in applying this sensitivity to science. This matter is discussed further in the next chapter.

Learning opportunities for lower juniors (7–9 year-olds)

Given the kinds of experience indicated in the infant-school years, children reach the lower-junior stage of schooling having made some considerable advances in their thinking. The major one is the ability to use thought instead of action, to think things through, to carry out what Piaget described as 'operational thinking'. The ability to do this develops gradually throughout the junior and middle years. It is very limited at first, restricted to those actions with which children are very familiar and which necessarily involve the real concrete objects they have been exploring. The main characteristics of children's thinking at these ages follow from the limited ability to carry out actions in thought. The advances over the previous thinking are that:

● they begin to see a simple process as a whole, relating the individual parts to each other so that a process of change can be grasped and events put in sequence
● they can think through a simple process in reverse, which brings awareness of the conservation of some physical quantities during changes in which there appears to be an increase or decrease
● they may realize that two effects may need to be taken into account in deciding the result of an action not just one (for instance that if a ball of plasticine is squashed flat it get thinner as well as wider, so it may not be any bigger overall than before)
● there is some progress toward being able to see things from someone else's point of view, as long as this point of view is one that the child could have experienced himself

- they can relate a physical cause to its effect and are less likely than before to say that, for instance, the leaves fall to the ground because the tree wants to get rid of them.

The limitations are:

- these kinds of thinking are carried out only on the familiar; they are no substitute for action and first-hand experience when new things are encountered
- thought about whether changes have really happened or are only apparent depends on how strong the visual impression is; thus apparent changes in volume of the same amount of liquid in different containers (which can confuse adults, after all) are less easily challenged by thought alone than changes where reasoning can more easily contradict perception
- the quantities that can be manipulated in the mind are those that can be seen and easily represented mentally, such as length and area; mass, weight and temperature are less easily grasped
- as might be expected, the complexity of a problem or situation influences the ability of children to approach it using rational thinking; they may be able to investigate the effect of one variable but if there are two operating together it is unlikely that their effects can be separated.

The implications for children's activities are that they should expand in two main ways. The range of content should be increased beyond the immediately familiar. The way in which the children interact with this new content might well be similar to their activity in the earlier phase, mainly finding out by observing, discussing, questioning and recording. In this way their experience of the variety of living things may be increased, through visits, books, films; their knowledge of different materials may be extended by making and handling collections of plastics, rocks, various kinds of wood, metal, fabric, building materials; their awareness of the way different things work may be expanded by investigating simple machines and mechanisms.

The second type of expansion in activities is a change in the way of finding out more about the already familiar things around them. The children can be helped to realize that some of the questions they ask can be answered by doing more than just observing things closely. They can see what happens when they do something to make a change and do this in such a way that they are sure that the effect they find *is* the effect of their action and not of something else. The idea of 'fairness' that is involved here is an important step toward investigation in a controlled manner. They also begin to make fair comparisons between things: to find out which toy car goes furthest, which paper towel soaks up water best, which paper dart is the best flyer, etc.

Again, the provision of activities should be such that opportunity is given for children to use the skills and ideas they have already developed and to extend them. Giving them more of the kinds of activities they learned from as infants is not sufficient; there has to be more challenge in the form of:

● a wider range of objects and events to observe and to relate to their existing experience

● tasks that require close observation of detail and sequence of events

● investigations of the effect on some object or system of changing a variable systematically, keeping other things the same

● tasks that require a search for patterns or relations in observations

● problems that demand fair comparisons between objects or materials

● encouragement to try to explain how things work

● expectation that they find answers to their own questions by systematic and controlled investigation rather than just 'do something and see what happens'.

A good example of the kind of activity described in the last of these points is the basis of a work card from the Learning Through Science (1982) Schools Council project's materials. As part of an investigation of containers (bottles, boxes and bags) it is suggested that the strength of plastic bottles is investigated as follows:

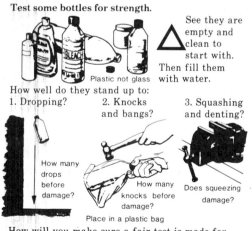

Test some bottles for strength.

See they are empty and clean to start with. Then fill them with water.

Plastic not glass

How well do they stand up to:
1. Dropping?   2. Knocks and bangs?   3. Squashing and denting?

How many drops before damage?

How many knocks before damage?

Does squeezing damage?

Place in a plastic bag

How will you make sure a fair test is made for each bottle?

Reproduced with the permission of Schools Council Publications from 'Materials' (Learning Through Science) Macdonald & Co. (Publishers) Ltd., 1982. (Original in colour).

Here the children are being asked to do something they will certainly enjoy, banging and squashing bottles until they break, but to do it in a controlled way. A quantitative element is introduced but this is in terms of counting rather than measuring. Careful measurement is best left until a little later, when it is more obviously needed. At this point the physical difficulties of making measurements are likely to obscure understanding of what is being judged or compared.

The process skills that are appropriately developed in these lower junior years, in addition to extending those already mentioned for the infant years, are the following.

- Observation: interpreting observations, identifying similarities and differences
- Interpretation of information: finding patterns, inferring, predicting, finding relations
- Raising questions: identifying science-related questions
- Hypothesizing: applying concepts, explaining
- Devising investigations: planning procedures for fair testing
- Communicating: making records, discussing, reporting, tabulating, using bar charts

The scientific attitudes are the same as those mentioned for the earlier years with the addition of perseverance (as a first step in respect for evidence). Also children should be testing out and rethinking ideas in all the main concept areas in the course of their activities.

Learning opportunities for 9–11 year-olds

The progression in children's thinking that continues throughout the junior years takes the form of consolidation and wider use of operational thinking rather than any major change in character. Given continued encouragement to extend the ability to think about a series of actions or changes as a whole, the child becomes capable of more mental operations. Although thought is still concerned with what can be perceived through the senses, appearances have less domination over reasoning. The upper-junior-school child can think through more complex actions and be more sure of the result. He can also entertain the idea that things can look different without affecting the rational argument that they have not changed. Behind this realization is the recognition that more than one variable has to be taken into account in many cases and that a change in one may be compensated by changes in others. This growing ability to handle the idea of more than one variable has a significant impact on the activities that the children can tackle at this time. Investigations can be carried out and problems solved in a more controlled manner than before. Children respond to the need for measurement in their investigations, the need for accuracy in observation and precision in the use of words and in recording.

So the strengths of the thinking of the upper-junior-school child are that:
- they can to some extent handle problems which involve more than one variable
- they can use a wider range of logical relations and so mentally manipulate more things
- they show less tendency to jump to conclusions and a greater appreciation that ideas should be checked against evidence
- they can use measurement and recording as part of a more systematic and accurate approach to problems
- they can think through possible steps in an investigation and produce a plan of necessary actions.

However, the limitations of the thinking are still considerable:
- The ability to separate and manipulate variables is confined to simple cases where the variables are obvious and can be physically separated. It may not extend to situations where combinations of variables have to be chosen such that one variable only is changed, as for instance in finding the effect of thickness on the noise made by a lathe of wood when it is held at one end and flicked at the other. Here different thicknesses but the same widths and lengths have to be compared.
- The things that can be manipulated mentally are restricted to those that have a concrete reality for the child. These are things the child can perceive as real and so represent in his mind; he does not have actually to have touched them for them to have this reality. The reality can be conveyed through books, pictures, television as well as first-hand perception of distant things such as the sun, moon and stars.

As long as these limitations are kept in mind there is a great deal that children of these ages are capable of doing to help their growing understanding of the world around them. They will not be able to think in terms of abstractions and theories. Their focus will be on how things behave rather than on why they behave as they do. Their conclusions will be limited and they should not be encouraged to generalize prematurely. 'All the kinds of wood I have tried float' is a more suitable, and accurate, conclusion than 'all wood floats'.

A very wide range of activities is now available for these children and the main problem of providing learning opportunities is ensuring that these cover all kinds of learning. It is possible for the children to keep busy devising tests to find the best colour for a car to be easily visible, the best polish for shoes, the strongest carrier bag, etc., and never to study the variety of habitats in the school grounds. Alternatively, the collection and study of 'minibeasts' and their habitats could keep children fascinated for so long that they never devise a test or attempt to construct something to solve a problem. Learning opportunity is opportunity to develop all the scientific skills and ideas according to the children's capability, so some of all the following types of activity should be provided:

● problems that can be tackled by detailed observation carried out for a recognized purpose and involving the use of instruments to extend the senses, such as magnifiers and a microscope, where appropriate and available

● discussions in which children raise questions about phenomena or objects in the surroundings, suggest how the answers to various types of question could be found and so begin to realize that science can answer only certain types of question

● practical problem-solving

● production of plans for investigations before they are carried out

● discussion of how problems have been tackled in practice, how to tackle new ones, how observations and results of investigations might be interpreted, how to report work to others

● the creation and testing of possible explanations of phenomena

● extension of knowledge through use of books or other sources of information.

The emphasis that there was in the infant and early-junior years on doing gradually gives way in the middle years to a shared emphasis on doing, planning, discussing and recording. During these activities all the process skills and subskills (p. 25) and all the attitudes (p. 44) will be used, so we will not repeat the list here. Progress in the skills and attitudes may well depend on children being allowed to try their skills in gradually more demanding and complex problems. So it is understood that the list of activities above indicates what the children should be doing for themselves, through their own thinking, not following instructions for actions devised by others. It is through trying, and sometimes failing, that, at this point as before, development takes place. A child who tackles a problem requiring the separation of variables, but who fails to keep other variables constant while varying one, will get results that do not make much sense. In the discussion of what he did he may realize his mistake and take a step toward a new way of thinking about such problems. Without being allowed to make the mistake he may well not have learned so much.

Learning opportunities for 11-13 year-olds

For most children the operational thinking about concrete things, developed in the previous 4 or 5 years, will be the main characteristic of thought throughout this further period. There may well be signs of change, however, shown in occasional speculation about hypothetical situations and abstract ideas. It may mean only one small step away from thought bound to reality, as in suggesting what might be the consequences for us if the earth stopped spinning, but it is a step toward liberating thinking from dealing only with representations of real things and events. Some children will be taking such steps by the age of 13 years; others may not do so; a handful will be using abstract thinking with some confidence. So this is a period of transition and it helps in describing it if we look at the kind of thinking that is developing, even though it may not be reached until later by most children (some probably not at all).

So what are they moving toward? The main changes will be in:
- the ability to manipulate abstract ideas in the mind instead of only representations of reality, as previously
- the use of logical relation at a general level, not just in specific cases (the difference between being able to see the flaw in the argument that 'If all cows eat grass and this animal eats grass, it must be a cow', but not in the general statement 'If X includes Y and Z is included in X, then $Y = Z$')
- the ability to envisage a variety of viewpoints and to realize that one's own is merely one of many, one's opinions not the only ones and that others' ideas can be as valuable as one's own.

To repeat, the great majority of children up to the age of 13 years will not have these abilities, but may be taking some strides in developing them. In providing activities we need to cater for children who are essentially concrete, not abstract, thinkers, but at the same time to provide challenges that may change their way of thinking.

An increased used of discussion and reflection is appropriate for this purpose. In planning investigations children can be helped to consider the possibilities there are even though all may not be represented in actual events. For example, in investigating the light and temperature conditions which living things favour, it is necessary to set up a series of conditions such as light and cold, light and warm, dark and cold, dark and warm, even though some of these combinations do not correspond with natural conditions. Similarly, biological controls require measurements to be made which appear pointless unless they are understood in terms of eliminating possible alternative explanations of events. Thus it helps development in thinking if children are encouraged to consider what might be and not just what possibilities actually exist.

Children who have not included all the possibilities that logically exist (but only those observed) in their plan for an investigation may be helped to realize its deficiencies by discussion after the investigation has been carried out. If the worms or woodlice could only choose between a place that was dark and damp and one that was light and dry, how do we know whether it was the dampness or the darkness or the combination that caused them to move? What other conditions should be provided to help decide this? Children who could not foresee this problem may well be prompted by such questioning to review their actions critically and anticipate similar problems in planning future investigations.

Discussion can also help in bringing together ideas generated separately in various experiences and abstracting more general ideas from them. For instance, the experience that sounds are made by vibration in the objects that have been studied can lead to the tentative generalization that sound is always caused by vibration (a generalization that should be tested as widely as possible). The association of sound with particular events (vibrations of parts of certain objects) will then be replaced by the association of sound with a condition that is independent of particular cases. Similarly, the notion of materials having properties (such as strength, mass, hardness), requires the abstraction of the idea of the property from the particular instances in which it is observed.

It would be wrong to give the impression that such abstraction and critical reflection on investigation procedures can be carried out only through discussion. It is the essence of the transition in thinking that there must be a firm footing in the continued exploration of concrete reality. This exploration is likely to require more accurate observation, careful distinctions and precise measurement than previously needed. Measurement must be refined and so the use of new techniques and instruments should be introduced and practised. Repetition of measurements and regard to accuracy should become part of a more careful quantitative approach to gathering acceptable evidence. Ideas must be firmly based on evidence at all points, so if there is an imaginative leap in thinking it has to be shown to be useful in understanding how things behave. When, and perhaps only when, children can make these leaps for themselves will they be able to take on board ideas about atoms and molecules and electrons which scientists find useful ideas in explaining how things behave.

Bringing these points together, the sorts of activities that provide for development in the middle years will include:

● tackling problems by applying and testing conclusions drawn from previous experience

● planning and carrying out investigations of the effect of combinations of variables

● setting up necessary control situations in cases where variables cannot be separated and investigated independently

● using procedures for measurement that give an appropriate degree of accuracy

● discussing possible explanations of simple phenomena (creating simple theoretical models) and testing their implications against further evidence

● drawing conclusions about general properties of materials from discussion of a range of specific examples.

The series of activities on springs shown in Figure 22 exemplifies some ways in which children can be encouraged to extend their thinking and their experimental skills at the same time. It is taken from the Science 5/13 unit *Structures and Forces Stage 3* which is written for teachers. The quoted section is introduced by suggestions for making the springs from a Slinky, with 5-, 10-, 15- and 25-turn coils.

The activities take children beyond the obvious investigation of extension of a loaded spring, which would be something most could do in the 9–11 year-old period, into a range of observations and measurements which can lead not just to wider knowledge but to a greater understanding of the behaviour of elastic materials as exemplified by springs. Note how a problem requiring fine measurement is introduced in point 5 and how some of the questions in 6 lead to the exploration of resonance as a general property.

The aims of such activities are the further development of all the process skills and attitudes which were considered in Chapter 2 and a more thorough grasp of the ideas listed in Chapter 4 (pages 78 and 79). This may at first appear to be a limited aim in terms of concepts, but understanding them as generalizations is a considerable challenge. At earlier points in development the ideas may be formed in relation to particular objects (that a hot teapot cools down, for example), but there is a big difference between this and the grasp of the idea that any object cools if it is warmer than its surroundings and the application of this idea and of its reverse in a range of situations (where the 'hot' object may actually be cold but can still lose heat if it is put in colder surroundings). Similarly, the understanding of life cycles can be developed beyond the realization that certain stages in the life of an insect fit into a definite sequence to appreciating that it is a general characteristic of living things, notwithstanding the variety of forms it may take. Thus the provision of opportunity to learn these basic ideas remains a worthwhile aim throughout the whole period of development from age of 5 to the age of 13 years.

Maximizing learning opportunities for individual children

It was acknowledged at the start of this chapter that providing a match, an activity in which progress is made, is a difficult task at the level of the individual child. All we have done in the last few sections is to suggest activities that are likely to be 'in the right ball park' and will avoid gross mismatching. We now return to the problem of 'fine tuning' to the characteristics of individual children that affect their learning.

Devising or selecting of an activity that matches an individual child is a process that requires knowledge about:
- the child's existing ideas, process skills and attitudes
- the size of step he is likely to be able to take at one time
- activities that are likely to provide the challenge to take this step and the motivation to make the necessary effort.

As soon as such a list is drawn up the enormity of the task of matching becomes apparent. For a start, it is not possible to know exactly the existing stage of any child's ideas, process skills and attitudes. These are things that are changing all the time in the dynamics of learning and living. Secondly, too little is known about the sequence of learning to be sure of the next step which is the 'right' one to take at any particular point. Thirdly, we cannot be sure that an activity will necessarily provide the right challenge for a particular child. There is so much that affects learning other than cognitive demand

The springs fit firmly into a saw-cut in a strip of wood.

Saw-cut

1. Load different springs by dropping three marbles in the container.

How many *kinds* of motion does a spring have when you do this?

Which of the springs (with different numbers of turns) stretches most with three marbles?

2. Take one spring and measure the extension each time that a marble is added to the container (not more than five marbles). Make a graph of number of marbles against extension.

Do this again using a spring with twice as many turns.

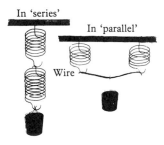

In 'series'

In 'parallel'

Wire

Draw the graph using the same axes as the first one. Are the stretch graphs similar? How are they different? Try a spring with a different number of turns and see where the graph fits in this time.

Do you get the same sort of graph if you use a rubber band instead of a spring? Try several sizes of rubber band. Would you choose a spring or rubber for making a weighing machine.

3. Compare the stretch graph for one 20-turn spring with that for two 10-turn springs (*a*) in series, (*b*) in parallel (see lower diagram).

4. Will a 5-marble load on a spring bounce more rapidly or more slowly than a 1-marble load?

Does a 3-marble load on a 10-coil spring bounce faster or slower than on a 20-coil spring?

With any particular load, do large bounces take a different time from small bounces?

In more detail, a graph may be plotted to show how rate of bouncing varies with the weight on a spring. Marbles (1 to 5) or washers may be used, or more accurate weights. Time, say, 20 bounces of the spring and make a graph of the time for 20 bounces against number of marbles (or washers or the weight in grammes).

How do the graphs for longer and shorter springs differ? Try several to see if there is a relationship.

Note: A bounce is a complete cycle of the spring, up and down, and the time for one bounce is called the *period* which in this case we would measure in seconds.

$$\text{Frequency} = \frac{1}{\text{period}}$$ ie the number of bounces per second.

5. When a spring is bouncing, does the 'trip down' take longer, shorter, or the same time as the 'trip back up'? It will be hard to observe. Use a spring with a long

period or match two springs and have one going down while the other is going up.

6. Resonance

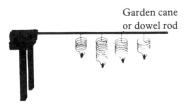

Garden cane or dowel rod

First hang a row of springs along the rod. Have some pairs which are equal in number of turns and several single springs which are different. Each should be loaded with one washer. Start each spring vibrating in turn and watch what happens.

Experiment just with two equal springs on the rod.

Does the number of turns matter as long as each spring has the *same* number?

Does the weight on the spring matter?

Does it matter where you hang the springs on the rod?

What happens if you clamp the beam at *both* ends?

What changes of energy take place when two equal springs are vibrating (with the rod clamped at one end)?

You may get some interesting things happening if the springs don't quite match.

7. Set up three springs 'in series', with washers between them as shown.

Start *A* moving.

Watch the movement of *C* against a fixed background.

Can you imagine what the movement of *C* would look like to a fly sitting on *A*? (Caution: Do not use too large springs for the second and third in the line or the first will be stretched beyond recovery.)

The work on springs will, in some cases, provide a starting point for an interest in waves and wave-motion, and open up a large new area.

A

B

C

Figure 22   Series of activities on springs (Science 5/13 *Unit Structures and Forces Stage 3)* Reproduced with the permission of Schools Council Publications from 'Structures and Forces: Stage 3', (Science 5—13), Macdonald & Co. (Publishers) Ltd., 1973.

(even if we could gauge this accurately): past experience, interests, likes and dislikes, preference for learning in certain ways. Finally, the thought of all this uncertainty plus the obligation of attempting a match for a class of 30 or more, all varying in past experience, existing ideas, etc., makes the task seem overwhelming.

It would indeed be overwhelming if we are expecting to be able to prescribe a matching activity for each child. This cannot be done, but it does not mean giving up all idea of matching. Instead it is possible to adopt a strategy for adapting and adjusting to the responses of the children as their activities proceed. The process has to begin by using as much information as is already available about the children and about the activities likely to be suitable, in making a 'best guess' about what is likely to match. It can be represented as in Figure 23.

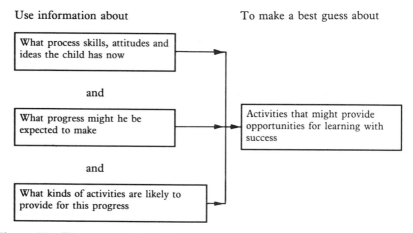

Use information about

> What process skills, attitudes and ideas the child has now

and

> What progress might he be expected to make

and

> What kinds of activities are likely to provide for this progress

To make a best guess about

> Activities that might provide opportunities for learning with success

Figure 23   The process of matching

The next part of the strategy, having brought the child and the activity together, is to gather some feedback about how the child responds to it. This does not have to happen straight away; children need time to come to grips with what they have to do and to try it their own way. Gathering feedback may not require any action by the teacher; a child who is bored or cannot cope usually makes this quite evident to those around. The information has to be more detailed than a general impression that there is some mismatching, however, for it has to serve as a basis for deciding how to improve the situation. Figure 24 shows the information that has to be gathered and the decisions to be made.

Gather information about   To make decisions about

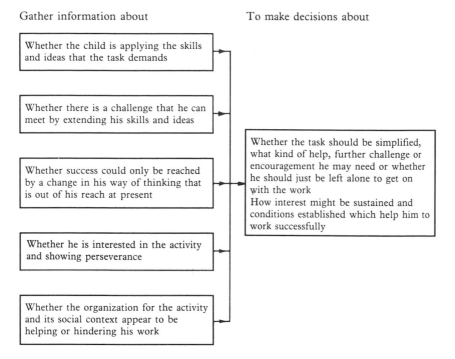

Figure 24   Information to be gathered and decisions to be made in matching

Gathering this information is valuable in two ways; as a basis for adapting the current activity so that expectations are neither too high nor too low and as an addition to the teacher's store of information about the child to use in subsequent decisions about activities. Once this process of gathering information relevant to matching becomes routine it does not require the conscious effort that the above analysis appears at first to imply. Here is an example of a teacher adjusting the level of an activity to 10 year old Martin's response to a new construction set which contained wheels and gears and a motor. It is clear that in practice the strategy for matching is much a matter of 'feeling the way' to find the right level of demand to make. It also shows how the child's reactions guided the teacher to keep the demands of the activity to the level where he experienced success. Perhaps he would return later to the challenge that he declined on this occasion.

> Martin surprised me with his enthusiastic reaction and wealth of ideas. He's always so quiet normally and more willing to follow than to lead. I didn't give them the motor at first, thinking that it might be too much the centre of

attention and prevent them seeing what they could do with the other components. It seemed that in no time at all Martin built a mobile crane which was really good to look at as well as working properly. He seemed to be able to pick out the pieces he wanted very quickly and fit them neatly, whereas the others were having to do much more by trial and error, and their results were unstable and rather messy. Some of the children have this set at home so I asked Martin if he had it, and he said no, he'd never done anything like this before.

I produced the motor and a battery and asked him if he'd like to try making his crane work from that. He mounted it on the body of the crane and arranged for a drive from the motor to turn the wheels so that the whole thing moved along. I thought perhaps he might like to make the crane hook move up and down with the motor, and said so. He needed some help to see what might be done, and it was soon obvious that the motor was going too fast and intermediate gears would have to be put in. I left him with this problem. When I came back he'd gone back to his first idea of using the motor to drive the wheels and was explaining it to the others. They asked to take it outside to give it a longer run in the playground. I agreed, and didn't return to the subject of gearing down the motor.

[Reproduced with the permission of Schools Council Publications from 'Match and Mismatch: Raising Questions' (Progress in Learning Science), Oliver and Boyd, 1977, p. 115.]

This episode would leave the teacher with an addition to her knowledge of Martin that helps in providing him with further learning opportunities. To put this in more general and more formal terms, gathering the information in Figure 24 has added a feedback loop to the decision-making process in Figure 23. The result is a dynamic strategy for matching, represented in Figure 25 (adapted from Match and Mismatch, 1977).

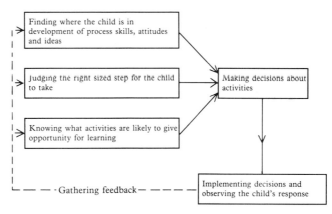

Figure 25 Dynamic strategy for matching

Cycles of decision-making and feedback are repeated so that decisions about activities respond to the ever-changing situation as children change and, hopefully, make progress. While it would be over-optimistic to suppose that the strategy invariably leads to optimum learning conditions it is at least likely to avoid the serious consequences of mismatching since action is taken as soon as the visible signs of mismatching appear.

Consideration of the responses of individual children in this way does not imply that they are provided with separate activities and learn on their own; far from it. Part of the learning environment of each child is made up of interaction with his peers and his teacher and these take as important a part in determining what he learns as the materials he uses and the task he engages in. Matching to individuals can be encompassed within a group working structure. While engaged in the same task there can still be differences between the experiences of individuals created by the teacher's expectations, the part he plays in the group work, the responsibility he assumes and, to some extent, the level at which he tackles the problem. It is through these subtle adaptations that a teacher caters for individual responses and encourages each child to attempt to take his own step ahead.

In considering how to improve the match of activities to children's cognitive development it has been necessary to go far beyond the choice of suitable content. The broad limits of the ideas that children can develop may be set by the content but, as was suggested at the beginning of this chapter, the organization of activities and the teacher's role also affect this learning. When it comes to the development of process skills and attitudes the teacher is even more important. The next chapter looks at the role of teachers in organizing opportunities for learning and encouraging children's progress.

CHAPTER 7

THE TEACHER'S ROLE

Introduction

Although the teacher's interventions during activities can have a considerable influence on children's learning, the role the teacher plays begins much earlier, at the stage of planning. Productive interventions don't just happen by accident; they take place in a classroom organization designed to bring children into contact with materials, with problems to solve, with information, with others' ideas to compare with their own; where time and space have been organized to allow teacher and children to talk and listen to each other. It is the intention in this chapter to look at the teacher's role, not just in helping children during their activities, but in planning, organizing and setting up the conditions for various activities to take place and for help to be given when needed.

It is not profitable, however, to discuss how teachers might plan their lessons without reviewing what it is they want to plan for. The kind of learning we want to encourage has been discussed in some detail in earlier chapters and the types of activities likely to be suitable at different points in development described in the last chapter. Now we have to consider what should happen during activities if the intended learning is to take place. What sorts of things will the pupils be doing to use and extend their process skills, attitudes and ideas? What will the teacher be doing to encourage progress and development? These are the questions we shall consider first and then come later to the planning necessary to translate the answers into practice.

Teacher's role in helping children to develop process skills

In describing the course of development of the process skills in Chapter 2 reference to the teacher's role could not be avoided. So some of the points to bring out here have already been made. We can therefore be brief in reviewing the opportunities required for process-skill development; indeed, it soon becomes apparent that there are patterns emerging which apply to all skills.

Observation

It may be recalled that the 'purpose of developing children's skill of observation is so that they will be able to use all their senses (appropriately and safely) to gather relevant information from their investigations of things around them' (p. 26). This describes what we hope will happen as a result of development. But of course children start by being unable to make a distinction between what we adults may see as relevant and irrelevant to an investigation. The focusing on relevant observations should not be forced, for it may end in children trying to see what they think they ought to see rather than what seems really relevant to them.

At the beginning of the development of observation the teacher's role is to provide opportunities for children to make wide-ranging observations. There are four main aspects of this opportunity:

● interesting materials or objects to observe and appropriate aids to observation (such as magnifiers)
● sufficient time to observe them
● invitations to observe
● discussion of what is observed.

Materials that can potentially interest children abound in their surroundings and can be brought into the classroom for closer inspection and for display. A little thought to what is displayed can, however, increase the information children can gather from their observations. Shells and pebbles might be displayed not only dry, but in water, so that their colours show more clearly. Snail shells of different sizes but of the same type provide a chance for children to find out through observation how the shell 'grows'. Children can also get some idea of mechanisms from observation of objects that can be taken apart, like a bicycle bell, torch or clock (preferably one made for this purpose!).

Classroom displays give children the chance to use odd moments for observing things and can provide fruitful starting points for activities without taking up formal class time. A headteacher noted the characteristics of a good display that attracts children in the following comment:

At the moment one of my staff has set up a display of fungi — tastefully laid out on a multi-level, fabric-covered background — and with them are lenses,

cards bearing single questions and two colourful and attractive books on fungi. Children are drawn to it, and whenever I pass there are children examining the fungi, comparing them and suggesting answers to the questions. The display is a way of directing children's learning, encouraging involvement and creating a meaningful environment.
(Ian Bennett, personal communication.)

If children have not had time to observe displayed material at their leisure it is essential, when new material is gathered or provided at the beginning of an activity, to allow a period of time for them just to look, touch, smell and perhaps listen, before suggesting a task. Time is also an important element at later stages in an investigation, so that observations can be checked, refined and extended. By watching a group of children with new materials it is interesting to see how they often appear to observe very superficially at first. This may well be just a first quick run through, however; given time and encouragement they start again, more carefully, sometimes using measurement to decide whether or not differences they think they have seen are real. If the teacher stops the activity after their quick tour of what there is to see, then the only observations they make are the superficial ones and they are prevented from going into depth. So providing time is an important part of the teacher's organization.

Some children need few 'invitations to observe' but others are more reluctant and may be easily distracted after a superficial glance. There can be many reasons for this; likely ones include the effective discouragement of detailed observation by allowing insufficient time, or the teacher plying them with questions too soon. Reluctant observers can be helped by a teacher making a comment that might encourage observation rather than a question, which can seem threatening. For example, 'Look what happens to the pebbles when you put them in water' is more of an invitation than 'What happens to the colour of the pebbles when you put them in water?'.

Discussion plays a major part in encouraging observation at all stages. In the early stages of development, talking about his own observations and hearing about what others have observed helps a child to make some sense of what he has found, to fit it into his understanding of the things just observed and of others like them which he may have encountered previously. He may find that what others report differs from his own view, so he will return to observe more carefully, focusing on the particular feature that will decide the issue.

The move toward focusing is a sign of progress in developing observation skill. It is then appropriate to help this development with questions: Do the snail shells all have the same number of turns?, Is there any connection between the size and the number of turns? These questions encourage the children to focus the observations for themselves. Problems in which objects or events have to be placed in some sequence are useful for this purpose, for they demand that the children find and focus on the feature that determines the sequence.

The narrowing effect of focused questions should be moderated by more open ones: What else is different about the shells of the same type of snail?, What things are the same about shells of different types? Answering these questions helps children to realize that their focused selective observation uses only part of the information that is available. It can prevent them becoming blinkered by existing ideas which lead them to observe only what they expect.

Discussion can provide a teacher with important information about whether children have observed what was there to find. It is otherwise difficult to know what has been registered by children. Just because certain features can be observed and may be noticed by the teacher does not mean that they are observed by children. The reverse may also be true, of course, the children noticing things unobserved by the teacher who may be applying a different focus. It is important for the teacher to know what has been observed and what has been considered by the children to be relevant to the purpose of the observations. Since she cannot be with children throughout their activity, she may not even know what features were observable. So when she comes to discuss with children what they have found it is important to begin from what they observed, before considering their results. If there is any doubt about the basis of their evidence an 'action replay' can be called for. Take the example of the teacher who left a group of 11 year-olds swinging pendulums to decide whether the weight on the end really did make a difference to how fast they swung (they were sure it must). On return she found them confidently reporting that the larger mass made the pendulum swing faster. Mystified, the teacher asked them to show her that they were right. They set two pendulums swinging and waited until one stopped. 'You see, this one stops first, but the other one goes on longer: it takes longer to stop 'cos it's faster.' The pendulums had in fact been swinging at the same rate but the children took no notice of this. The influence of the children's ideas on the focus of their observations is very obvious here.

In summary, the teacher helps the development of observation skill by:

● providing opportunity (materials and time) and encouragement for children to make wide-ranging *and* focused observations (by comments and questions)

● enabling children to talk informally about their observations, to each other and to the teacher (discussion)

● finding out what they took notice of and what interpretation they made of it (by listening)

● arranging for observations made in small groups to be shared in a whole-class discussion.

Interpretation of information

One of the important basic aspects of this process skill is looking for patterns or relations which link together observations or data which might otherwise remain unconnected. The ability to do this helps children to make sense of a great deal of information which would be difficult to grasp as isolated events or observations. But patterns are often obscured by features which vary unsystematically (for example, there is a pattern between the incubation time of birds' eggs and their size but this might not be noticed if attention is directed at the pattern of the shells). It is useful therefore in helping children to search for patterns to provide some activities where the patterns can easily be picked out (as suggested on p. 29). Discussion and hearing what others have found will help those who have difficulty at first. So it is necessary to arrange for the children to talk about the patterns they find.

It helps children's grasp of patterns if they use them to make predictions, but this is not something they often do spontaneously. The teacher will have to suggest this by 'What do you think will happen if ...' questions, in discussion, either with a group or the whole class. Interestingly, children can often use patterns predictively without necessarily being able to describe the pattern very well [the APU results show this very clearly (DES, 1981 a, 1983 a, 1984)]. The problem may be one of language use (to which we shall come later) but it may also be that the pattern is grasped intuitively rather than at a rational level. If the teacher listens carefully to the way children express their patterns she will be able to give the appropriate help. For example, children often describe the relation between the length and pitch of a plucked string in these ways:

> the longer the string the lower the note
> the longest string gives the lowest and the shortest the highest
> a long string gives a low note
> if you change the length the note changes.

Each is correct, but the last three give less information than the first. The teacher's problem is to find out whether children who give an incomplete account of the pattern have actually grasped it as a whole but cannot express it as a whole, or whether they do not see the pattern that links all the information, as done in the first statement. There have to be opportunities therefore for a great deal of talking about patterns and about different ways of describing them. Generally, much too little time is used in this way.

Checking of predictions against evidence is an important part of 'pattern finding' work, as well as contributing to an attitude of respect for evidence. So the organization of this work has to allow for to-ing and fro-ing between making observations or finding information and discussing it. Children might also be encouraged to speculate about the patterns they expect to find, before gathering data and checking carefully to see if there is evidence to support their ideas.

As children's ability to detect and express straightforward patterns becomes established their experience can be widened, taking in situations where the relation between two quantities is not an exact pattern. For example, there may well be a general relation between the size of people's feet and their height but there will be people who have larger feet than others who are shorter than they are. Discussion of these cases is useful in encouraging caution in drawing conclusions from patterns. Clearly, with foot size and height there is no cause–effect relation; the pattern shows only that these are features which tend to go together, though not invariably. This is probably because they are both related to other features, ones which determine growth. It often happens that a pattern is found between two things which both relate to a third variable, or a string of other variables, but have themselves no direct cause–effect relation. (Success in school and month of birth is an example, winter-born children tending to be more successful than summer-born children. There is nothing about the time of year that itself makes any difference, but it is related to time in school and time in school in turn is related to measured success in school.)

This digression has been made to show that there are good reasons for resisting the temptation to draw conclusions about cause and effect from observed relations. Causes have to be established through controlled experimentation. Children cannot be expected to realize this but when interpreting findings or information they can, and should be expected to, make statements which keep to the evidence.

It requires a delicate touch on the part of the teacher to encourage children, on the one hand, to try to relate together different pieces of information but on the other hand not to assume a type of relation for which there is no evidence. We also want children to try to explain the patterns and associations they find but to realize that when they do this they are going beyond the interpretation of evidence and making use of previous knowledge, or imagination, in their hypotheses.

Before going on to discuss hypothesizing, we can sum up the actions a teacher can take to encourage interpretation of information. It involves:

● providing opportunities in the form of activities where simple patterns or more general trends can be found (practical work)

● enabling children to talk about their findings and how they interpret them (by questioning and listening)

● asking them to make predictions, explain how they arrive at them and check them against the evidence (discussion and practical work)

● expecting them to check interpretations carefully and to draw only those conclusions for which they have evidence (discussion and practical work)

● organizing for interpretations of findings to be shared and discussed critically.

Hypothesizing

As defined in Chapter 2, this process skill includes the application of concepts and knowledge in the attempt to explain things. The difference between application of something already learned to explain a new phenomenon and generation of an explanation from hunch or imagination, is not as great as it may at first seem. Both ways of attempting to explain should be encouraged. For, although it is important to help children use information or ideas learned previously in making sense of new experience, it could give them a closed 'right answer' view of science if this were the only approach used. The question put to children in asking for an explanation should more often be 'What could be the reason?' rather than 'What is the reason?'. For instance, what could be the reason for:

● some pieces of wood floating higher in the water than others?

● apples turning red when they ripen?

● pigeons sometimes puffing out their feathers?

● snow melting on the footpath before it does on the grass?

● Julie's salt dissolving more quickly than David's?

To all of these questions there could be more than one answer. Thinking of all the possible ones they can is a worthwhile task for children to undertake in small groups, where their combined ideas will be richer than those of any individual. Furthermore, in groups the children are less worried about contradicting each other and turning down far-fetched ideas or ones that would not explain the phenomenon. For example (about the snow melting on the path):

John: People walk on the path and not on the grass, so that took it away
Peter: But it was on the path as well at the start and went before anyone walked on it, didn't you see? Can't be that. I reckon the path was wet — wet sort of dissolves the snow...
Mary: They put salt on roads...
John: Yes, that's it

Peter's idea, too, was later challenged but he stuck to it because there was no convincing evidence against it so it went down on their list of possibilities. It was noteworthy that as this discussion went on the children began to talk in terms of what might be happening instead of the more certain earlier claims of what was happening. Another feature of the situation was that what they were trying to explain was a shared experience and one which provided the chance for them to check some of their hypotheses. Other ideas needed information from further observations or tests, depending in this case on the co-operation of the weather. The important thing was that they were not trying to advance grand theories to explain a whole range of phenomena (e.g. heat energy is needed to cause a change of state), but making sense of particular things in their immediate experience. Success and enjoyment in doing this would help the development of the ability to hypothesize which might well serve them well later when they might have to entertain alternative grand theories.

As well as the ideas generated within a group the children should have access to ideas from others outside the group. Listening to what other groups have proposed is one way, but they should also be able to consult books and other information sources. Part of the teacher's role is to make relevant books, posters and pictures available, selected so that the children can easily find ideas in them. For lower juniors it helps to place appropriate books next to the aquarium or the display or have them ready when a particular topic is to be discussed. Older children might be expected to find books for themselves.

The provision for development of hypothesizing therefore involves the teacher in:
- selecting or setting up phenomena which children can try to explain from their past experience
- organizing groups to discuss possible explanations
- encouraging the checking of possibilities against evidence to reject those suggestions which are inconsistent with it
- providing access to ideas for children to add to their own, from books and other sources (including the teacher and other children).

Raising questions

An aim of helping children to raise questions is to lead to the identification of the kinds of question that can be answered by investigation. In the first place, however, as was made clear on p. 33, children should be encouraged to raise all kinds of questions. Opportunities for this require interesting and thought-provoking materials to explore, time to handle, examine and wonder about them, encouragement to ask questions and to discuss ways of finding the answers.

Some questions children ask are comments expressed in question form (Why is it raining today?); which these are soon becomes evident in discussion, for the children may hardly pause for an answer. Others require simple factual answers (Does it rain more often in England or in Wales?) which the teacher can supply either directly or by directing the child to a source of information. Questions with complex answers (or no answer at all, such as philosophical questions) have to be treated differently. They may be less clearly defined than other types of question but it is important not to brush them aside in favour of more straightforward questions. A useful approach for the teacher to adopt is 'Let's see what we can do to find the answer', rather as suggested on p. 35. The question may then be able to be turned into one, or a series of questions, which can be answered by investigation. 'Why is the soil brown?' can be tackled in this way. The first stage is 'Let's find out what is in it that might make it brown' which might be followed by 'Is soil always brown?', 'What's the difference between soils of different colours?'. These are all questions that can be answered by enquiry.

The process of turning questions into ones that are investigable not only helps children to realize that they can find out answers for themselves, but to begin to appreciate the kinds of question that are tackled in science. This should not prevent them raising all kinds of questions but help them to use a scientific approach to answer the ones that science can handle.

The teacher's role in this development can be summarized as:

- providing opportunities for children to study things which can provoke questions and be used to answer some of them through enquiry
- listening carefully to and studying children's questions to decide whether:
  - they require an answer, or just an encouraging comment
  - they can be answered briefly in a way the child can understand
  - the children could find the answer for themselves by enquiry
  - the question could be turned into one that is answerable by enquiry
- discussing children's questions and involving them in deciding how they could be answered
- making sources of information available.

Planning investigations

As with other process skills, the key factor in development here is opportunity to use the process skill. Unless children sometimes take a problem and work out for themselves all the steps in solving it practically (listed on p. 37) they have little chance of knowing what is involved. They may not even realize that planning by someone has gone into the activities that they carry out by following instructions. When they come to plan for themselves for the first time they may have little idea of what to think about and put into their plan.

Planning is, however, a complex skill and to do it well takes a great deal of time. Two things follow. First, that planning should begin with simple problems, with no greater demand than just 'tell me what you're going to do'. Gradually, more can be expected, such as the planning of a fair comparison, followed later by discussion of variables and eventually the notion of control at a more sophisticated level. The second point is that children do not have to plan out every activity for themselves, though they should have the chance to do so quite frequently. It is particularly useful to help children plan in those investigations where they have only one chance to make the observations and mistakes cannot be easily rectified by starting again (such as in gathering information during visits or using materials that are strictly limited in availability).

The kind of help in planning which children require changes as their skill develops. The supporting structure the teacher provides can be gradually reduced as children grasp what is involved in planning. At first they may need to be reminded to go through the steps of planning, at both a general and a specific level, that have been outlined in Chapter 2 (p. 38). Planning skill can be aided at all stages by reviewing the steps after the investigation has been carried out, whether or not the children planned the investigation for themselves. This is best done during discussion when the equipment is still at hand. Questions which probe how decisions were made, whether fair comparisons were made, how measurements or observations could have been made more accurately, etc., can be asked without implying criticism. Children will gradually be able to take over responsibility for reviewing their work if the teacher introduces it as a regular part of the discussion that should follow any practical activity.

The role the teacher takes in developing planning skills therefore consists of:

● providing problems but not instructions for solving them, thus giving children the opportunity to do the planning
● supplying a structure for the planning appropriate to the children's

experience (questions to take them through the steps of thinking about variables to change, to control and to measure)
- sometimes discussing plans before trying them out and considering different ideas
- always discussing activities afterwards to consider how the method of investigation could have been improved with hindsight.

Communication

The points made in Chapter 2 about this process skill encompassed communication as a means of giving or gaining information and as an aid to thought. This dual role makes this skill a particularly important one. Its development may be neglected, however, in teachers' plans since communication seems to be going on all the time with no special effort required to cater for it. A closer look may reveal, though, that the opportunities for development are limited. For instance, the claims made for the value of informal talk in small groups are summed up by John Darke in the following words. But as we read them we should ask ourselves, when do children actually have a chance to argue, to clarify their own ideas by trying to make them explicit to others?

> We talk ourselves into our own understandings by sharing our insights and problems with others. Most of us argue to find out what we ourselves think rather than to persuade another to our point of view. During the course of argument, new slants are put on a particular idea so that it begins to grow in another direction, or perhaps to have certain aspects cut off it. The net result of this activity is a slow change in our view of the world. A need to be explicit to other people results in being explicit to oneself.
> (ASE, 1980)

Teachers who subscribe to this role of language in learning must see part of their role as making sure that there is opportunity for children to use language in this way. Some of the consequences for class organization are obvious; there must be group work, for example. Others are found out only from experience. Jane Glover describes her attempts to find a satisfactory organization for science work with top infants:

> I have tried a number of ways of organizing practical science in the classroom — with varying success. For many activities the class is split into groups. One possibility would be to have one group of 4 to 6 children doing some practical science while the rest of the class are involved in other things. I find that this does not work well. Children are often very stimulated by practical science and discuss their observations excitedly with their co-workers. I certainly do not

want to discourage this enthusiasm and the exchange of ideas, but the noise can be distracting for another child involved in a piece of creative writing! Another disadvantage of small group work is that the time for teacher/group interaction is limited, particularly for the important initial discussion and the discussion of results at the end of the session.

A second possibility is to have all the class doing practical science, but to keep the group system and give each group its own set of experiments. This can work well, particularly if the separate investigations are all different aspects of a single theme — group results can be pooled, and discussed by the class at the end of the session.

(Jane Glover, 1985, 'Science and Project Work in the Infant School' in The Open University (1985) EP531 Primary Science: Why and How, Block 1 Study Book).

Equally strong arguments are made for the value of writing to learning. But, as with talking, the fact that some kind goes on all the time does not necessarily mean that children have opportunities for the kind of writing that is most useful for their learning in science. The use of a personal notebook, which was mentioned in Chapter 2 (p. 41), and keeping a diary, are devices for encouraging children to use writing to aid their memory and to help sort out their thoughts. Teachers who wish children to use these things have to arrange to supply not just the materials, but the incentive and the time to use them.

More formal written communication in science often involves use of non-verbal forms: graphs, charts and tabulated numbers. The techniques of using these are usually not difficult to learn; what is more difficult and more important is the selection of the appropriate form to suit particular purposes and types of information. Skill in selecting among possible symbolic representations comes with experience, but experience is more likely to bring development if it is discussed. The critical review of activities could, with advantage, include discussion of the form of presentation of findings. The teacher can also help in this matter by displaying in the classroom good examples of information appropriately and clearly presented.

From these points the teacher's role in developing communication skills can be summarized as:

● organizing the class so that children can work and discuss in groups
● providing a structure in the children's tasks that encourages group discussion and the keeping of informal notes
● introducing a range of techniques for recording information and communicating results using conventional forms and symbols
● discussing the appropriateness of ways of organizing and presenting information to suit particular purposes.

Looking back now over what has been said about the role of the teacher in regard to the development of process skills a great deal of repetition is apparent. There are certain things the teacher has to do to enable children to use and develop all the process skills: provide opportunity for children to encounter materials and phenomena to explore at first-hand; arrange for discussion in small groups and in the whole class; listen to their talk to find out what processes of thinking have been used in forming their ideas; encourage them through comment and questioning to check that their ideas are consistent with the evidence available; encourage critical review of activities and findings as a habit. For many process skills the teacher has, in addition, to provide the children with access to ideas from books, displays and other sources, and to teach them techniques of using equipment, measuring instruments and conventional symbols.

The common factors in the approach to teaching for development of all the process skills constitute both an advantage and a disadvantage. The advantage is that if the teacher does put all these things into practice then the conditions exist for the various skills to be developed in step with each other. Observation advances at the same time as interpretation and communication, for example. Each activity therefore contributes to several areas of development, though to each one only in a small degree. Gradually, the cumulative effect of successive activities builds up the skills. This creates what might be considered by some to be the disadvantage, that opportunities for process-skill development have to be provided frequently, if not continuously. It is no use allocating one or two sessions to developing 'raising questions' or 'devising investigations' and then forgetting about these process skills. Not only will the skill drop out of use but it will probably be actively discouraged if an approach to teaching is adopted which excludes children raising questions and doing their own planning.

Table 1 attempts to bring together the components of the teacher's role in developing process skills and the purposes that each is designed to serve.

Development of scientific attitudes and the teacher's role

Attitudes are more generalized aspects of people's behaviour even than process skills. They can be said to exist only when a general pattern of reacting in certain ways to certain types of situation has been established. One observation of a child spontaneously checking a suggested conclusion by seeking more evidence is not a sufficient basis for assuming that he has the attitude of 'respect for evidence'. But if he did spontaneously check so often

Table 1   Components and purpose of the teacher's role in process-skill development

Role	Purposes
Providing the materials, time and physical arrangement for children to study and interact with things from their environment	For children to have the evidence of their own senses, to raise questions, to find answers to them by doing things, to have concrete experience as a basis for their thinking and to be able to check ideas they develop against the behaviour of real things
Designing tasks that encourage discussion among small groups of children	For children to combine their ideas, to listen to others, to argue about differences and to refine their own ideas through explaining them to others
Discussing with children as individuals and in small groups	For children to explain how they arrive at their ideas; for teachers to listen, to find out the evidence children have gathered and how they have interpreted it, to encourage children to check findings and to review their activities and results critically
Organizing whole class discussions	For children to have opportunity to describe their findings and ideas to others, to hear about others' ideas, to comment on alternative views and to defend their own; for teachers to offer ideas and direct children to sources that will extend the children's ideas
Teaching the techniques of using equipment and conventions of using graphs, tables, charts and symbols	For children to have available the means to increase the accuracy of their observations and to choose appropriate forms for communication as the need arises
Providing books, displays, visits, visitors and access to other sources of information	For children to be able to compare their ideas with those of others, to have access to information that may help them to develop and extend their ideas, to raise questions that may lead to further enquiry

that one could confidently predict that he would do so in further instances, then he might well be described as having this attitude.

The nature of attitudes means that there is a great deal that is common in encouraging their development. They cannot be taught, for they are not things that children know or can do; rather they are 'caught', for they exist in the way people behave and are transferred to children by a mixture of example and selective approval of behaviour that reflects the attitude. Indeed, quite frequent reference has already been made to the encouragement of certain attitudes during the discussion of opportunities for process-skill development and it must already be obvious that there is much in common in the approaches required to foster attitudes and skills. Therefore, one example of the teacher's role in developing an attitude is sufficient to establish the approach which would be similar for all. We shall consider flexibility.

Points about the importance of this attitude for scientific development were made in Chapter 2 (p. 48). It was suggested there that young children are often more successful in modifying their ideas than older ones (which is not surprising when many adults are quite inflexible in their thinking). For a continued development of ideas, however, a preparedness to change them in the face of new evidence is essential. This applies to ideas of all kinds, but it is perhaps necessary to stress it particularly in science where it seems rather too easy to give the impression that its principles and concepts exist as correct ideas to be handed on and learned. So somehow we have to find a way of preserving the flexibility that enables young children to develop their thinking.

A useful start to thinking about what can be done is considering why children may become less flexible about their ideas. This may happen because:

● they cling to an idea because it is 'theirs', part of them, and some self-confidence would be lost in relinquishing it
● they may have no better idea to replace the existing one
● they fear being thought to be wrong if they admit the inadequacy of an existing idea
● they need more time to make the mental adjustment required by a possible change.

Teachers can do much to avoid circumstances arising which are unhelpful in encouraging flexibility. Some relevant points have been made in discussing process-skill development. Provision of access to a range of alternative ideas goes part of the way to making sure that there is no shortage of different ideas to consider. As well as making these generally available, however, the teacher also has to consider the children as individuals. What may seem a reasonable alternative idea to one may not appear so to another with different existing ideas and experience. There has therefore to be time for the teacher to talk to, and to listen to, children individually and in small groups.

Individuals also vary in their reaction to group pressures. For some children the small group discussion provides an invitation to 'play' with ideas; they do not feel personally associated with any one and so lose no self-esteem if one idea is changed for another. For others the position may be quite different; they become identified with an idea and so feel a personal rebuff if it is rejected. This situation can be exacerbated by a teacher who reinforces this identification by interventions such as 'Let's try Daniel's idea' or 'Who agrees with Jane?'. The deliberate dissociation of ideas from the people who suggest them helps everyone involved to consider them more objectively and more flexibly. This helps, too, in the use of ideas from books (which are not always accurate). Children should be encouraged to consider these on the same footing as any other ideas and not be overawed by the authority behind them.

Children can also be helped by the suggestion of ways of dealing with conflicting views; for example, by drawing up a list and agreeing first of all on what each item really means. Once this is done it might be appropriate to help them to see the difference and to identify the way they can decide which suggestion is 'better'. Alternatively, the best thing may be to leave them to talk and think things through for themselves. It is not always necessary to supply new data to bring about learning. As children become older, particularly, they may learn by reflecting on things they already know about, finding some new significance in them. Encouraging this is encouraging a mature form of flexibility.

Probably the most important role of the teacher, however, is to provide an example of flexible thinking. She can take part in discussion in a way that shows her own thinking has changed: 'Yes, I used to think that, too, but then I realized ...'. She can also deliberately throw in an idea that the children can readily challenge with evidence. But in addition to these contrived examples there should be a genuine readiness to be flexible and to admit mistakes and changes of mind in small matters as well as in scientific explanations. The teacher is the dominating figure in creating the social climate of a classroom. To encourage flexibility this climate has to be one in which differences in views are respected and it is not a matter of shame to have the ideas one suggests disproved by evidence.

The main features of the teacher's role that emerge are:

● showing an example

- creating a classroom climate that gives approval to the behaviour that demonstrates the attitude
- providing opportunity for the attitude to be shown, in this case exposing children to alternative ideas
- making allowances for individual differences
- encouraging children to dissociate ideas from their sources.

If we now look at the other scientific attitudes (p. 44) it is fairly clear that the teacher's role in developing them would have all the features just listed. Opportunity, example, encouragement and a supportive classroom atmosphere are required in all cases. Provision of these should be as much a part of teachers' plans as the selection of content, if we are to take seriously the aim of scientific attitude development.

Teacher's role in developing children's concepts

Although this chapter has been concerned so far with the circumstances that may encourage process skills and attitudes, there have been references throughout to children's concepts. This underlines the interrelation between these three types of learning goal. We wish children to develop process skills so that their concepts develop and we wish them to develop concepts to help them make sense of further experience using process skills. So it is not necessary to go over the ground again to consider how the teacher can help children's concepts develop. It has already been covered in considering how to develop their process skills and attitudes. There is, however, one aspect of the teacher's role which causes teachers particular concern and which remains to be considered: the words used in science.

Introducing 'scientific' words

The main issue is when teachers should introduce the technical language of science and expect children to use it correctly. Should this be done, as it were, from the beginning? Or should we allow children to describe things in their own words even though more precise terms are available? What do we do about those words which have both an 'everyday' and a 'technical' meaning, such as 'work', 'force', 'power', 'condensation'? These are not separate but related problems and opinions differ as to how to deal with them.

Many of the words used in science label a related set of ideas or characteristics. The word 'solution' is a useful example. For the scientist it means a system in which one substance is distributed at the molecular level in another without being chemically combined with it. It includes the solution of solids in solids as well as in liquids, liquids in liquids and gases in liquids. For the secondary-school pupil the meaning will be much less extensive, probably being restricted to solids in liquids but still bringing with it the notion that there is a limited amount of solute that will dissolve in a given amount of a solvent, that solutions are clear but may be coloured and are different from suspensions. Younger children will use the word 'solution', however, as if it had an even more restricted meaning. It may not include a coloured solution or a solution in which some solid remains undissolved. As their experience increases the meaning they have for the word changes; if they study science in the sixth form it may approach the meaning of the scientist; if not it may stay at the level of their 13 year-old experience, or it may become a word they only use for the answer to a crossword puzzle!

It would be unreasonable to insist that the word 'solution' should only be used with its full scientific meaning (indeed it would never accumulate this meaning without being used in a more restricted sense first). But it is equally unreasonable for the word to be used the first time a child experiences a solid disappearing into a liquid. A good argument for this point of view has been put forward by Brenda Prestt (ASE, 1980). She compares a word to the wrapping of a parcel, which obscures its contents (its meaning).

> Words introduced too soon are part of that 'verbal wrapping paper' of science.... Many teachers say that children 'like' to use technical words even though their understanding of them is very limited. I would suggest that wrapping paper can be very gaudy and attractive but it still covers and obscures the contents of the parcel.
> (ASE, 1980; p.79)

If the 'right' word is not to be introduced too soon but in time to help children begin to attach to it the package of ideas it stands for, how can the best time be judged? Brenda Prestt suggests that the answers to the following questions will help in this judgement:

Does the word matter?

Does it add to the child's understanding if he uses it?

Does he have to know the word *now*?

Would insisting on the use of the word be useful to the child?

There is probably no single guideline that can be used for all children and all words. Reflecting on these questions could certainly help in specific cases. When the answer to most or all of them is 'yes' then the child must have had experience relating to the ideas it represents and may be already expressing its meaning in his own words. This really is the 'right' point to introduce the word, when it fills a gap and fits into the child's vocabulary with meaning. A simple example is of supplying the word 'sinking' to a young child who is describing an object as 'falling to the bottom' of the bowl of water. The word 'solution' might be offered to the older child with plenty of experience of putting various solids in water who wanted to describe how the liquids 'that you can see through' are different from the liquid before any solid was put in.

The most persuasive argument for waiting until the child seems to need the word before introducing it is that there is then more chance that the 'package of ideas' that it represents to the child will be not too far away from what it represents for the teacher or the author of the books the child might read or other people with whom the child may communicate. It does children no service to provide words which they cannot use to convey meaning because they do not realize what meaning the word has. Of course we cannot prevent children collecting words, like stamps, and showing off their trophies by talking about black holes, radioactivity, cloning and such. But we accept this for what it is, mere imitation of adult language, not intended for communication.

The same argument can be the guideline for the words that are used not only in science but have a more precise meaning when used as a scientific term than when used in everyday life. It is pointless to try to prevent the word 'work' being used for occupations, like thinking, which involve no 'work' in the physicist's understanding of the word. When the word is required in its scientific meaning, that is, when children have some notion of the concept, then is the time to say 'the word 'work' is used for this in science and not for other things that are called work'. The everyday use of the word can be discussed as well as the scientific use to clarify the distinction (cf. the suggestion about the meaning of 'animal' on p. 82). Thereafter, the teacher should be careful to notice how the children are using the words, by listening and reading what they write, so as to find out the concept that is conveyed by the children in the words they use.

Concern about the special vocabulary of science should not take all the attention. Normal non-scientific words can also present a barrier to communication if they are put together in complex structures. When we say warm air is 'rising' (instead of going up), light is 'travelling' (when we could say that it is going from one place to another), a balloon is 'expanding' (rather than getting bigger), we should stop to ask ourselves: Do we really need to use these words? Do they help the children's understanding or are they just another layer of verbal wrapping paper?

Planning and the teacher's role

Looking at the complex and subtle nature of the teacher's role in the last sections has served to underline what was said at the start of this chapter: opportunities for learning and for teachers to play a part in it do not happen by chance. They require planning, but planning of a different kind than, and additional to, the selection of content. At the same time the planning does depend to some extent on the content because some topics lend themselves more naturally to treatment that emphasizes certain process skills than others.

Although in theory almost any activity could be used to develop all the process skills and attitudes, to do this would often involve a rather artificial treatment of the subject matter. It might also impose restrictions on the choice of subject matter. For example, activities concerning the weather or the sun, moon and stars must be observational rather than experimental; understanding simple circuits depends largely on experimentation; the investigations that can be carried out on living things are limited by ethical considerations as well as the complexity of the factors that influence outcomes. The level of development of the children is another factor, for although older children may be able to make necessary measurements with sufficient precision to provide reliable evidence, this may not be so for younger ones. So we must accept that in practice content influences opportunities for process-skill development as suggested in Figure 20 on page 123.

At the same time, not every topic is different from every other in this respect. It is easy to see, for instance, that the same approach can be used for comparing fabrics for flammability, comparing woods for hardness, comparing colours for visibility at a distance, etc. All would involve devising relevant tests for making fair comparisons. These topics would give plenty of opportunity for observing similarities and differences, identifying variables and discussing and recording results, but less for predicting, finding relations, raising questions and hypothesizing. Similarly, there are other types of topic that are more rich in opportunities for some process skills than for others. The four main ones can be described in terms of the process skills that form a natural focus, as follows:

● comparing topics
● pattern-finding topics
● hypothesis-generating topics
● question-raising topics.

Planning in every case has to ensure that there are the opportunities for the children to learn from interaction with objects and materials, from each other and from other sources, and for the teacher's role in this learning. The organization that provides this for the different types of topic has a different 'shape'. The notion of shape here describes the succession of events as the topic proceeds. In sketching the shape of each type it will be useful to use a set of symbols:

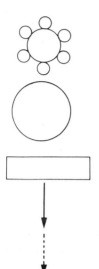

means children working in groups, all at the same time

means whole-class discussion, usually groups reporting, followed by comments on each others' findings

means teacher setting groups to work, describing task and arrangements for obtaining equipment

means a move from one phase to another

means a possible extra step or detour

The topic shape is a planning structure which ensures opportunity for various kinds of interaction in the classroom but allows flexibility to suit a variety of arrangements for time allocation. The movement from one phase of activity to another and how long might be spent on one phase would also depend on the children. Younger ones would probably spend less time at any one phase than older ones with a longer attention span and more ideas to argue about. There are various places where natural breaks can be made. It would clearly be best not to have to break in the middle of a phase or between a [   ] and a ☼ ; other arrows provide possible break points. We shall now look at the basic shapes of the four main topic types in turn.

Comparing topics

These are topics involving fair comparison between objects where the purpose of the comparison is clear in the problem but the operational form has to be worked out. The general form is which *x* does *y* best? Which detergent washes the clothes best? Which fertilizer is best for the plants? Which polish is best for shining shoes?

A useful sequence for these topics allows children to work out how to decide which is 'best' during an initial period of free interaction with the materials.

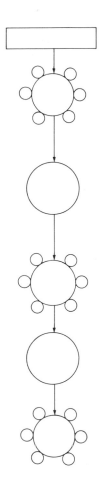

Teacher sets the scene, briefly describes problem of deciding 'which is best'

Groups have equipment to explore and use while defining what 'best' means, what they have to do to decide it and what tests are necessary. A group record of their suggestions is drawn up

Suggestions are collected from groups on the blackboard or large sheets of paper. Comments are invited about whether the suggested tests will show what they are intended to show, whether one test will be enough to decide 'best', etc. In some cases tests may already have been carried out roughly; suggestions should be made for improvement. Ways of recording results discussed

Children carry out tests (probably different ones by each group or similar ones carried out in different ways). Teacher reminds them about recording; helps by showing techniques where necessary

Groups' results reported to others, possibly by demonstrating what was done and showing results already drawn up in a table, graph or chart. Discussion of meaning of results, whether enough testing done to justify selection of 'best', etc. Critical review leading to suggestions for improvement

Groups act on suggestions for extending and improving tests. May modify results and conclusions. Possible preparation of classroom display of results

These 'which is best' problems are essentially 'real' problems, of interest to others (just in the way 'Which?' tests of goods are to consumers). Advantage can be taken of this intrinsic interest to encourage the children to refine their tests and repeat results so that they are sure of them and then prepare a 'report' which can be in the form of a demonstration, poster or display put up for children from other classes to see.

Pattern-finding topics

Some of these are topics where the related variables are easily identified. Examples are found in the note given by a bottle when you blow across the top (or strike it) and the amount of water in it, in the direction of a shadow cast by the sun and the time of day, in the number of turns given to a wind-up toy and how far it will go. Other topics require more investigation of the variables to see which ones give a pattern and which do not, such as the floating of the wooden blocks described in Chapter 1 or finding what makes a difference to how far a paper dart will travel. There is more value for developing the skill of finding patterns if the variables that are related are not pointed out and the children have to distinguish them from those where there is no regularity. For instance, children running toy cars down a slope could be told to measure how far they go for different heights to the end of the slope. Alternatively, the activity could go as follows:

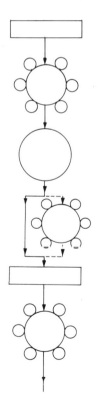

A period for free exploration with the cars, the only guidance being to try different cars, see what happens if the slope is changed and find as many things as possible that are the same and are different about the cars. The children have to decide what observations to make, but to agree in their group on what they think they have found and be prepared to report it to other groups.

Each group reports their observations which are collected together by the teacher on the blackboard, perhaps listing 'things that were the same about the cars' and 'things that were different about the cars'. Conflicts in observations from groups are discussed and sorted out using the equipment

A more focused task is then set, designed to make them use their observations in finding patterns, e.g. what things make a difference to how fast the cars go?

Children return to groups. Teacher discusses with each group, listens to their ideas, provides help as required, reminds them to come to an agreed result.

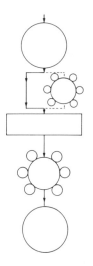

Groups share their ideas about the patterns they have found. Teacher accepts all the relations offered and invites comment from children when all ideas collected. Groups asked to describe how their results were obtained, leading, perhaps, to checking where there is doubt

Teacher introduces a task involving the use of the patterns, e.g. a prediction to be made

Groups work out prediction and then check it. Teacher discusses basis of prediction with each group; may set further challenges according to needs of different groups. Written report may be prepared by some groups at this stage

Ideas shared about how good predictions were, how they could be improved. Ways of testing predictions reviewed critically

Several different objects could be substituted for the cars and the slope in this example, leaving the basic shape of the topic the same. The following topic shapes are described in general terms that could relate to any suitable subject matter.

Hypothesis-generating topics

These topics begin with a problem whose solution may take the form of an explanation, the production of an artifact or a way of making something happen. The ones requiring an explanation can arise from the observation of some event or phenomenon in daily experience, such as the appearance of dew on grass overnight or the misting of windows of warm humid rooms, or the behaviour of a 'Cartesian diver', or why footsteps echo in some places but not in others. The hypotheses that are made and tested out are ones concerning the effect of variables in the situation rather than the general scientific principle. In other types of problem the hypothesized solution is constructed physically: a model bridge to carry a given load, a way of making a floating object sink or vice versa. These latter problems are on the fuzzy border between science and technology.

The sequence of events in all such topics would begin with the study of the phenomenon or the problem in a wide-ranging and open-ended manner. If it concerns a phenomenon that can be readily reproduced (for instance by observing water condensing on the cold surface of a tin can with ice in it, to replace the dew on the grass) then this part of the activity can be carried out in the classroom. Otherwise it may be necessary to go to the phenomenon to study it, particularly if it concerns living things in their habitat.

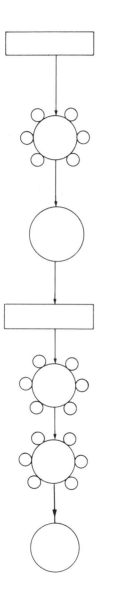

Teacher arranges for children and problem to come together. Open-ended task is to observe what is happening and think of as many things as possible that might explain it or lead to a solution

Children observe the phenomenon and explore the factors affecting it (e.g. what makes the thing that we want to make float sink at the moment?). Teacher listens to their ideas and helps them to distinguish between observations and inferences (such as 'it sinks because it's heavy')

Observations are shared, discussed, checked against evidence. Teacher collects observations separately from inferences. The latter are turned into hypotheses and added to the list of suggested explanations (or possible solutions). The suggestions are discussed; some may be eliminated by appeal to logic or evidence, others added from the teacher or from books

Tasks are assigned to groups to test out (or try to make) the various suggestions. (There is opportunity here for children to plan before carrying out their tests)

Groups each test one of the hypotheses or try to produce the result in one of the ways suggested. Whether or not a written plan is asked for by the teacher, the children's ideas about what to do should be discussed to help them think ahead and anticipate difficulties

Having reached an answer to their own satisfaction and discussed it with the teacher, groups work on a report or prepare a demonstration of their solution for others

Children share accounts of what they have found and demonstrate solutions. From the combination of findings ideas are reached about the best explanation or way of solving the problem

It may well be appropriate for the combined reports or artifacts to be displayed and further time allowed for the necessary 'tidying' to be done. There is value in spending time in this way on occasion, it helps in consolidation of ideas, but it is better if it does not become a routine, when it can lead to children seeing the purpose of their work in terms of producing something to go up on the wall instead of the satisfaction of understanding.

Question-raising topics

These require the most open-ended treatment of all types if they are to achieve the aim of eliciting questions from children which they answer for themselves. In theory they can concern any object or phenomenon about which children are likely to be curious, but in choosing the subject matter some thought has to be given to whether the materials which may be needed by children in attempting to answer some of the questions can be provided. It will also help if teachers are prepared for the kinds of questions children might ask (from background reading, such as Nuffield Junior Science and Science 5/13 *Teachers' Guides*). Living things, natural materials (such as log sections) and materials with unexpected properties are good question raisers.

As with other topic types this one also is best begun with a period of free interaction with the material. In this case it enables children to make observations that will answer some of their initial superficial questions while they are deciding what other things they would like to find out.

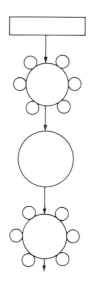

The teacher arranges for the children to handle, observe, explore the material

Children interact with the material; they look, handle and explore it for a short period without any direction. Teacher then suggests that each group draws up a list of the things they are most interested to find out about it

Questions from different groups are collected and combined into one list. The teacher leads a discussion of how to find an answer to each one. Those that can be answered by the children's investigations might be shared out among the groups

Children plan how to find the answer, discuss plans with teacher, then carry out their investigation

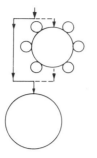

Children report their investigations to the class, demonstrating when possible, and answering questions asked by other children. (This may lead to another set of questions being raised and a further round of investigations)

Teacher leads a general discussion on how they might put together findings of various groups; she makes suggestions and assigns tasks for a report on what has been found by the class as a whole.

Planning decisions

Many things are common to the suggestions for treating these four types of topic. Some common features are considered essential: for example, starting with children observing real things, events or phenomena and providing tasks that demand genuine collaboration of children in groups. Other features are optional or can be varied, indeed some must be carried out to suit the type of material, its location and its availability. In the general descriptions that have been given all the variations cannot be included, so some should be mentioned now.

If the material or equipment the children have to use is only sufficient for one or two groups at a time then having all groups working simultaneously will not be possible. The group working will then have to be staggered, some groups working on their science activities while others are involved in other activities. But the whole-class discussions can still be held, being planned to take place when all the groups have completed a particular phase of the group work. Staggering group work may also be necessary if the use of the equipment requires careful supervision for reasons of safety or for the teaching of a particular skill. However, if there are no good reasons for staggering, then having all the groups working together on activities related to the topic has many advantages. Jane Glover mentioned some in the quote on p. 156. Others arise from the value of having a recent experience that is of interest to others and being able to hear what others have done while the work is fresh in everyone's mind. A great deal more learning with understanding is then likely than if each group works on its own topic and has no shared experience to talk about with others.

The suggestion of distinct phases in the activities gives rise to some objections that slow groups will be hurried and quicker ones bored if they are expected to keep in step with each other. In practice this is not often a problem, partly because groups have children of mixed ability within them, and partly because there are always more lines of enquiry than time to pursue them. For example, groups who find the answer to their question very quickly in a question-raising topic can readily find another one to tackle, even if it is one that another group is already attempting. Part of the teacher's role during group work is to keep an eye on the progress of groups and to suggest extensions for groups that can make progress more quickly than others. If children are really interested in a topic, however, it is rarely necessary for the teacher to make these suggestions. Indeed, the more able children often appear to work more slowly than the others, since they pay more attention to detail and accuracy and go into greater depth in their group discussions.

The discussion the teacher has with groups has also an essential part to play in preparation for a useful whole-class discussion. By taking part in the discussion of each group, and by listening, the teacher can pick up the points of interest and concern, the ideas and the problems, that can usefully be shared between groups. Bringing out these points when the whole class gets together for discussion is then likely to lead to exchanges between pupils which are of interest and benefit to all of them. This helps to avoid the whole-class 'discussion' being of interest only to a few at any time and more a question and answer session between teacher and individuals in turn than a genuine discussion.

A final point refers to the balance between the various types of topic and the order in which they are introduced. For children who are new to using process skills in practical investigations, the order in which the types have been listed and discussed here is the best for their introduction. Fair testing is an idea easily grasped, even by 6–8 year olds, and pattern-finding topics can be structured to give the focus that children may need in their activities at first. Hypothesis-generation is something that depends on previous experience and is more suitable for junior-age children than for infants. Question-raising topics demand the most from both teacher and children. The children have to have some experience of answering questions by investigation before they can appreciate the difference between these and other kinds of questions. The teacher requires confidence to deal with questions as they arise; she can pre-plan only to a certain extent with regard to likely questions but not for all the questions. However, having the 'shape' of the topic in mind can help considerably, for it provides a flow of activities and indicates the next step once the children have offered their questions.

Thinking in terms of the shape of the topic provides the organizational structure for the teacher to play her part in children's learning and for the children to learn from their interaction with materials and with others. It adds a further dimension in the planning of activities. Decisions about content and shape have to be taken together so that opportunities are provided for development in children's process skills and attitudes which help their understanding of the world around them.

CHAPTER 8

ASSESSING CHILDREN'S PROGRESS

Introduction

In earlier chapters there have been several references to teachers' need of information about children's thinking and abilities. This information is needed for planning activities at the level likely to provide a challenge that children can meet, for deciding how to help individual children's ideas and skills to develop and for keeping records of progress to use in future planning. How can a teacher do this? How detailed has the information to be, to be useful? How often does the assessment have to be made? These are the questions this chapter attempts to answer. It is concerned with how information can be gathered about children's current thinking, such as is required for matching as described in Chapter 6. When used for making day-to-day decisions about children's activities the information will probably be stored in the teacher's head, but if occasionally summarized on paper it forms a record of progress which can be used for other purposes.

The word assessment is used here with a broad meaning and it is important to make clear that we are not assuming that assessing is the same as testing. Assessing is one of the possible ways of gathering information about children; testing is one of the possible ways of assessing. Just as there are many ways of gathering information about children's progress other than assessment (e.g. collecting samples of work, tape recording their spoken language or even videotaping) so there are many ways of assessing other than by testing. Assessment differs from other ways of gathering information in that it involves a description of what children have done rather than a collection of the actual evidence. It replaces the real thing by a summary of it: a comment, a mark, a spoken word; even a smile or a frown or other gesture can be the result of assessment.

An important feature of assessment is that it is a process involving the making of a judgement about the evidence. There are always some criteria, or standards, applied in making the judgement, just as there are in the process of evaluation. The same arguments about the selection of criteria made in Chapter 5, pages 101 and 102, apply to assessment. There is an element of arbitrariness in the result in that it is always possible to use different criteria in judging what a child has done, each probably leading to a different assessment result. For example, when a teacher writes the word 'good' on a child's written work this is the result of applying a certain criterion of what is to be expected. A more stringent level of expectation applied to the same work might well lead to a less favourable judgement.

The aim in devising methods of assessment is to minimize the arbitrariness of the results and one way of doing this is to spell out the criteria being used as unambiguously as possible. But it is not possible to eliminate all arbitrariness and subjectivity in assessment; some always remains. This is true for all kinds of assessment including so-called 'objective tests'. These tests are objective only to the extent that they can be marked with 100% agreement between markers (and even marked by machine). But there is still subjectivity in the process, not at the stage of marking, but at the earlier stage of deciding what items are included in the test. It is fairly certain that a change in the selection of items, and there are always many just as acceptable as those chosen, would produce different marks for individual children even though the overall level of difficulty might be the same.

Purposes of assessment

The purpose of assessment has important implications for how it is carried out, in particular for what information is required and how it is gathered. We are concerned here with one main purpose, assessment for helping learning. The approaches appropriate for this purpose will not necessarily be so for others. It may help in keeping this restriction in mind to put the purpose of present interest in the context of other possible purposes as in the following summary of purposes and implications for the 'what' and 'how' of assessment (Table 2).

The most detailed information is required for the first of the purposes in this list, the only one we shall deal with here. Information about testing in primary science, which is more appropriate for some of the other purposes, has been given elsewhere (Harlen, 1983).

Table 2   Types of purpose of assessment

Purposes	Implications for 'what' and 'how'	Limitations
Diagnosis: identifying problems, matching activities to development, planning by teacher, record keeping	A wide range of information needed about progress in developing skills, attitudes, concepts. Methods must be capable of being applied frequently and repeatedly without interfering with normal work. No need for all pupils to be assessed in exactly the same manner since no comparisons are being made	Information rich in detail but often arising from specific activities and not always generalizable
Making comparisons: with earlier performance to show progress, to compare groups, to give information about individuals in relation to group or class	Emphasis must reflect the basis upon which comparisons are made (which of necessity must be restricted). Methods are required to be such that pupils are all treated similarly and comparisons are fair	May not be possible to find methods which allow for comparisons to be made *and* relate to all major types of goal. Often development of attitudes and skills is neglected for this reason
Reporting achievements: to parents, pupils, other teachers interested in the progress of individual pupils	Range of information should reflect all major goals but in summary rather than in minute detail. Methods must provide straightforward, readily grasped judgements which are reliable. The criteria used in the assessment must be made clear	As above, existing methods may not cover all types of goal. Hence unless new methods are devised information tends to be about what is testable but not necessarily educationally important
Research and curriculum evaluation: comparison of teaching approaches, materials, investigation of differences among pupils	Information will reflect aspects which are the focus of the investigation, probably not the whole range of what is thought important. Methods must suit this focus without any in-built bias against particular approaches or pupils	Information will be limited to what can be assessed in the short term, but this may not be a fair indication of progress towards longer-term goals
Monitoring at national or LEA level: looking for differences related to school variables, for trends over time	The assessment has to reflect a basic set of general goals which are valid for all schools even though their programmes vary. Methods must be able to be used with reliability in a large number of schools	Results will be derived from assessment which is not tailored to the particular curriculum experienced by the pupils. Methods limited by their feasibility for large-scale use

Harlen, 1983

What information does the teacher require?

The short answer to this question is that to help children's scientific development a teacher must know where the children have reached in all the process skills, attitudes and ideas discussed earlier. The arguments put forward about matching, in Chapter 6, make this conclusion unavoidable. It is most unlikely that the teacher can even begin to make a 'best guess' at the sorts of activities and encouragement that will take children a step forward unless she has some idea of where they start from. Furthermore feedback about individual children's responses is central to the 'fine tuning' that is needed for matching (see p. 144). If we are seriously working toward progress in all areas then it must be possible to obtain feedback about all the process skills, attitudes and ideas.

This is a tall order, particularly when we recall the nature of these attributes. Process skills are used in making sense of experience by trying out ideas and modifying them as new evidence comes to light. Each skill has an influence on performance in many activities but in no one activity to such an extent that one could say: if a child can do this then he knows how to interpret information, or how to hypothesize, or whatever. Process skills have to be built up by continued use in a wide range of activities. Similarly, their development has to be assessed by gathering information about their use in this wide range of activities.

The same arguments apply to the assessment of attitudes, which are even more generalized aspects of behaviour. There must be many pieces of evidence drawn from activities where a child might show curiosity, respect for evidence or respect for living things, etc., before we can reach any conclusion about his development of these attitudes. In any one activity attitudes play a part in determining a child's performance but only a small part beside other factors related to the content, level of difficulty, process skills demanded and so on. Again this points to having to bring together evidence drawn from a large range of activities to look for a pattern relating to attitude development.

Although concepts are specified to a greater degree by the content of activities there is here, too, a case for looking at more than a few instances of their application to assess development. The basic concepts that are the aims of primary science are developed gradually by a process of cautious generalization about knowledge of specific instances. To see where children are in this development it is necessary to assess not just the knowledge of isolated facts (such as whether particular materials float or sink in water), but rather the grasp of broader ideas that have wider application (such as that size on its own makes no difference to whether a material floats or sinks).

The whole list of process skills, attitudes and concepts defined as relevant to science amounts to some 23 items. This seems a large number to add to a list of aspects of learning in other subject areas that a teacher has also to keep track of. However, because of the overlap with other subject areas, many of the skills and attitudes are common and their assessment would serve to help learning in those as well as learning in science. Indeed, a combined list of process skills and attitudes in science, mathematics, history, geography, social and environmental science would only be a little longer than that required for science. This economy would work well where the same teacher is responsible for the children's learning in all these areas; it would not be possible where science is taught by a different teacher.

How can the information be gathered?

By implication the use of tests for the purpose we are considering has already been dismissed, but perhaps we should make the reasons for this explicit. Testing means putting children into special situations (often, but not necessarily, answering a given question on paper) so that their response can be assessed. From the discussion in the last section about the nature of what we want to assess in science, it emerged that it would be necessary to assess each skill, attitude and concept by looking for clues in a range of situations. Test questions can be created to do this but a large number of them would be needed. Such test questions have been developed and used by the APU science project for the purpose of surveying national performance levels. These surveys can overcome the problem of requiring a large number of questions for a valid and reliable measure of children's performance because they are not concerned with individuals' performance but with estimating the performance of the age group. So a test composed of over 300 questions can be used (spread over six main process skills; attitudes cannot be encompassed in the test format) by giving different questions to different subsamples of pupils. All the subsamples are randomly selected in the same way and are therefore equivalent as far as their representation of the population is concerned (DES, 1981a, 1983a, 1984).

The contrast between what is done in a national survey and what is appropriate in the classroom illustrates the importance of tailoring a method of assessment to its purpose. The APU can use tests because a large number of pupils can share the testing and the purpose of the assessment can still be achieved. But to give different children in a class different tests would not achieve the purpose we are considering, of obtaining the information about each one's development needed for helping their learning. It would be equally absurd to suggest that each child should be given all the test questions; this would take more time than the average child spends on science in a whole term.

Further disadvantages of the use of tests become apparent by considering the 'ideal' features of a method of assessment for the purpose we have in mind. The Schools Council project Progress in Learning Science, set up to consider the problems of matching, described what is required for finding out about children's development as follows:

> What is needed is a method which, ideally, would have these features:
> — can be used frequently and repeatedly,
> — can be used for individual pupils as necessary without affecting others,
> — does not require special equipment or preparation,
> — does not take up time from or interfere with learning activities,
> — does not disturb pupils or make them anxious,
> — provides a valid assessment, not one arising from a snap judgement,
> — gives information about the wide range of behaviours which is encompassed by the aims and objectives of education.
>
> Reproduced with the permission of Schools Council Publications from 'Match and Mismatch: Raising Questions' (Progress in Learning Science) Oliver and Boyd, 1977.

A test cannot be repeated on several occasions, so it does not provide the continuous monitoring that is required for helping learning. Although individually administered practical tests can be devised to assess skills and attitudes which are not easily assessed by written questions, the time and organization needed for them would never be available to the classroom teacher. Even if it were, frequent testing might well induce anxiety in children.

There are probably enough reasons here to accept that, although tests have their place in assessment for other purposes, they are not a viable solution in the present case. What teachers can do instead of putting children into test situations is to gather information about their development from the skills, attitudes and concepts they display in normal activities. After all, an activity which gives children opportunity to use a particular skill is at the same time an opportunity for a teacher to assess this skill. This method of gathering information is one that teachers already use in other areas of the curriculum, in helping children's reading for example. It can easily be extended to science if two conditions are met: first, that opportunities are provided for children to use the attributes to be developed and, secondly, that the teacher knows how to recognize and interpret the evidence in what the children do. Assuming, for the moment, that the first condition is met, what help can be given with the second?

Defining criteria for use in assessment

We have seen that assessment involves judging information against some standards or criteria. When assessment is carried out to tell us about the development of various abilities of individual children the most useful judgement is about what the individual child can do. The judgement is therefore best made by comparing what the child does and says against criteria which describe what children do and say at certain points in development of skills, attitudes and ideas. An alternative basis of judgement is to compare the child against the average, or norm, for his age group. The result in this case would indicate more about how the child compares with the average than about what he can and cannot do. Such a result has much less diagnostic value, which is what we want for the present purpose, than more direct information about the child's abilities, particularly as this must take the form of a profile rather than an overall result. As we shall see later, however, the criteria are not independent of norms (p. 185)

Some first steps have already been taken toward establishing criteria in Chapter 5, when some examples of indicators of the use of process skills were proposed in the context of evaluating opportunities for learning (p. 112). These described the kinds of things children would be doing if they were using process skills. They are some help in focusing attention on the features of children's behaviour which have to be observed for assessment but do not go much further than this. The element of development is missing; we need to know how to judge the level at which children are observing, for example, rather than just whether they are observing or not.

The problem of defining criteria at different levels of development was tackled in the Match and Mismatch materials (Schools Council, 1977). The work was carried out with the help of several groups of experienced teachers 'to try to describe how progress in each ability, attitude or concept would show in children's observable behaviour' (p. 234). After various drafts and classroom trials it emerged that the most convenient format was to have descriptions at three progressive points in development. This format has been followed in the examples on page 182. The statements describe the development of the particular selection of process skills we have considered in this book, but they draw heavily on the content of the checklists in Match and Mismatch.

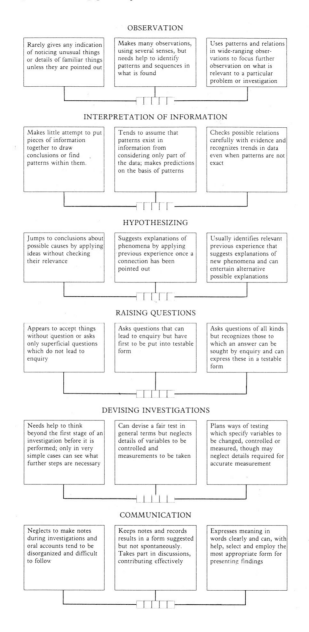

OBSERVATION

| Rarely gives any indication of noticing unusual things or details of familiar things unless they are pointed out | Makes many observations, using several senses, but needs help to identify patterns and sequences in what is found | Uses patterns and relations in wide-ranging observations to focus further observation on what is relevant to a particular problem or investigation |

INTERPRETATION OF INFORMATION

| Makes little attempt to put pieces of information together to draw conclusions or find patterns within them. | Tends to assume that patterns exist in information from considering only part of the data; makes predictions on the basis of patterns | Checks possible relations carefully with evidence and recognizes trends in data even when patterns are not exact |

HYPOTHESIZING

| Jumps to conclusions about possible causes by applying ideas without checking their relevance | Suggests explanations of phenomena by applying previous experience once a connection has been pointed out | Usually identifies relevant previous experience that suggests explanations of new phenomena and can entertain alternative possible explanations |

RAISING QUESTIONS

| Appears to accept things without question or asks only superficial questions which do not lead to enquiry | Asks questions that can lead to enquiry but have first to be put into testable form | Asks questions of all kinds but recognizes those to which an answer can be sought by enquiry and can express these in a testable form |

DEVISING INVESTIGATIONS

| Needs help to think beyond the first stage of an investigation before it is performed; only in very simple cases can see what further steps are necessary | Can devise a fair test in general terms but neglects details of variables to be controlled and measurements to be taken | Plans ways of testing which specify variables to be changed, controlled or measured, though may neglect details required for accurate measurement |

COMMUNICATION

| Neglects to make notes during investigations and oral accounts tend to be disorganized and difficult to follow | Keeps notes and records results in a form suggested but not spontaneously. Takes part in discussions, contributing effectively | Expresses meaning in words clearly and can, with help, select and employ the most appropriate form for presenting findings |

There are several points to make about the use of these developmental criteria. We now look first at the practical aspects of what they are, and are not, intended to do and at how records can be kept, then at a more theoretical side of the use of criteria of these kinds and at the difficulties teachers have reported in using them and how these might be overcome.

Use of developmental criteria

If teachers were asked just to observe their children to 'see how well they interpret information', for instance, it is inevitable that a number of different notions of this skill would be used. The criteria define the skill in operational terms at different points in development as well as directing attention to behaviours that are significant in its development. Thus gathering information for assessment by observation can be made more efficient, by knowing what to look for. This means that a teacher using the criteria must already have them in mind before observations are made. The criteria should affect, and help, the information gathering and not merely be used at the point of making judgements.

There is some danger in focusing too narrowly, of course, and this must be guarded against both in the way the criteria are expressed and in their application. The statements have to be in sufficiently general terms to apply to a particular skill in a wide range of contexts but sufficiently specific to indicate the characteristic of the behaviour that is significant. When they are used it must be borne in mind that evidence has to be gathered about behaviours in a variety of situations; a snap judgement should not be made on too little evidence.

A further point, the criteria for each skill (and attitude and concept) should be applied separately. It is easy to allow knowledge about a child's ability in one skill to influence judgement of another. This can be avoided by using the criteria meticulously and consciously. If a teacher says 'I don't think Joe is very good at hypothesizing' she should ask herself 'What have I seen Joe do or heard him say that supports this judgement?'. It may be that Joe is not very good at some other process skills and this has influenced the teacher's judgement of his hypothesizing without there really being any evidence for it. Behaviour relevant to each skill should be observed and assessed by using only the appropriate criteria.

It is useful to regard the use of the criteria and this approach to assessing children as a way of extending, and adding rigour to, something that is part of teaching. The list is not a new instrument that can be brought out when wanted, requiring no thought at other times. The information has to be gathered as often as there is opportunity for the children to display the skills, attitudes and concepts. So, as we have said, the criteria have to be in teachers' heads, carried around as part of their professional tool kit, rather than existing on a piece of paper to which occasional reference is made.

Keeping records

Much of the information gathered will also be stored in teachers' heads and used in the day-to-day decisions about matching activities to children's development. It is not necessary, nor hardly possible, for every observation of a child to be recorded. A record should be made occasionally, however, so that what is known about a child at one particular time is brought together. Once a term or twice a year is about the best frequency for this.

One way of keeping records is incorporated in the layout on page 182. For each skill each of the three statements is linked to one of five boxes beneath. These boxes can then be used to record the development along a scale from left to right. The second and fourth boxes allow for some interpolation between the statements. Teachers have devised their own ways of completing the record to incorporate some indication of how sure they feel of it. For example, ▨▨☐☐☐ means 'this child is beyond the first statement and has shown some behaviour relating to the second' or ☐☐▨▨▨ means 'this child operates mainly between the second and third statements, sometimes showing behaviour at both higher and lower levels'.

The diagrammatic representation has an advantage as it can be used as a cumulative record. Further information can be added on the same record, simply by increasing the shading when there is more certainty about what a child can do, or making subsequent records in a different colour. For example, the cumulative record for the six process skills for a child might look like this:

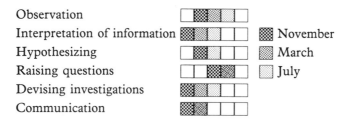

Observation	☐▨☐☐☐	
Interpretation of information	▨▨☐☐☐	▨ November
Hypothesizing	☐▨☐☐☐	▨ March
Raising questions	☐☐▨▨☐	☐ July
Devising investigations	▨▨☐☐☐	
Communication	▨▨☐☐☐	

This would mean that the child was making many observations and beginning to detect patterns in them. Putting the 'observation' information together with the 'interpretation' record suggests that he needs help in understanding what may be behind a pattern and in using it. This is supported by the 'hypothesizing' record; he has been slow in coming to the point of suggesting explanations and still needs help in seeing the connection between one experience and another related one. He has asked questions freely throughout the year and is beginning to sort out for himself the ones that can be answered by investigation. In 'devising investigations' he has made steady progress as far as setting up a fair test is concerned but needs help in controlling variables and planning what to measure. He needs considerable help in communication, particularly in organizing his thoughts to present to others.

Note that the meaning of the record comes from the criteria used in making it. If a record is made which simply records a rating of a child's ability on a five-point scale, then a rating of 2, say, does not give information about what the child can do. A change from a rating of 2 to 3 would show that a child had made progress but would not describe the quality of the change or suggest what he can now do that he could not do previously. The record therefore has to be read with the same criteria in mind as used in making the observations. For this reason it is essentially a personal record for the teacher using the criteria. Its meaning could be ambiguous if passed on to another teacher who was unaware of the criteria which had been used.

Criteria and norms: some theoretical considerations

When criteria of the kind which have been proposed are used a question can arise about the level at which they are interpreted. The criteria for skills and attitudes are expressed in general terms and are not specific to any content. But in practice skills and attitudes are always shown in relation to some content which influences their deployment. It is not difficult to show, by considering extreme cases, that the influence could be quite large.

For example, an 11 year-old who is able to find and use patterns in data concerning the girth of trees and their height might not be able to pick out patterns in the chemical properties of elements that explain their arrangement in groups. It would be unreasonable to judge the 11 year-old's pattern-finding ability in the latter context, but quite reasonable to do so for a sixth former studying chemistry.

What we are saying is that we judge the 11 year-old's skill in pattern-finding in contexts where the skill would be reasonably expected to be used.

What can be 'reasonably expected' is different for an 11 year-old and a sixth former. Thus to some extent a consideration of what can be expected, what is the 'norm' for the child, is brought to bear.

In this case the interaction between the process and the content helps to make the point, but a similar interdependence of criteria and norms emerges even if we consider the process criteria alone. How is the span of development encompassed by the criteria chosen? Could it start at a lower level? Could it reach a more sophisticated level? Again the answer is that these things are determined, not by theoretical ideas of development that pay no heed to what real children actually do, but by a pragmatic approach. The teachers who helped to develop the Match and Mismatch criteria did so by carefully observing children in their own classes and reflecting on how they would interpret what they saw. Through examples they described development over a range that they judged to be appropriate for children of certain ages. Indeed, from this work there emerged two lists, one of criteria for early development (roughly 5–9 years) and one for later development (roughly 9–13 years).

In development of criteria of any kind there always is some implicit reference to a norm. This conclusion has emerged clearly from research: 'When almost any specific example is looked at in detail, it will be found that information about norms influences the setting of criteria. It is also true, although perhaps less evident, that criteria affect norms.' (Black *et al.*, 1984). However, in use of the result, in the criterion-referenced assessment discussed here, the behaviour being judged should be assessed against the criteria and not against the norm. In this way we should avoid limiting our goals to the level of development that is the norm for a particular age by allowing 'what is' at present to become 'what ought to be'. The criteria describe the course of development but do not suggest that a particular level is the best one for a particular age group.

Using the criteria: problems and some solutions

When the Match and Mismatch study materials were produced they included the two lists of developmental criteria mentioned above. Each one contained three sets of statements for 24 goals. These checklists were included as examples of what teachers could produce to help in matching, for they were produced by teachers and used by those who produced them. The study materials were devised to help the teachers create checklists for themselves, as it was considered that this is the best way to 'internalize' the criteria. However, inevitably the example checklists were taken out of context and many teachers were encouraged to try using them without any chance to internalize the criteria. Not surprisingly they found the task almost overwhelming.

Some teachers found that they did not have enough time to give attention to individual children to make the necessary observations. This was a particular problem for middle-school teachers who were specialists and taught several classes. Two general issues are raised by these reactions. First, the lack of time to take account of individual children for the purpose of assessment implies lack of time for dealing with children as individuals in their learning. If this is really the case, then matching has no place in this way of teaching. But if the teacher genuinely does wish to take account of individuals then there has to be some change in the organization of teaching which would give the opportunity for observation of individuals. Covering less content but spending time on what is included may actually lead to more, not less, learning.

Secondly, the root of the specialist science teachers' problem is not the number of children they encounter, as might be supposed. The specialist has the chance to observe each child in science activities for the same time as the general teacher if science occupies the same proportion of the children's time regardless of the organization. So, given that the specialist would have the same set of criteria to apply to all the children, while the generalist would be concerned with other criteria relating to other areas of the curriculum, the task should be no more difficult, perhaps even easier. That this does not appear to have been the case suggests that the function of the criteria was not recognized.

Seen out of the context of matching and only as a way of recording, the checklist is certainly unwieldy and unnecessarily detailed. If it is regarded as an end in itself the burden of filling in the record can be seen as likely to encourage superficial judgements, quite the opposite of what was intended and defeating the purpose. Separating the assessment from its purpose gives rise to this reaction. There really is no point in making detailed observations of children unless there is some intention and some known way of using this information to help children's learning. Match and Mismatch did provide help with making decisions about choosing activities and creating the organization for matching for those who wished to use it.

In the face of these difficulties are we to say that assessment that helps teaching (and is needed for diagnosis and matching) is not practical? There is little to be gained by looking for alternatives to gathering information by observation, since other methods would be more time-consuming, less valid for the whole range of skills, attitudes and concepts and would not provide the immediate and regular feedback that is required. The solution to the difficulties teachers have found might well be to turn the problem on its head. Instead of asking 'What is wrong with the way of assessing?' we might ask 'What is wrong with the way of teaching that prevents assessing and teaching going together?'.

Let us go back to the last chapter, where the teacher's role in developing skills, attitudes and concepts was spelled out in some detail. Among the things it was suggested that teachers should do were:

● to allow children to talk, to argue and to refine their ideas through explaining them to others

● to listen to what children have to say, to find out the evidence they have used and how they have interpreted it

● to watch what they do (sometimes as a 'replay' to find out what has been done when the teacher could not observe)

● to take part in discussing their work with individuals and small groups

● to organize whole-class discussions so that children listen to each other and the teacher can find out how they present their ideas and their products.

It was suggested that these were part of good teaching, certainly essential to teaching that aims to involve children in learning by generating and testing ideas. These particular items are, however, exactly the things that a teacher has to do to gather information by observation. They were expressed in Match and Mismatch as:

> dialogue with children
> questioning
> listening
> watching actions and working processes
> looking at the products.
> (Match and Mismatch, 1977; p.45)

The overlap between these two lists is quite striking and indeed there is hardly anything left to say about what observation for assessment means in terms of the action teachers have to take since it has already been discussed at length. It may only be necessary to explain that by dialogue is meant:

> an exchange of views in which the participants, in this case teacher and pupils, express their ideas freely, listen to each other and feel able to ask or answer questions. In such circumstances children are more likely to show how they think and feel about their experiences and to give the teacher an idea of their way of looking at things around them.
> (Match and Mismatch, 1977; p.45)

Questioning means the use of open and person-centred questions which encourage children to give their ideas without the feeling that they have to give the right answer. Watching means looking at how children go about their work, not just at the products at the end of it. But looking at their products is included as well, with emphasis on taking a diagnostic view. There is particular value in noting the apparent errors or mistakes a child makes when drawing or writing about something. Apart from genuine slips of the pencil, the mistakes can tell a great deal about the way things seem to a child; indeed 'mistakes' are relative to our view of what is accurate, but they may represent accurately how the child saw things. The examples of children's drawing in Chapter 4 illustrate this point.

So there is consistency between the features of a teaching style which uses feedback about individual children's development and the conditions required for gathering this feedback. The problems in carrying out the appropriate assessment seem to be brought on by thinking about it first, before thinking about and arranging the conditions for the learning we want to take place. When attention is given first to learning, making provision for the development of children's ideas, concepts and attitudes creates a need for assessment, which then has a definite purpose. Assessment carried out without a clear purpose is almost certain to seem difficult and pointless.

It has to be admitted that it takes an initial effort to undertake assessment in the way suggested. The main effort is in recognizing, in real life, the behaviours that the criteria describe on paper. To bridge the gap between the words and the reality it can be useful to select some activity which provides a particularly clear opportunity to pick up information about a certain skill or idea and then to make a point of looking and listening for specific clues. Thinking out what is significant beforehand in these special situations means that observation at the time is sharpened. After a little practice in this way it becomes clear that special situations are not needed; things of significance can be seen happening in all activities.

One of the team which produced Match and Mismatch describes how she helped a group of three infants' teachers and a helper to use the Checklist for Earlier Development:

> I brought plenty of material in here [one of the home bays in the co-operative infant unit], and then one lunch hour we brought a cup of coffee in here and we asked Robin in, and I said, 'We'll watch how he reacts to the material, and then I'll break in and start to talk to him about it and try to draw these points out.' So this is what we did. They saw that all the way through, and we discussed where we would place the child according to the checklist statements from that information. Then they went through the actions themselves with other

children. Then it seemed that they then knew much more clearly what they were looking for. They said they had come to terms with what they were looking for, also with what the statements were meaning. Afterwards they said they had previously been mistaken about a child and changed their minds from when they first tried to use the checklist last term — you know, they've said 'I know I made a mistake from what I have heard him say and what I have seen him do this term,' — which is an indication that they are working with their eyes open now. One teacher also said that 'they're doing things that either they didn't do before or else I didn't notice them doing them before.' We couldn't decide whether it was because she was providing new ideas for them to explore or whether she hadn't looked at those clues in that light before.

Then they said that they wouldn't need to go through these special activities again. Before they couldn't relate the checklist statements to the children at all, and now they could do this and they are trying to match the children's activities to the development which they now see.

Reproduced with the permission of Schools Council Publications from 'Match and Mismatch: Raising Questions (Progress in Learning Science), Oliver and Boyd 1977, p. 201-2.

Using the results of assessment

The results of assessment are either kept in the head or recorded on paper. Although much of the information gathered by observing children will be used immediately and not recorded, there is more value in the information which can be exploited if a record is made. Also, creating or updating records occasionally is itself a useful process. It helps the collection of information since it forces a review of what has already been obtained and highlights what is missing. It is very easy to notice the attention-seekers in the class and those at the extremes of the ability range but to overlook, in some aspects, those who do not stand out in the class. Bringing together information also reveals patterns in the profiles of individuals and perhaps in the class as a whole which should be taken into account in planning further activities. Cumulative records can be summarized for other purposes, such as discussions with parents or completing school record cards.

An important consideration in deciding how to keep records is that the form can distort the message. Imagine the profile of the child on page 184 being recorded, instead of diagrammatically, as 4 for Observation, 3 for Interpretation, 3 for Hypothesizing, etc. The message conveyed would be somewhat different. It would sound more precise and definite than we know this information actually to be. The form of a record should not give the appearance that the information is more definite than it really is. Neither should we try to force a child into one category or another; there should be room for flexibility and for indicating a range of behaviour if this is what the child displays.

With these warnings sounded it is not necessary to go into the varieties of forms that records can take. It seems best for teachers to devise methods which they find easy to use and which lose as little meaning as possible in the making; after all these are personal records for teachers' own use. More important than the niceties of record sheets is the use that is made of the information.

The chief use is in matching, which has been discussed in earlier chapters; most of the information will have been used for this purpose before being committed to paper. When a record is kept there are other purposes it can serve: for reviewing the progress of individual children, for reviewing the progress of the class as a whole and for reflecting on the learning opportunities provided in the class.

A cumulative record, that shows how the profile of a child's skills, attitudes and concepts has changed, can be a considerable help in longer-term planning as opposed to the day-to-day management of activities. A clue to how to help a child who has made little progress in some facets of development might be found by looking at progress in other areas. Development in communication skills, for example, can be helped by using ability in raising questions and devising investigations to provide motivation for describing events in an ordered way either in talking or writing. The teacher's planning should include activities of the kind that might help the areas of slow progress and interventions that ensure the child takes an active part in them, not leaving the thinking and generation of ideas to others. The link between attitudes and skills is particularly relevant here and points to the importance of including scientific attitudes in the records.

Looking across the profiles of all the children in the class can also alert a teacher to factors to be considered in planning. Suppose there is very little progress by any child in 'devising investigations' or in 'critical reflection'. The first thing to check would be whether there was any opportunity in the activities provided for any progress in this area to have taken place. If there was in theory, then perhaps in practice the children did not take advantage of it because an activity was not well matched to them. Possibly, however, the learning opportunity was minimal and reasons for this should be sought. The lack of opportunity can then be compensated in the activities and organization planned in the future.

The children's development can only be assessed by observation if there are the opportunities provided for them to display the ideas, skills and attitudes we are interested in. If we find no change from a low level of these attributes or, worse, no information that gives any idea of what the children can do, this must raise questions first about the children's experiences. Thus the assessment of pupils and the evaluation of learning opportunities become connected. It is not a simple matter to decide which should come first. On the one hand, one could say that it is necessary to evaluate the opportunities for learning and establish their existence before it is worthwhile looking to see what the children have learned. On the other hand, the notion of opportunity to learn is not independent of the children; it depends on their existing ideas, skills and attitudes. These therefore have to be assessed before suitable experiences can be provided.

The conclusion must be that neither evaluation of experiences nor assessment of children has priority. Both should be seen, not as one-off events, but as part of a continuous review of teaching and learning which can help us to come closer to 'the right match to the stage of learning the child has reached'.

CHAPTER 9

CURRICULUM ORGANIZATION FOR CONTINUITY AND PROGRESS

The freedom teachers have in a decentralized system to decide what, when and how to teach is of great potential benefit to children's education. It can mean that they use and study their own environment in the development of process skills, attitudes and concepts, that the scientific aspects of their study are not cut off from other aspects, that each child's activities are suited to his interests and capabilities and that each can progress at his or her own rate. But in practice this is often not what it means with regard to science. Sadly, evidence suggests that activities may be provided without consideration of whether they contribute to building ideas and skills; teachers may have few records to show where individual children have reached in their development and so cannot arrange to match activities to the needs of individuals; science activities may receive scant and superficial attention within an integrated topic and children may encounter the same activities year after year. This contrast between the ideal intended and the reality as it sometimes turns out, is not an argument for abandoning the curricular freedom of teachers, but rather one for recognizing the difficulty of the decisions they have to make and for providing a structure of support.

Science causes many teachers more concern than other areas of the curriculum. It has been pointed out by Symington & Osborne (1985) that experienced teachers, confident in handling other activities, behave as inexperienced teachers when it comes to science. The root cause, they suggest, is overconcern about teaching 'correct' scientific ideas and too little concern with the children's present views. This may be an important part of the problem, though probably not all. Science does undoubtedly present more difficulties in planning for progress and continuity than, for example, the other basic subjects of language and mathematics where the course of development has been better mapped.

By and large, teachers are also much better prepared in their initial training courses to cater for progress in mathematical and language skills. Even then, most teachers do not develop their own programmes from scratch but follow the framework of activities within a set of teaching materials or the guidelines agreed within the school. It is not reasonable to expect teachers to do for themselves the job that teams of curriculum developers have laboured over for many years. Various activities, ways of organizing them in the classroom and ways of managing them at the school level have taken years to devise and evaluate and teachers cannot produce these for themselves. Projects such as the Nuffield Junior Science, Science 5/13, Learning Through Science, etc., have created and collected together a wealth of ideas and information for teachers, but it is teachers who have to make the difficult choice among the range now available. If they are left to make the choice as individuals, in isolation, there will inevitably be less continuity and provision for progress than if they exercised choice within a framework which reflects decisions made at the whole-school level. This means less freedom for individual teachers as far as their own classes are concerned, but it need not mean less freedom for the staff as a whole if they are involved in working out the framework agreed at the school level.

Similarly, there are decisions to be made in devising the school's framework, or policy, for science which would be very difficult and time-consuming without outside guidance. Moreover, the freedom of individual schools to do exactly what they might prefer, even to the point of deciding not to teach science, is not in the interests of the children. So schools must be able to obtain help, and at the same time accept some restriction on their decisions, from the local authority. But the participation of schools in developing the local authority guidelines should minimize the loss of freedom for schools to make decisions which they feel are their own.

So the decisions that influence children in the classroom are taken at three different levels: the teacher, the school and the local authority. In countries with centralized systems, decisions are also made at a further level of the state.

The questions now to be considered concern which decisions are most appropriate at the different levels and what guidance in making them should be expected at each level from the ones above. There are various criteria which can be applied in deciding 'appropriateness'. The view taken here is that the aim should be to preserve maximum freedom for the teacher while giving as much help as possible in using this freedom effectively. It is a view informed by experience of educational systems which take most freedom from teachers by providing detailed centralized syllabuses. When teachers are told what to do, topic by topic, sometimes activity by activity, the responsibility for bringing about learning shifts from the teacher to the syllabus and the textbook. Teachers become a medium for passing on a message which is not theirs. They have not had to think about the point of the activity and so are less likely to have thought out the role they should play in it. The resulting experience for children may make little contribution to their science education.

Guidelines at the local authority level

The purpose of documents produced by local authorities, usually under the guidance of local inspectors or advisers, is essentially to help schools form their own policies and to collect together information which would be time-consuming for each school to find for itself. In meeting the first part of this purpose therefore the LEA document should indicate what a school policy should contain and how it might be drawn up. To serve the second part of the purpose there should be lists of useful books for teachers, pupil books and work cards, essential equipment, with addresses of suppliers, information about local educational facilities, places to visit, etc., and some ideas on developing the school and its grounds as an environment for scientific enquiry.

A review of some of the LEA documents on primary science (a survey of LEAs in England in 1983 revealed that 66 of the 73 LEAs responding to the enquiry had published or were in the process of producing primary-science guidelines) shows that most do contain sections on what should be included in a school's own policy statement and on resources, materials, equipment. The following sections give a few brief examples of the kind of advice offered and some comment on what is omitted as well as what is included.

Advice about the aims of science

There is considerable variation in explicitness of statements about the aims schools should adopt. Whereas some, for example the documents of Devon and Oxfordshire, lay out a series of issues and alternatives for teachers to consider in forming their own ideas, in others there is a tendency for the LEA to adopt a quite strong line on what it wants the schools to do. For instance, the Avon document emphasizes the point that primary science 'should not consist of an easier version of secondary school practice' and continues:

In support of this view of primary science, schools will find it useful to consider the following framework in formulating or restructuring their policy for science.

Science must include: 1. Basic scientific skills
2. Development of concepts
3. Encouragement of positive attitudes

and these should be fostered within a structure which ensures progression.

1. SKILLS   The basic scientific skills are:
— observing
— comparing and classifying
— predicting
— estimating and measuring
— testing
— communicating
— critically interpreting information.

2. CONCEPTS   These are the core ideas or principles of science (termed 'key scientific notions' in the HMI Primary Report).
Children should be encouraged to acquire concepts through mastery of the above skills and the acquisition of knowledge. Concepts should include:
— living things and their processes
— interdependence of living and non-living things
— cause and effect
— change
— matter
— time
— energy

3. ATTITUDES The attitudes children should be encouraged to develop should include:
— curiosity
— originality
— co-operation
— perseverance
— open-mindedness
— self criticism
— responsibility
— independence in thinking
— self discipline

The development of these skills, concepts and attitudes, has value for young children not only in science but as a stimulus in the development of literacy and numeracy, as a unique opportunity for creativity with materials and ideas, and as a preparation for life in a technological society.

(County of Avon Education Service, undated)

There is a remarkable consensus in the LEA documents as to the meaning of science at the primary level, in general aims and in the attitudes and process skills to be developed. There is more diversity in the statements about concepts, however, perhaps reflecting an uncertainty at LEA level as much as at school level over just what are the 'basic concepts' of science. For example, Cheshire restricts its proposals on this matter to a list of 'fundamental ideas' which is admitted as being incomplete, as a basis for schools' consideration in drawing up their own list. The items suggested are:

mass	floating	speed
volume	sinking	pressure
temperature	food chain	force
solid	growth	electric current
liquid	life cycle	shape
gas	reproduction	size
mixture	conservation	strength
solution	length	light
evaporation	time	dark

(Cheshire County Council, 1982)

In some contrast Avon provides a much longer list of 58 generalizations (such as 'Certain changes are irreversible, e.g. cooking and burning') grouped under the seven concept headings quoted on page 196. Many documents take the approach adopted by Oxfordshire of quoting various lists of concepts or ideas published by HMI, the APU and curriculum developers.

It is interesting to contrast, on the one hand, the general agreement on attitude and skill goals and the confidence with which they are recommended to teachers with, on the other hand, the diversity in the statements about concept goals and the unwillingness of most LEAs to dictate concept aims to schools. If concepts were less important than process skills and attitudes this situation might be understood. But they are equally important and, because of the interdependence of the different types of goals, which has been discussed at length in the earlier part of this book, they are essential to the development of process skills and attitudes as well as to children's understanding of the world around them. If the reason for not stating them is that LEAs consider that the basic concepts are things that schools should decide for themselves, while attitudes and process skills are not, then this position should be justified. If the reason is that those preparing the LEA documents are less sure about what the basic concepts are than they are about the other types of goal, then a justification for this should also be given. In reality the second of these is usually the case and the reason for the uncertainty is that identifying and defining basic concepts in science is very difficult and time-consuming. It should be recognized, however, that in leaving the decision to teachers we are expecting them to do the difficult job that others have not yet been able to do.

Advice about methods and organization of teaching

In the matter of organizing science within the school the LEA guidelines generally urge that a range of methods of organization have to be used and they offer some pros and cons about each one. These often draw heavily on the summary table provided by the Learning Through Science team, reproduced on page 199 (Table 3).

There is room for more discussion than is generally found in the LEA documents of the implications for children's learning of these different forms of organization. Most points for and against refer to the convenience of the teacher, the demand on materials and so on. Such things do have to be considered and curriculum developers have ignored them at their peril. But it is one thing to take these practical problems into account and quite another to allow them to be the only consideration in deciding the organization. Such a course of action tends to lead to a single type of organization (e.g. Mr Baker's, described in Chapter 5). Instead, if the type of learning is considered first, we can identify what organization would provide the learning opportunities intended and then how to work from the 'ideal' to the practicable.

Pros and cons of topic work

Many LEAs recommend that science is included as part of topic work. Oxfordshire's document, for example, states that:

> One effective way of ensuring a balanced programme of science activities within topics is to suggest three themes for the year (one each term). One of these should give particular opportunities for science investigations. The other themes might give a more general emphasis on science, e.g. 1. Castles 2. The river 3. Flight.
>
> (Oxfordshire County Council, 1983)

Other LEA documents go into more detail of what this might mean, reproducing pages of 'topic webs' to show the different activities of all kinds that can be linked to a theme such as food, bridges, keeping warm, etc. There is often a sharp contrast between statements made earlier in the documents about the importance of development of skills and broad concepts and the focus on content in these webs. Moreover, these topic webs give no indication of progression. The considerable difficulties of catering for development in science skills and in ideas within an integrated theme are hardly acknowledged. Catering for development in a topic in fact makes much greater demands on a teacher's skill than it does in other forms of organization which may be better suited to providing learning opportunities in science. The HMI comment on integrated topics is worth noting:

Table 3   Organization of school science

Method of organising	Advantages	Limitations
Whole class Teaching by 'chalk and talk' and demonstration	Minimum organisational demands Economical on time and equipment	No first-hand experience. No allowance for individual ability of pupils. Difficult to involve whole class
Class practical Children work in small groups doing similar tasks	Relatively easy to plan ahead. Children can work at own pace if extension work available. Equipment demands known in advance. First-hand experience for pupils	Preparation of extension work. Follow-up lines of enquiry difficult. Quantity and duplication of apparatus. Involves much clearing away
Thematic approach Small groups working independently to contribute to the whole	High in interest and motivation. First-hand experience for pupils. Pupils work at own pace. Builds confidence in communication skills when reporting back	Difficult to arrange balanced cover of science experiences. Difficult to ensure coherence and understanding from report back
Circus of experiments Small group rotating around prescribed activities	Easy to plan ahead, less demanding on apparatus and all can use specialist items. High interest or motivation	Activities cannot be sequential Occasional pressure on completion time before change-over. Difficult to organise report back on whole circus. Method of briefing essential
Small groups or individuals Areas of study chosen by themselves	Allows variety of interests. High on motivation. Children work at own pace and to own potential	Demanding on teacher. Structured framework necessary. Stretches school's equipment and resources

Reproduced with the permission of Schools Council Publications from 'Learning Through Science: Formulating a School Policy', (Learning through Science), Macdonald & Co., (Publishers) Ltd., 1980.

It is sometimes thought that all or most of the science experience children need can be included in or extracted from a whole range of activities which have other and different objectives. Unfortunately it is seldom that such an approach leads to good science education. The reasons lie in the fragmentation of the subject; the labelling of parts of an activity as science when they may not be scientific at all; and the use of unsuitable science topics because they seem to fit the general topic.
(DES, 1983b).

As the HMI document goes on to say, the topic approach can lead to good science but requires 'outstanding knowledge, expertise and insight from the teacher'. Probably the LEA documents are created by groups which include, or represent, such teachers. It is a pity that they ignore the evidence in research and inspectors' reports that makes it clear that the needs of the average teacher are quite different. When teachers do not have as part of their own thinking a framework of children's development in mind they are unlikely to promote this development in topic work. For them a more appropriate organization for science is one which enables them to identify and focus on more clearly the activities which promote children's learning in science.

Advice on who should teach science

The integrated or topic approach automatically has implications for organization of science within the school; it is taken for granted that science is taught by every teacher to his or her own class. The justification for this, often implicit rather than explicit, is to be found in the notion of 'science across the curriculum' and its converse, the value of science to the development of language, mathematical and other skills. There is little hint in the LEA documents of thinking along the lines that science HMI indicated in *Science in Primary Schools* (DES, 1983b). Not only do the inspectors suggest that 'the position of the teacher with special responsibility for science is crucial' but take a step toward specialist teaching:

A specialist system for science may not be appropriate but it seems reasonable to assume that there will be some teachers who will not wish, or who feel themselves unsuited, to teach the subject. The advantage of placing science in the hands of a relatively small number should be looked at. Certainly this would reduce in the short-term the problems of in-service training and support from the advisory service.
(DES, 1983b; p.20)

With such ideas being offered at the national level it seems appropriate for the LEAs to help schools consider them, even if the result is rejection, in developing their own policies. One of the findings of the HMI survey of 1978 was that a post of responsibility, used effectively, was associated with greater success in matching work to the abilities of children in other areas of the curriculum. There seems no reason to suppose that the effect of a post in science would be any different from this. The number of such posts has increased considerably over the last few years. The APU age 11 science survey in 1980 reported 30% of schools in England had a post of responsibility for science (DES, 1981a) but 3 years later this had almost doubled to 57% (DES, 1984). Yet few LEA documents go into any detail about the value of a post of responsibility. One of those that does include this is the document from Devon, which summarizes for schools what the ASE (1981) has proposed in its Science and Primary Education Paper No. 3: *A Post of Responsibility in Science*. We refer to this document again later (p. 214).

Advice on the role of the headteacher

Most documents contain a section on the role of the headteacher. This is to be welcomed and is in the right place in a document at this level. It need only be brief but it is essential to remind those in schools of the responsibilities and powers of headteachers in determining the curriculum. They must see that a school policy is drawn up, determine how it is to be decided and ensure that it is more than an exercise on paper. The headteacher's recognition of science as part of the basic curriculum of the school is a key element in a successful science programme. It will ensure that science has a share of time and resources that reflects its contribution to primary education. At present it occupies, on average, about 5% of curriculum time and consumes 5% of the school's capitation allowance (DES, 1984). As many heads committed to science are raising these values to at least 10%, many others must be allowing them to fall below 5%.

Advice on pupils' and teachers' records

Many LEA documents make some reference to the links between science and other areas of the curriculum, particularly language and in some cases mathematics. These points are often linked to ones about the records that children might make of their work. Generally, teachers are urged to extend the range of ways of recording beyond writing to tape recording, drawing, photography and various graphical representations. Unfortunately, most of the examples of children's recording used to illustrate LEA documents are of transactional writing.

Given the general lack of records of science activities (Clift *et al.,* 1981; DES, 1978) the inclusion in many documents of a section on record keeping, assessment of pupils and evaluation of programmes is to be welcomed. There might well be more, however, about ways of teachers using assessment to help individual pupils rather than just compiling records. Some ideas for teachers on evaluating learning opportunities in their classrooms (along the lines of Chapter 5) might also be offered.

While urging teachers to cater for children's development there is a marked absence of any practical guidance from LEAs for schools in attempting to do this. HMI have offered some ideas for catering for progress. They claim that 'It is not difficult to list, in order, statements about a particular topic and then rearrange them in a suitable progression' (DES, 1983b; p. 8). Ironically, the examples they provide are so easy to criticize that they illustrate that indeed it *is* difficult to do this well. One major shortcoming of the approach they propose is that it apparently pays no attention to the ideas children have, but only to a logical structure of development seen from an adult view. A second problem is one that the HMI point out themselves, that identifying different content is not sufficient to indicate what is appropriate for matching children's development. What ideas children will take from an activity depends on their existing ideas and the skills and attitudes they bring to bear in making sense of the experience. A great deal more thinking and research has to be done before we can give teachers definite guidance about the sequence of activities.

Advice on resources

Useful additional information in LEA publications for schools are sections on resources and their storage. The Avon document provides photographs of how science equipment is organized and stored in some schools in the county and gives a brief but pertinent list of equipment that can be found already in the school, collected ('junk'), or obtained from science-equipment suppliers. Their list is supplemented by references to the most useful books which go into more detail concerning equipment. They also list establishments in the locality that can provide information or be visited (study centres, museums, gardens, zoos, arboretum, etc.). In addition to these resources, the Cheshire booklet includes ideas for developing an outdoor resource area in the school grounds where animals can be kept, plants grown and simulated habitats created.

To sum up, the role of the LEA document can perhaps best take is to provide schools with help in producing and implementing their own policies.

The most helpful subjects that it can cover are:
- what a school's own policy should contain and to provide some issues to be considered in deciding this policy; laying out alternatives seems more appropriate than laying down a line to be followed
- the importance of the role of the headteacher
- suggestions for how a post of responsibility for science may be used
- information about useful materials and ways of obtaining, and storing, them
- books useful to teachers and pupils
- suggestions for developing the use of the school environment for science
- ideas for when and how to review the school's policy for science
- notes on safety and relevant aspects of law and local regulations.

Schools' policies

The areas that a school policy should cover have been helpfully laid out by the Learning Through Science (1980) project. The main points are that a policy should:
- be an account of the school's understanding and interpretation of 'science'
- indicate the importance the school attaches to science
- specify the goals it hopes the children will achieve and the overall plan for achieving these goals
- include reference to methods of teaching and how these change for younger and older children
- say how records of development and. activities covered will be kept and collated
- lay down guidelines to ensure that there is continuity in children's experience from year to year
- serve to prevent unnecessary repetition of activities.

We now look at how the policy could be produced and what might emerge from the process.

First the process of production. Involvement in producing the document is the most important factor in its subsequent acceptance and use by the school staff. However, anything written by a group is likely to be at once disjointed and repetitive. So one person (or two at most) might be assigned to put the policy on paper after a series of discussions involving the whole staff. The document is likely to go through several drafts, each discussed by the whole staff. Even when the final draft is produced, the difficulty of expressing complex intentions in words generally leaves everyone with the feeling that there is room for improvement. This is a healthy sign for it means that thinking about the issues raised in developing the document will continue even though formal meetings on its content have temporarily ceased. Such a result is unlikely if a ready-made document is handed to teachers. Hence the importance of participation.

There is no call for lengthy prose in a working document, which is what a school policy is. Questions should be raised and answered as succinctly as possible. The structure of Why? What? How? and When? is a useful one. It represents a gradual change in focus from the general view of science to the particular features of work in each class.

The function of the policy statement should be kept in mind in producing it. It should serve to give a unity of purpose and a basis of coherence to the science work in individual classes. It should not take away the freedom of teachers any more than is thought necessary in the interests of continuity and consistency in the children's learning. Exactly where the line is drawn in relinquishing power at the individual teacher level and investing it at the collective school level is a matter for headteachers to decide, by agreement with the other teachers if at all possible. To see how this may work out in practice, we take examples of two schools, both given pseudonyms.

Hollybush Primary School

The school's document begins as follows:

Hollybush Primary School Policy for Science
Why science?
Science is included in the curriculum at Hollybush because we want our children to:
 — begin to understand the way things work in the world around them through their own investigation and observation of them
 — develop skills of enquiry and of dealing with information that are useful in other subjects as well as science
 — become caring people who respect living things and the non-living environment and who will not wish to waste natural resources
 — be able to create simple devices to do a given job and so begin to develop some understanding of technology
Science is organized so that children have:
 — plenty of first-hand practical explorations of living and non-living materials
 — expeditions and visits which give them the chance to explore things outside the classroom and extend the variety and range of their experience
 — time to discuss their work with the teacher
 — opportunity for co-operation in groups

— encouragement to construct things both at home and in school
— experience of different ways of recording and reporting their work
— experience of success in their activities coupled with an awareness that certain aspects could be improved.

The first three of these four statements refer to the main aims of developing certain concepts, skills and attitudes. The fourth adds a commitment to introducing children to technology. This was included after an earlier draft was criticized by one young member of staff for excluding any direct reference to technology. Many staff members were resistant to the idea at first. It emerged that they were quite uncertain in their own minds about the meaning of technology. The young teacher did not feel able to convince them from his own experience and asked the head to invite to their next meeting an LEA advisory teacher known for enthusiasm in this area. The advisory teacher brought along several devices made by children and convinced the teachers that primary technology was rather more homely than its title suggests.

For the answer to 'What science?' the teachers chose the list of attitudes, process skills and concepts published in Match and Mismatch (1977) and quoted in Learning Through Science (1980). These were chosen after several other lists had been considered, mainly because Match and Mismatch provided a checklist for the assessment (see p. 208) and it was felt that there should be some consistency between the formulation of the goals of teaching and what was assessed.

The question How? was answered in a manner which gave individual teachers the maximum freedom in respect of organization and teaching methods as long as agreed learning experiences were provided. It was taken for granted that each teacher would be responsible for the science work in her own class. There was no question at the time of a grade II post being made available for someone taking responsibility for science. The fourth-year teacher was, by mutual agreement, the one who kept an eye on the small central pool of equipment that was not duplicated in every class and ordered equipment, but her sphere of influence was not seen as extending beyond attending to these resources.

The Hollybush staff spent a great deal of time over the question of When? This meant when to study which topics or to carry out various activities. They were prepared to restrict the choice for each class to avoid topics being repeated for the same children. However, they could find no rationale for allocating topics to classes on the basis of some being more difficult or complex than others. It seemed possible to carry out any activity at a range of levels of sophistication. Eventually, they hit on the idea of using a framework of the child's expanding world. They saw the focus of interest as expanding out from the children themselves and their classroom, to the school, then the school grounds, etc., and so on to the earth as a whole and its place in the universe. In the fourth year, however, they felt that there should be some revisiting of topics touched on earlier so as to go into more detail about human needs, senses and interaction with the environment. So apart from this 'rounding off' the plan was concentric rather than cyclic. There was an understanding that the skills, attitudes, concepts and experience of technology listed earlier would be gradually built up through all the topics. The relevant section of the policy ran as follows:

When?
Topics are selected for each year group to suit the gradually expanding world of our children. The suggested subjects are a focus of the work not an artificial boundary. For example, we expect the children to make use of the school grounds in all years, but in Junior 1 they will study it more thoroughly and systematically. The idea is to prevent repetition of the same activities as children go up the school.

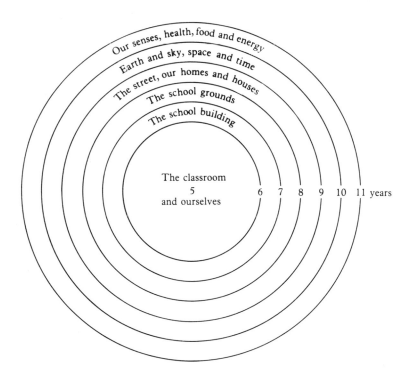

Some of the topics that might be taken in each year are as follows. Related activities can be found by using the index to Science 5/13 (in Learning Through Science, Macdonald) and the Learning Through Science cards (LSc)

Lower infants	Early experiences (5/13), Ourselves (5/13)
Upper infants	Materials (LSc), Metals (5/13), Wood (5/13), Plastics (5/13), Things that float, Coloured things (5/13)
Junior 1	'Out of Doors' (LSc), Trees (5/13), Minibeasts (5/13), Birds, Weather
Junior 2	Change (5/13), Part of 'All Around' (LSc), Science from Toys (5/13), Pets
Junior 3	'Earth' (LSc), Sky and Space (LSc), Time (5/13), Moving I (LSc)
Junior 4	Our senses (LSc), Moving II (LSc), Electricity (LSc)

As a further safeguard against repetition the teachers agreed that they would keep records of activities carried out each year to pass on to the children's next teacher. But a list of topics encountered does not necessarily give any information about what the children have gained from their work. A useful suggestion for a solution to this problem was found in Learning Through Science (1980), which they studied carefully as a guide to drawing up their policy. This led them to Match and Mismatch (1977) and to drawing up record cards for each pupil relating to the list of attitudes, skills and concepts which they adopted in their policy. The record cards were as shown below (cf. Chapter 8, p. 182). They added 'Manipulative skill' and 'Invention' to the original list of 24 items to cover the technological component of the science work.

Record keeping
Two forms of record are kept for science. The Activities Record shows what the activities were about. If LSc cards have been used these are recorded, otherwise the activity is briefly described. Where activities vary among children the record is on an individual basis, otherwise the record applies to the class as a whole.

The Progress Record is an individual record for each child. It keeps cumulative record of progress towards the various goals of science using the check-list in Match and Mismatch. Each teacher has a copy of the check-list and a record card is kept for each child. The record of each child is reviewed once a term using information about progress observed throughout the term.

Both forms of record are passed on at the end of the summer term to children's next teacher to use in planning the next term's work.

Curiosity	Curiosity
Originality	Originality
Willingness to co-operate	Willingness to co-operate
Perseverance	Perseverance
Open-mindedness	Open-mindedness
Self-criticism	Self-criticism
Responsibility	Responsibility
Independence	Independence
Observing	Observing
Problem solving	Proposing enquiries
Raising questions	Experimenting/ investigating
Exploring	Communicating verbally
Finding patterns in obs.	Communicating non-verbally
Communicating verbally	Finding patterns in obs.
Communicating non-verbally	Critical reasoning
Applying learning	Applying learning
Cause and effect	Cause and effect
Classification	Measurement
Weight	Volume
Length	Force
Area	Energy
Volume	Change
Time	Interdependence of living things
Life Cycle	Adaptation of living things
Manipulative skill	Manipulative skill
Invention	Invention

The final sections of the policy document listed:

(a) the books for teachers on science and science books or work cards for children which were available in the school

(b) the equipment stored centrally and other school resources, such as the aquarium in the entrance porch

(c) local places of interest and areas for study

(d) arrangements to be made and rules to follow in organizing visits out of school

(e) notes on safety in science work.

The document was dated and ended with the statement: 'The wording of this policy will be reviewed after one year when a decision will be taken about any changes to be made.'

Windbury Junior School

The second example comes from a junior school which produced its science guidelines 'following many discussions with staff and a year's in-service course held jointly with Windbury Infants' School and Blackwood Primary School'. It begins with a brief statement of the staff's view of science at the primary level, followed by a section on aims, which follow those of the Science 5/13 project. The main part of the document comprises suggestions for teachers to follow in planning their lessons and is supplemented by a series of Appendices:

Achieving our aims and planning a topic

We have decided that science will be integrated with other areas of the curriculum and taught under topic headings. Lists of these and their science content will be given in Appendix 3.

In order to develop a topic and still achieve aims the following sequence of suggestions might be useful:

1. When the general topic has been decided upon draw out a flow diagram of possible areas of study across the curriculum.
2. Select some ideas for practical scientific investigation and produce an extended flow diagram.
3. Use Appendix 1 taken from Science 5/13 'With Objectives in Mind' and draw up a list of objectives for development of skills, attitudes, abilities and concepts appropriate to that topic. This may seem time-consuming but should help you decide on 'Where am I going?' and will later help with evaluation and help with deciding what has been achieved.
4. Check the availability of appropriate resource material:
    a. Apparatus — is it in school or do we need to order it, borrow or ask the children and parents to begin collecting.
    b. Books — in classrooms, school library, project library (give them $\frac{1}{2}$ term's warning).
    c. Museum service — also best to order early and don't rely on exhibits for the beginning of a term.
    d. Check appropriate T.V. and radio programmes and look at the details. 'One off' programmes may be appropriate to what you are doing, and won't only be included in science programmes.
    e. Plan visits or visitors who can be invited in to talk to the children.
5. Refine the flow diagram in the light of 4.
6. Decide on appropriate areas for pupil investigations and a) collect work cards from various schemes available. b) Make your own cards or large charts, audiotapes appropriate to your children or group of children. (Remember to provide material for the less able and extension activities to stretch more able pupils.)
7. Decide on how the activities will be organised. Do they need to be in a sequence or can they be used as a 'circus' of experiments? Will they be

carried out by the whole class, a group, a pair or an individual or combinations of these? (Pros and cons given in Appendix 2.)

8. Anticipate evaluation.
9. Assemble the materials and prepare an initial display to evoke curiosity. This can include pictures, charts, short written questions and possibly some simple activities for the children to perform and objects they can handle. (Extension of 'Nature Table'). As the project proceeds the children's work can gradually replace the initial display. Then Go!

(Remember that however carefully you have planned and prepared the science content of the topic there should always be room for incidental science activities even if they are unrelated to the work in hand. Find time to discuss with the children 'What do you wonder about?').

Time allocation, teacher's role
It is envisaged that each child will spend approximately half a day a week on science. This may include work in other areas of the curriculum related to the science activity or more time will need to be allocated for recording work and discussion.

As each class in a year will probably be working on the same topic in the same term the staff will need to agree over timetabling in order to share resources. Apart from this organisation will be left to the individual teacher. (Again refer to Appendix 2.)

The importance of children carrying out their own practical investigations cannot be overstressed but equally as important is the discussion between teacher and pupil and pupils' discussion amongst themselves about their work.

The teacher asking leading questions can improve the child's observation and thought, introduce the correct terms where appropriate, test the child's understanding, check whether or not the children have considered whether or not the test is fair and give 'leads' with specific questions to further investigations. Investigations and results of a group discussed with the class can help to develop constructive criticism, lead to decisions about the work and help to clarify misunderstandings.

No teacher is infallible in his/her ability to answer questions. In response to a question we don't feel confident to answer, we must say that we don't know but say that we will find out and encourage the child to try other sources as well.

Teachers' plans

Experienced teachers can plan and carry in their heads the details of lessons that inexperienced teachers have to plan on paper. Even the most successful teachers produce some notes, often very brief and schematic, to remind themselves of their intentions which are envisaged in their minds in much greater detail. Since, as noted earlier, many teachers, experienced in other areas of the curriculum, are inexperienced in science it is necessary for them to plan science activities in some detail. It is a mistake to assume that because we want children to do the thinking and exploring and testing that the teacher's role is a minor one, not requiring forward planning. On the contrary, to give children opportunity for these things requires very careful thought about the organization, the questions the teacher might ask, how the work of various groups will be co-ordinated, how the children will record their work and so on. Spur of the moment decisions can lead to disjointed work unless the teacher has thought out a range of possibilities and knows their implications, that is, has plenty of experience.

Once a topic has been decided teachers' planning for science activities should include decisions about:

● particular process skills, attitudes and concepts which the activity should help to develop (it is not necessary to list all the ones that might be involved)

● the overall 'shape' of the activities (see Chapter 7)

● the organization of each phase of activity, i.e. individual, group or whole class

● the timing, i.e. whether all will work at the same time

● the equipment required, which will depend on the above decisions

● the kinds of questions the teacher might put to the children at various points in the activities

● the forms of record that children might be asked to make of their work.

Some teachers develop a personal 'short-hand' to write plans. This means they can convey many decisions in a brief list or even diagram. The overall shape of the activities is readily seen and such plans are more easy to use than ones expressed in prose.

The following example shows how a series of activities, spreading over half a term, were planned on a single side of paper. The topic was on making sounds. The children were 8–9 year-olds. The symbols used by the teacher were ◯ for group work and ⬜ for whole-class discussion. The six working groups were friendship groups of four or five children.

Topic: making sounds
Main idea: sound comes from objects when they vibrate
Main process skills: observation (listening and looking), finding patterns, predicting and checking predictions
Equipment: 5 similar bottles, water jug, cigar box and fine string, rubber bands, chime bar, ruler, guitar, recorder

Week:
1.

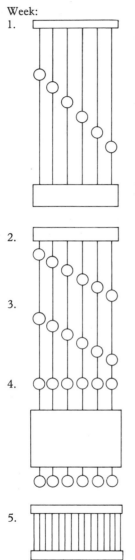

5 minute introduction. Each group to work on equipment in turn. Explain task (also on card by equipment). Groups work at convenient times throughout morning. Prepare for discussion at beginning of afternoon

Group work questions. What do they think is different/same about sounds from different things? What different sounds can they make from the same things? How do they describe the differences? What ideas do they have about where the sound comes from?

Groups in turn demonstrate the sounds. Make list on board of words used to describe sounds.

2.

Recap. Discuss ideas about how to change loudness and pitch
New task: check ideas and find other ways for each 'instrument'

Staggered group work

3.

Questions: How to make a note higher than a given one (predict before trying)? How to make a note lower than a given one (same)? Any other ways of doing these? What patterns?

4.

Groups prepare results for presenting to whole class

Exchange of reports (keep each group to one instrument to avoid repetition). Discuss differences; check using equipment
Discuss ideas about how sound is produced. Use word 'vibrating'
Groups tidy report on one instrument for class display

5.

Set individual task. Listen to sounds around. 20 minutes (quiet) in school grounds. Decide or find out what is vibrating
Discuss, then write or draw for class display

As a second example, the teacher of the children investigating the floating wooden blocks, described in Chapter 1, was following a plan of this kind:

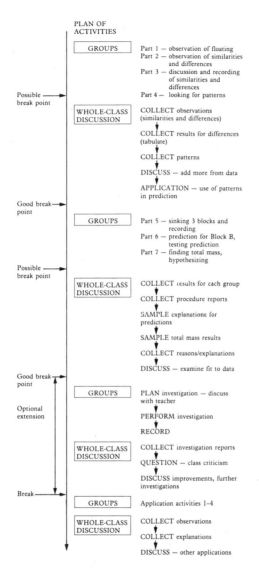

PLAN OF
ACTIVITIES

GROUPS	Part 1 — observation of floating
	Part 2 — observation of similarities
	and differences
	Part 3 — discussion and recording
	of similarities and
	differences

Possible →
break point

Part 4 — looking for patterns

| WHOLE-CLASS | COLLECT observations |
| DISCUSSION | (similarities and differences) |

COLLECT results for differences
(tabulate)

COLLECT patterns

DISCUSS — add more from data

APPLICATION — use of patterns
in prediction

Good break →
point

GROUPS	Part 5 — sinking 3 blocks and
	recording
	Part 6 — prediction for Block B,
	testing prediction
	Part 7 — finding total mass,
	hypothesizing

Possible →
break point

| WHOLE-CLASS | COLLECT results for each group |
| DISCUSSION | |

COLLECT procedure reports

SAMPLE explanations for
predictions

SAMPLE total mass results

COLLECT reasons/explanations

DISCUSS — examine fit to data

Good break →
point

| GROUPS | PLAN investigation — discuss |
| | with teacher |

Optional
extension

PERFORM investigation

RECORD

| WHOLE-CLASS | COLLECT investigation reports |
| DISCUSSION | |

QUESTION — class criticism

DISCUSS improvements, further
investigations

Break →

| GROUPS | Application activities 1–4 |

| WHOLE-CLASS | COLLECT observations |
| DISCUSSION | |

COLLECT explanations

DISCUSS — other applications

Here the words 'collect', 'sample', 'question', etc., are used as a short-hand;
each recalls a whole set of actions on the part of the teacher which do not have
to be spelled out each time.

The post of responsibility for science

The difficulty and the importance of stimulating and co-ordinating science activities in a school certainly justifies headteachers using some of the points at their disposal to create a post of responsibility for this work. The post may not be dedicated only to science; it may cover science and mathematics or environment studies and science, but clearly includes the obligation to help the headteacher ensure that science takes its place in the curriculum.

The teacher with the post for science will take a leading role in developing the school's policy and reviewing its working, but there are many other ways in which the other staff can be helped by the post-holder. The main ones are:

● providing support for teachers who lack confidence to make a start; this may involve giving specific ideas for topics, class organization, displays, etc.

● sharing the teaching in a class (when the post-holder is able to leave her class in the hands of someone else, perhaps the head) or inviting another teacher into her own class to observe science in action

● acting as a source of information to other teachers, being available to discuss science content as well as teaching approaches

● collecting and organizing books, materials and information useful to teachers including audio-visual aids, radio and television programmes, microcomputer software and safety regulations

● making proposals for enriching the school environment as a resource for scientific investigation (growing interesting plants, making habitats, places for weather observations, bird watching, etc.)

● being the link between the school and sources of help such as advisory teachers, services provided by museums, zoos and industry

● compiling useful information on places of scientific interest for class visits and a list of interesting people willing to visit

● extending the staff's competence in teaching science by school-based workshops, discussions on specific issues or the study of current reports and relevant research

● generally keeping the school in touch with new thinking and new developments in the field of primary science.

Some of these points are expanded in the pamphlet produced by the ASE Primary Schools Science Sub-Committee entitled *A Post of Responsibility in Science* (ASE, 1981). This document comes down heavily against the use of the post-holder to teach science in other classes, describing the role as that of a consultant in the school. The person who holds the post requires 'qualities of leadership, tact and enthusiasm for science learning' as well as 'a good background of scientific knowledge and understanding of science as a way of working'. The document goes on:

However, the attitude of the holder of the scale post is of far more importance than traditional knowledge and qualifications. Teaching methods and subject matter constantly change. Somebody willing to admit, at times, to not knowing, but alert to the need for finding out and for keeping up to date, is likely to be active in seeking the help that science advisers and advisory teachers can provide. Such a person will also use in-service training, meetings at Teachers' Centres and relevant books and articles, and encourage other members of staff to take advantage of the same opportunities.
(ASE, 1981; p. 39)

Evaluating and reviewing guidelines and policies

Science is still struggling to take its place as a basic part of the primary curriculum and ideas about how to arrange for this to happen are fairly new. For this reason, then, some rapid changes in curriculum organization for science can be expected. In addition there are other developments in the curriculum which have an impact on science, as well as some other areas. Examples are the rapid introduction of computers into the primary school, the growing interest in including elements of technology in pre-secondary education and the further light that research and surveys, such as the APU science work, can throw on the nature and practice of science at this level.

There are several reasons therefore why documents at LEA and school level should be regularly evaluated. Many of the general ideas given about evaluation in Chapter 5 are relevant and so it is only necessary here to consider some points specific to the documents considered in this chapter.

At the LEA level information might be collected by questionnaire from all primary and middle schools in the authority about:

● whether they have used the LEA document
● if so, who used it, how often and for what purposes
● which parts were of most help/least help
● whether there was any dissension from the advice offered.

The subjects covered by the document might be listed and schools asked to comment on whether the points made were thought useful/not useful/not appropriate (i.e. a matter for the school to decide). There might also be a list of subjects not covered by the document, for schools to decide whether it would be useful to have these in further editions of the guidelines. For example, not all guidelines cover:

● time to be spent on science
● integration and relation with other subjects
● safety precautions and matters covered by local or national laws

- dovetailing primary and secondary work
- the role of a post-holder
- problems of particularly fast and slow learning children
- use of TV and radio programmes.

It is important to gather information from as many schools as possible and certainly for the review to be carried out independently of the group who drafted the document. As already mentioned, these people are inevitably experienced in science teaching; they may well have forgotten the feelings of anxiety and helplessness which often consume the inexperienced. The guidelines should be of use to schools at a variety of levels of development with regard to their science work.

Similar types of information are relevant at the school level, but can be gathered less formally. The use that teachers have made of their school's policy could, however, be pressed a little harder. If the policy is to have more than a window-dressing function it must be adhered to by the teachers. Thus the review of the policy should take teachers into the evaluation of their work, for not only should they have agreed to provide the opportunities for the kind of learning expressed in the document, but they should also have done so as far as possible. If this is found not to be the case it may point to various kinds of action. The policy may be at fault in being too ambitious, perhaps too general, too easily misinterpreted, or there may be real disagreement on fundamental points about the nature of science education. Inservice support, perhaps just for some teachers or perhaps for the whole staff, may be indicated.

Another feature of the review at the school level is that consistency with the LEA document should be checked. Where obvious differences occur the reason should be sought. If the school disagrees with the LEA document it should make its objections known so that these can be taken into account when the latter is revised. If there is no disagreement but just a wandering off target then the school might reconsider whether its policy could be brought into line in the interests of the children's learning.

Finally: a national statement?

In discussing the planning which seems appropriate at the various levels mentioned at the beginning of this chapter, the general principle of maximum freedom for those closest to the children has been applied. Those who know the children are in the best position to provide the activity or the question or piece of information that will help them from one point to another in development of ideas, process skills and attitudes. At the same time it has been argued that teachers must relinquish some of the freedom to do exactly what they want; to pursue completely different types of goals of learning from their fellow teachers would be disastrous for the children. In the interests of the children teachers agree to an overall school policy.

So, too, at the school level, it serves the children best in their future science education for there to be some common aim in teaching science among schools in the LEA. The most important freedom that schools relinquish in conforming to the LEA policy is the freedom to decide not to include science in their programme.

Is there, then, any need for a statement at national level? Since responsibility of the secular curriculum in schools rests with the LEA (1944 Education Act, section 23) a national statement can in any case only be advisory as the law stands at present. If there were such a statement it should not concern itself with the content of the curriculum, which is being very effectively worked out at LEA and school level. A national statement on this matter would stifle initiative at other levels. Local officers and teachers implement best the policies which they help to define; participation brings commitment, and the reverse can also be true. All that a statement at national level should do is to advise LEAs against the neglect of scientific development as a goal of primary education.

CHAPTER 10

RESOURCES FOR TEACHING AND LEARNING SCIENCE

Introduction

The kind of learning discussed in this book cannot take place without there being the materials necessary for children to observe, investigate and actively engage with. Both tools to use in inquiry and objects for study or experimentation are essential at some time. These living and non-living resources for children to use in their learning take some effort to obtain, organize and store: some of the problems to which attention is turned in this chapter.

Handling and investigating material at first-hand are not the only experiences children need to help their learning, however. We have frequently referred to the value of access to ideas of others which can come through various channels. As well as discussion with other children and the teacher, it is valuable for children to have access to suitable books and non-book sources of information such as posters, photographs, slides, films, television, radio and microcomputer programs. This may appear a long list but it is not unmanageable. The key factor is setting up a system for organization and control of the resources which is kept up to date and known to all those who use them, children as well as teachers. Indeed, it can be seen as a significant part of the children's experience to help in the care of living material and the organization of other resources.

At the beginning of Chapter 1 it was noted that in many schools there might well be resources unknown to most if not all teachers and largely unused. The collecting together of existing materials and books can often form a useful nucleus for a central store of resources. There are many good reasons why the science resources in a school should be collected in a central store to which all teachers have access. It enables maximum benefit to be had from scarce resources and allows all teachers to know what is available. A little more will be said later about setting up such a central store. The co-operation among teachers needed to share the material is likely to be fostered by the kinds of collaboration and discussion involved in developing a school policy for science. Indeed, the resources should be closely related to the policy and the teacher with responsibility for science should take a central role in establishing and maintaining both.

'Resources' is a wide term, so in the following sections it will be broken down under four main headings: resources in the school, including both non-living and living materials; out-of-school resources; written materials; non-written materials including radio, television and the microcomputer.

Resources in the school

Planning and provision of equipment

Rarely does a school have the task of drawing up a shopping list of requisites for science starting from scratch. Invariably, it is a matter of augmenting an existing collection which has often been assembled in an unplanned way. But at some point it is useful to draw up a list of the basic needs for implementing the programme for science which is envisaged in the school policy. Comparing what is desirable with what is available will then enable any purchases that can be made to build up the collection in a systematic way.

It is not difficult to find suggested lists of equipment. Most teachers' guides to curriculum materials contain lists required for the activities they describe [e.g. Nuffield Junior Science Project, 1967; Brown & Young, 1982 (Exploring); Learning Through Science, 1982] and the science HMI have also provided an equipment list (DES, 1983b). A school might readily adopt one of these lists, especially if it is making use of the corresponding curriculum materials. On the other hand, unless a published course is being followed rigorously, it is likely that selections will be made and extensions added which adapt activities to the needs of particular schools and the opportunities provided in their environments. The given list of equipment might not then match the schools' requirements all that well.

It might be worthwhile therefore for a school to draw up its own list of necessary equipment. A considerable amount of material used in science will be common with other areas of the curriculum and so need not be listed. This includes paper, paint, Plasticine, Sellotape, string, scissors, glue, rulers, etc. If we restrict attention to the science-specific items it is helpful to identify

Table 4 Basic equipment for science work

Concept area	Equipment required for younger children	Additional equipment for older children
Sight and light	Torches, plane mirrors (preferably plastic), metal foil, shiny spoons, coloured transparent material	Curved mirrors, glass blocks and triangular prisms, coloured acetate sheets, hand stroboscope
Hot and cold and temperature changes		Spirit thermometers, polystyrene blocks, candles, spirit burners
Hearing and producing sound		Wire for making home-made sonometer, tuning forks
Movement and forces	Wheeled toys, inclined plane, springs, weights, marbles, balls, timers	Stop clocks & watches, balloons, model rockets, pulleys, retort stands or frame for suspending pendula, springs, pulleys, etc.
Air and breathing		Balloons, candles
How things behave in water	Washing up bowls, sponges, drinking straws, bubble pipes and bubble mixture, droppers, plastic funnels and tubing	Blocks of different woods all the same size, heavy washers, filter paper, test tubes and racks, plastic guttering, mini-fans
Ourselves and other animals	Bathroom scales, animal cages, (and equipment for cleaning), insect cages, aquarium tank, sheets of glass (taped), hand lenses, binocular microscope	Pooter
Soil and growth of plants	Flower pots, small trowels, (large old spoon), watering can, hand lenses, binocular microscope	
Sky, seasons and weather	Wall thermometer, outdoor thermometer	
Materials and their properties and uses	Collections of pieces of metal, wood, plastic, ceramics, fabrics, shells, stones, etc., hand lenses	Woodworking tools, magnets, compass, screws, nails
Simple electric circuits		Screw-in bulb holders, wires, bulbs to suit batteries used, crocodile clips

what is needed for activities relating to the basic ideas, such as those suggested in Chapter 4 (pages 78 and 79). Table 4 attempts to list the items which might be found useful. Fewer science-specific items are required for younger children and those listed for older ones are in addition to the list for the younger ones. The list omits common domestic items which can be readily collected and are useful for a wide range of activities, e.g. jam jars and all other types of container including saucers, pans and buckets, boxes, plastic bags, tins.

In addition, there may be the need at various times for consumable materials, not used in other subjects, including the following: Plaster of Paris, seeds, sand, cement, clay, sugar, salt, flour, talcum powder, animal foods, oil, dried foods, fresh foods, cotton wool. There will also be call for some tools for use by the teacher only: metal shears, for example.

The list of science-specific equipment is not in fact very long, the reason being that many activities can be carried out with materials already in the school. For example, no specialized equipment is required for the wide range of activities young children can engage in that help their awareness that there is air all around (they can 'feel' air moving as they rush through it or fan it onto each other, make paper gliders, parachutes, kites, windmills, make bubbles in water, try blowing a pellet of paper into an 'empty' bottle) all without using any materials other than those which can be collected at school or home. Similarly, there are many activities concerning sound and hearing which make use of everyday objects or containers, rubber bands and any musical instruments already in the school.

There is virtue in keeping the specialized equipment to a minimum and not merely on grounds of economy. Special equipment that is used only in science and not found in other parts of children's school or everyday experience can isolate science from the 'real' world around children. If a special set of instruments has to be used for weather observations, for example, the impression may be given that useful measurements depend on that set. It can come between the things being measured and the child. A better understanding of what is being measured may come from a home-made rain gauge, a windsock made from a stocking and an anemometer made with yoghurt containers rather than from more sophisticated equipment. These will be designed by the children to do the job that they have defined; they will not be starting with an instrument whose function they have to learn. The more children help in designing the ways they interact with their surroundings the more they will realize that they can investigate and learn about the world around through their own activity.

Storage of equipment

Storing equipment centrally in the school is an obvious way to make best use of items which have to be purchased. Items such as hand lenses, mirrors and magnets need only be obtained in sufficient quantities for one class or for two in a large school. The disadvantages of keeping equipment in a central store can be overcome by systematic labelling and indexing, keeping records and providing easy access and ways of transporting equipment. Before dealing with these points, however, there may be the prior question of how and where to find space. In some cases ingenuity may be required, but there are many examples (some published in the Learning Through Science project's excellent book *Science Resources*, 1982) of under-used store rooms or corners partitioned off which have been most successfully transformed into resource storage areas. Often parents are only too willing to clean and paint and put up shelves and hooks. Sometimes these activities can be encouraged to extend to constructing multipurpose frames for equipment that needs to be supported and even purpose-built trolleys for particular sets of equipment.

The organization of equipment in the store requires some thought. The notion of 'topic boxes' has been adopted in some schools, particularly where the work is organized round workcards used throughout the school (cf. Mr Carter's class, p. 95). It seems wasteful, however, for materials to lie in boxes when they could well be of use in topics other than that for which they are earmarked. Further, this organization would not suit more open-ended activities where equipment demands cannot be anticipated. The opposite extreme is to have all items stored in separate sets and for the collection needed at any time to be gathered by the teacher. This could be wasteful of time, too, since it could be anticipated that bulbs, bulb holders, wires and batteries would probably always be used together.

A compromise is probably possible, in which some equipment is kept in topic collections and other more general equipment kept in separate sets. Careful cataloguing is the key to the success of this, or indeed any, system. A listing of every item should be available to all staff showing where it can be found if stored as general equipment or in which topic box it is stored, e.g.

Items in alphabetical order	General equipment	Topic box
balloons	Shelf B, position 5	—
droppers	Shelf A, position 2	—
metal cylinders, etc.	—	'Metals'

In addition the contents and storage position of each topic box should be listed. This may seem a great deal of cataloguing but almost every school now has a microcomputer which should be used for this purpose. Not only is it very much easier to create a list by using the computer, which will order items alphabetically or by topic, by shelf or whatever is desired, but it can also be easily kept up to date. New lists can be printed whenever new equipment is obtained and distributed to staff. In large schools the computer may also be used to 'book' equipment at certain times, so that a planned lesson involving the microscope, for instance, is not frustrated by finding it already in use in another classroom. For transporting equipment a trolley, or preferably more than one, is almost a necessity. If several can be obtained, some can be converted as the permanent and mobile store for certain commonly used materials, or for particularly heavy topic equipment. Most often, though, a teacher will load the trolley with the collection needed at a particular time. When a chosen collection is in use in a classroom for a few days or longer, details of what is there should be left in the store.

In setting up a store it is well to remember that collections of material generally grow quite rapidly, they rarely diminish. Items brought to school to add to a display or to the range of materials being investigated are generally donated. In this way useful items such as an old camera, clock, clockwork or battery-driven toys, metal and wood off-cuts are added to the store and room has be be available for them. The store should also house a range of containers and other general equipment that is above that required in each classroom for activities other than science. This collection can swell quite quickly, too, once parents are aware that squeezy bottles, yoghurt pots, foil pie tins, and plastic and glass bottles are all useful for school activities.

Living things

Animals kept in the school for an extended period of time require specialized housing and regular care. It is worthwhile planning the provision of these non-human members of the school so that they make the most contribution to children's experience of the variety of living things. In one school there were terrapins and turtles in one classroom, fish in another, gerbils in another and so on. Each year the children changed classroom, so that they lived with each type of animal in turn. In other cases an agreed rota for exchanging classroom animals might be more appropriate, with teachers planning children's activities to suit the animals in residence at different times.

As well as captive animals in the classroom it should be possible to provide access to animals in natural habitats set up in the school grounds. Many schools are now using a small part of the grounds for an outdoor study area, where plants are grown and where birds, insects or other 'minibeasts' can find food and shelter. Few schools are unable to find the few square metres where plants can be grown, even if it is only in a chequerboard garden formed by taking up one or two patio slabs. Generally, much more can be done, so that nesting boxes can be provided, shrubs planted to attract butterflies, a bed for planting seeds with larger areas of garden for planting out seedlings and, quite important, a semi-wild area where wild flowers and grass can grow up round a pile of stones, giving shelter to a range of insects and other invertebrates. A good example of such an area is given in *Science Resources* (Learning Through Science, 1982; p. 30).

An outdoor resource area provides a valuable opportunity for children to study creatures without disturbing them too much. But if brought into the classroom for further study, temporary housing can be improvised from a variety of clear plastic containers.

Display

A great deal of attention has been given to storing equipment and materials tidily away, but not all of it should be always out of sight. As mentioned in Chapter 7, page 147, displays can provide starting points for activities and give children a useful way to pass odd moments. Displays can feature anything from a collection to tools, measuring instruments, or materials taken from the store, to special items on loan from the museum, local craft centre or industry. There should always be information provided about the exhibits in a suitable form and if possible invitations for children to handle and explore them or to inquire further in other ways.

Out of school

Since the overall aim of science activities is to help children understand the world around them, getting out into that world has an important part to play. This is not to deny that the classroom and school and all that is in them are part of the child's environment, but this is a selected and controlled part and to make connections between children's activities in school and the larger environment it is necessary regularly to observe and interact with parts of it at first-hand.

There are good practical reasons for taking children out of school. Visits are highly motivating to children, they bring back to school many vivid impressions which sustain follow-up work and often persist over several weeks.

They contribute, of course, to work in other areas of the curriculum and this is not being forgotten in concentrating here on the science work. A most successful teacher of primary science (incidentally not trained in science) always began every topic with a visit; he said it was the equivalent to charging a battery, giving the work for 5 or 6 weeks energy and vitality. Each visit was chosen to suit the programme planned and to provide opportunities for children to develop science concepts during follow-up investigations. It is not difficult to select a site for a visit in this way since most venues provide opportunities for development of any of a whole range of ideas. Figure 26 illustrates this, showing just some of the links between the possibilities for visits and the main areas of basic science concepts. (This does not include museums or special exhibitions which could relate to any or all of the concepts; these have a valuable role in children's learning in addition to and not as a substitute for visiting places which are more a part of everyday life.)

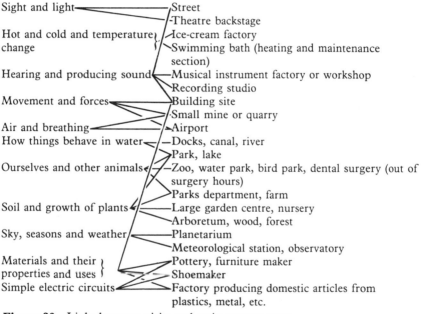

Figure 26   Links between visits and main concept areas

A considerable amount of work for the teacher is involved in planning and organizing a visit but this is rewarded several times over by the quality of the ensuing work of the children. Apart from the necessary correspondence and communication of plans within the school, a prior visit by the teacher is an essential part of the preparation. This is an opportunity not only for the teacher to find out what the children will experience but to tell anyone in the place to be visited who may be acting as guide, demonstrator or informer, something about the children. In some cases those involved may have little idea of the level of background knowledge, length of attention span and interests of primary school children. The teacher can help them with their preparation by suggesting some of the questions the children might ask and the sorts of things that will need to be explained in simple terms.

Some useful hints for preparing visits of primary school children to industry have come out of the exploratory study of schools–industry work for the age range 8–13 years carried out by the Schools Council Industry Project [Jamieson (ed), 1984]. Primary school teachers may be more familiar with visits to parks, woods and streets than with visits to factories or small industries. However, many of the guidelines have relevance for visits of all kinds. The study identified these points as helping to make a visit successful:
(i) It should not be an isolated event, but the centrepiece of extended work which begins beforehand and continues afterwards.
(ii) The type of industry visited should preferably be one producing something which children recognize and relate to, for example bicycles, toys or domestic utensils. It was found that complex processes involving huge machinery, often very noisy, did not make for successful visits.
(iii) The best size of group to take round a work place was found to be six to eight children, so to break a class down into groups of this size requires the help of parents or people from the industry being visited.
(iv) When children were issued with worksheets, either by the school or the place being visited, it was found that these:

> tended to unduly narrow the observational powers of the children. Many children were observed spending most of their time buried in their notebooks (or even worse, other children's notebooks!) rather than listening to and observing the operation of the factory or workplace.
> [Jamieson (ed.), 1984; p. 12]

The approach that appeared to be a useful compromise between too much and too little prior instruction was to indicate to children beforehand the main areas of interest and enquiry and to leave the children scope to frame their own questions. The value of this approach for process-skill development is shown clearly in the report that: 'Several schools dealt with this problem by preparation time on the development of questioning and observational skills.' [Jamieson (ed.), 1984; p. 12]
(v) In many cases it was useful follow-up work for the children to create a model of the place visited. As well as the problems of scale and construction to

be overcome, the activity helps children to realize the sequence of events. For older children flow diagrams would have similar benefits.

(vi) Inviting someone from the industry back to the school to talk to the children some time after the visit gives them opportunity to pose questions which have occurred later during reflection on the visit. The double benefit here is that the adult from the industry has the chance to learn about the children's work and the school environment, which can improve school-industry communication to the good of later visiting groups.

Written materials

Reference materials

Children need information, which frequently goes beyond that which the teacher can supply, to satisfy their curiosity and sometimes their appetite for collecting names and facts. There are many excellent books, some in sets (such as the Observer's Books published by Warne) which are suitable for children and adults to use for reference. A most comprehensive list of titles is given in the Learning Through Science (1982) Book on resources. The important qualities of books for children are that they have large and clear coloured photographs and an easily used index or other way of locating information.

Reference books can usefully be kept together in a central school library and borrowed by classes, perhaps for an extended time such as half a term, on those occasions when they are likely to be in constant demand for the topic in hand. With this type of use in mind it may be preferable to purchase smallish books restricted to one topic rather than large encyclopaedic volumes.

Not all reference material is in book form. Wallcharts, although less durable than books, have some advantages over them. Several children can consult them at one time and each can see all the information available: useful either for identifying a specimen by matching or for seeing the parts of a process linked together in a large flow diagram.

Activity books or cards

Some of these are written for teachers, some for children; some constitute a set course whereas others provide a menu a là carte. It may be supposed that the set-meal variety has been planned to provide a balanced diet but whether or not this is in fact the case is a matter to be checked rather than assumed.

All activity materials, whether intended for teachers or pupils, can be useful to teachers as sources of ideas. However, there is a great deal of such published material now on the market and it would be a tremendous task to comb through it all. It may be best to have in the school the full range of at least one extensive set of materials [such as Science 5/13, Learning Through Science, Exploring and, for the older-age group, Nuffield Combined Science Themes for the Middle Years (1977–1980)] rather than a selection of parts of several, which can mean some repetition and some gaps. The school programme and the planning of individual teachers can then draw on ideas from across those published.

The selection of activities and the development of a programme is an extremely difficult and time-consuming matter and there is every reason for a school not undertaking this from scratch. A planned series of activities throughout the 4 years of the junior school has many attractions; the decisions about suitable content and approach for different ages have already been taken and there is an intention, at least, for these activities to add up to a coherent and progressive series of learning experiences avoiding repetition and discontinuity. If full advantage is to be taken of these virtues of the course then it has to be used throughout those years of the school for which it is devised. It is not helpful to step into a course at year three if the work is dependent on years one and two. It requires the full commitment of all the teachers, which they will (and should) only give if they consider the course is better than they could provide in other ways and allows sufficient flexibility to match children who may vary in their development even though they are in the same class.

Teachers are often reluctant to agree to adopt a course whole-heartedly since, despite the apparent advantages, there are many disadvantages. In the first place the course may not achieve the aims they themselves consider to be important. The method of evaluating workcards given in Chapter 5 (pages 111–114) can be adapted for use on any material for the purpose of assessing the extent to which particular aims can be achieved. This analysis gives attention both to the methods of working as well as to the content. A second point is that adopting a set science course separates science from other areas of work more than a teacher might wish. If there is integration, it will be the other work which has to fit into the science framework. The notion of topic work spreading across science and several other subjects would be difficult to reconcile with the adoption of the course. Thirdly, there would be some pressure to cover the ground at a pace necessary to finish the prescribed activities within a certain time, for otherwise the continuity in the programme might be in danger. Finally, there is the problem of catering for a range of interests, abilities and rates of working.

Many teachers find these points strong enough to deter the adoption of a set course, particularly one based on children's workcards. Workcards designed to keep children 'on course' are inevitably somewhat closed and give little opportunity for the development and use of some process skills. There is an ironic conflict between the set meal and the balanced diet! But the materials in the course are not without value to teachers even if they are not used with children. They are sources of ideas, just as any other materials, but in addition they give operational examples of how treatment of content differs for the younger and the older children. This is a valuable function, given the great difficulty teachers have in matching science activities to children (see Chapter 6, p. 124 and 141–145.)

Teachers' guides

It seems that attempts to reduce dependence on teachers' decisions, by providing a preplanned series of activities, tend to constrain the children's experiences, particularly their opportunities for the kind of learning we have been discussing here. This kind of learning depends essentially, as we have seen in earlier chapters, on the teacher's role. To produce more carefully structured materials is not the answer; instead, we should give teachers more help to take their unavoidable role. Inservice work is a major source of such help, but teachers can now also find more books and articles which help them in their curriculum decision-making as well as in their day-to-day classroom work.

It underestimates teachers to regard them as wanting only to be told what to do. This approach does not develop teachers' own skills but rather cuts them off from consideration of the purposes of the activities and of the ways of advancing children's learning. Fortunately, it is now easier for teachers to have access to various ideas about primary science [the collection of short articles edited by Richards & Holford (1984) is an example], to suggestions for improving the reading skills particularly required in science [another collection, edited by Harlen (1985b) is an example] and to suggestions for developing programmes (Learning Through Science, 1982). At last, attention is being turned to the broader curriculum issues and to pedagogy, which are probably better routes to helping teachers with content than the narrow concentration on classroom activities.

Non-written materials

Use of the media of slide, radio and television, like everything else, has its pros and cons. The idea of children sitting restlessly in a darkened room looking at slides of things they could easily see for themselves out of doors, and which they would then find intriguing, is not in harmony with good practice in science teaching. On the other hand, slides or films can enable children to see things which it would be too difficult or dangerous for them to see for themselves, can extend their knowledge of the variety of things in the environment and may be used to stimulate rather than substitute for enquiry. It is not the medium that may be faulted but the way it is used.

Radio and television programmes for schools, as distinct from programmes for a general audience which may be of value to school work, are used by about one-quarter of the schools in which children of age 11 years are taught, according to the APU survey of 1982 (DES, 1984). Not all of these follow through a whole series and the decision facing a school or teacher as to whether to do this depends on much the same issues as discussed for adopting a programme of written materials. There are additional points to consider, however. The programmes use only very carefully selected and tried-out activities and audience-reaction evaluation during development of a series has been used to ensure that both the content and its treatment will be interesting to children. [This is not to say that writers of written materials may not go to similar lengths, but it is nonetheless possible (and does happen) that activities are included which do not work in practice, whereas this would not happen on a television programme.] Furthermore, television programmes can, and often do, show children engaged in investigations, so they can indicate methods of working as well as content.

On the negative side, apart from any problems raised by arranging television viewing conveniently, the main additional point is the danger of science becoming a spectator sport. To avoid this the programmes require careful building into the curriculum. As isolated events, constituting the children's only activity labelled 'science', they may be as readily forgotten as last week's *Blue Peter*. Fortunately, the most popular programmes are accompanied by written guides for teachers which give detailed suggestions for the essential preparatory and follow-up work.

The introduction of the microcomputer into the primary school and its possible use in science can be another mixed blessing. In the forefront of planning the use of this technology in teaching should be that it must not take children away from contact with the real world and the investigation of things around them. Whereas simulations and models can be useful applications of microcomputers in science at more advanced levels, for the under-thirteens they may well be regarded as games, with no more relevance to real life than

'Space Invaders'. However, it is possible to avoid this pitfall and for the computer to take a useful role in learning science if we take advantage of its potential to:

● extend the range of children's activities, for instance making available to them data which they would not have time or opportunity to gather at first-hand but which they decide they want and can use

● extend their ability to try out different approaches to a problem or to display data in different forms at a speed which can be attained in no other way

● respond to the children but leave them with a great deal of the control of the activity in their own hands

● encourage genuine collaboration between groups.

No computer program can do these things 'single-handed', as it were, and realizing the potential value of the computer requires that its use forms only part of an activity or of the work on a topic. It should feature in those parts where it has most to offer in increasing children's opportunities to gather information, to test ideas and to communicate effectively at all stages of an enquiry. Programs which meet these aims are only now being developed and there is room for a great deal more research and experiment into the roles that the computer can take.

At present the most useful programs for science activities are ones which help in data processing. This is, however, only one of the possible roles of the computer. Others include:

● helping in making measurements and recording data

● guiding children's thinking about identifying investigable questions and designing investigations which the children later carry out in practice

● extending the range of subject matter that can be investigated, as distinct from being observed, by simulations linked to the children's own observations

● short-circuiting time-consuming data collection by providing additional data to supplement those collected by children

● posing questions to help children apply the ideas and methods of working they have gained from past enquiry work to new problems.

There may well be other roles, as yet unsuspected. It is appropriate for science educators to keep an open mind about the kinds of learning that the new technology may make available. With such a powerful force at hand we should not restrict use of it to replacing aspects of a teacher's role. It may be that children's undoubted ease in communication with computers facilitates modes of learning not tapped and made accessible in any other way.

That is for the future. For the present, one of the pleasing, and perhaps surprising, features of having a microcomputer in the classroom is that it can stimulate children to discuss ideas and work together. A group of three is ideal, according to teachers' experience. To agree on their response at each point where they interact with the program the children have to argue their case with each other. They obtain immediate feedback as to their success at each step and observation shows that they use this in later responses. The construction of ideas and reasoning about ways of working can be rapid, given a suitably challenging program. Perhaps it is no more than a teacher could do by giving undivided attention, combined with endless patience, to three children for a considerable time, but the teacher is too busy doing the things a computer cannot do.

Conclusion

Resources for teaching include all the materials, objects and aids that can be used in helping children learn. In science the use of resources is essential to helping children to explore and to develop ideas about their environment; it is not just a matter of making learning more interesting. There is a variety of resources that are needed; some to be investigated, some to be used as tools in investigations, some to give information, some to give ideas of how to tackle problems, some to pose questions and challenge children to justify and support their own ideas. A well-informed teacher is the best resource of all, but he or she cannot be all things to all pupils at the same time, nor replace the children's own investigations of things around them. For science, then, resources of the kind discussed in this chapter are indispensable. If the provision of such resources is not to become a burden, however, it is essential that the resources are well organized, maintained and easily accessible. Perhaps the measure of the extent to which a school takes science seriously is the extent to which useful materials have been gathered and arranged so that teachers know of their existence and use them regularly with the minimum of organizational problems.

References

ASE (1966) *Science for Primary Schools. 1. Children Learning Through Science* London: John Murray.

ASE (1971) *Science for the Under-Thirteens* Hatfield, Hertfordshire: Association for Science Education.

ASE (1980) *Language in Science* Study Series No. 16. Hatfield, Hertfordshire: Association for Science Education.

ASE (1981) Science and Primary Education Paper No. 3: *A Post of Responsibility in Science* Hatfield, Hertfordshire: Association for Science Education.

Avon Education Committee (undated) *Primary Science. A Policy for Science* Bristol: Education Department.

Barnes D. (1976) *From Communication to Curriculum* Harmondsworth: Penguin.

Bell B. (1981) *Video: Animals* Working Paper No. 51. Science Education Research Unit, University of Waikato, Hamilton, New Zealand.

Bell B. & Barker M. (1982) Towards a scientific concept of 'animal'. *Journal of Biological Education* **16** (3) pp. 197–200.

Bennett N., Desforges C., Cockburn A. & Wilkinson B. (1984) *The Quality of Pupil Learning Experiences* London: Lawrence Erlbaum Associates.

Biddulph F. & Osborne R. (1984) Pupils' Ideas about Floating and Sinking *Research in Science Education*, 1984, Vol. 14 pp. 114–124.

Black P.J., Harlen W. & Orgee A.G. (1984) *Standards of Performance: Expectations and Reality* APU Occasional Paper No. 3. London: DES.

Brown C. & Young B.Y. (1982) *Exploring Primary Science: Teachers' Handbook* Cambridge: Cambridge University Press.

Bruner J.S., Goodnow J.J. & Austin G.A. (1966) *A Study of Thinking* New York: John Wiley.

Cheshire County Council (1982) Cheshire County *Primary Science Guidelines*, County Hall, Chester.

Clift P., Weiner G. & Wilson E. (1981) *Record Keeping in Primary Schools* London: Macmillan Education.

Davis B. (1983) The problems of starting and continuing primary science, Advanced Diploma Thesis, Department of Educational Studies, University of Oxford, Oxford.

DES (1967) *Children and Their Primary Schools* Plowden Report. London: HMSO.

DES (1977) *Education in Schools. A Consultative Document* London: DES.

DES (1978) *Primary Education in England* London: HMSO.

DES (1981a) *Science in Schools. Age 11* APU Report No. 1. London: HMSO.

DES (1981b) *Environmental Education: Sources of Information* London: HMSO.

DES (1981c) Circular 2/81. *Falling Rolls and Surplus Places* London: DES.

DES (1982) *Science Education in Schools: a Consultative Document* London: DES.

DES (1983a) *Science in Schools. Age 11* APU Report No. 2. DES Research Report. London: DES

DES (1983b) *Science in Primary Schools* A discussion paper produced by the HMI Science Committee. London: DES.

DES (1984) *Science in Schools. Age 11* APU Report No. 3. DES Research Report. London: DES

Duckworth D. (1972) The choice of science subjects by grammar school pupils, unpublished PhD Thesis, University of Lancaster, Lancaster.

Exploring Primary Science Units 1–4 (1982–5) Cambridge: Cambridge University Press.

Galton M.J., Simon B. & Croll P. (1980) *Inside the Primary Classroom* London: Routledge and Kegan Paul.

Gloucestershire Education Committee (undated) *Gloucestershire Activities for Primary Science.*

Glover J. (1985) Case Study 1. Science and project work in the infant school. In *Open University (1985) EP531 : Primary Science — Why and How?* Block 1 Study Book, Milton Keynes: Open University Press.

Harlen W. (1975) *Science 5/13: A Formative Evaluation* London: Macmillan Education.

Harlen W. (1980) Matching. In *Primary Education* (C. Richards ed.) London: A. and C. Black.

Harlen W. (1983) *Assessment in Schools : Science* London: Macmillan Education.

Harlen W. (1985a) Science education : primary school programmes. In *International Encyclopaedia of Education* Oxford: Pergamon Press.

Harlen W. (ed.) (1985b) *Primary Science: Taking the Plunge* London: Heinemann Educational.

Harlen W. & Symington D. (1985) Helping children to observe. In *Primary Science: Taking the Plunge* (W. Harlen ed.) London: Heinemann Educational.

Jamieson I. (ed.) (1984) *We Make Kettles: Studying Industry in the Primary School* London: Schools Council.

Kelly P.J. (1959) An investigation of the factors which influence grammar school pupils to prefer science subjects, unpublished MA Thesis, University of London.

Learning Through Science (1980) *Learning Through Science: Formulating a School Policy* London: Macdonald Educational.

Learning Through Science (1982) *Science Resources* London: Macdonald Educational.

Lovell K. (1962) *The Growth of Basic Mathematical and Scientific Concepts in Children* London: University of London Press, London.

Martin M.D. (1983) Recent trends in the nature of curriculum programmes and materials. In *New Trends in Primary School Science Education* (W. Harlen ed.) vol. 1, pp. 55–67. Paris: UNESCO.

Match and Mismatch (1977) Materials include three books: *Raising Questions, Teacher's Guide, Finding Answers* Edinburgh: Oliver and Boyd.

Nuffield Combined Science Themes for the Middle Years (1977–1980) London: Longman.

Nuffield Junior Science Project (1967) *Teachers' Guide I, Apparatus and Animals and Plants* London: Collins Educational.

Ormerod M.B. & Duckworth D. (1975) *Pupils' Attitudes to Science* Windsor: NFER Publishing Co.

Osborne R.J. (1985) Children's own concepts. In *Primary Science: Taking the Plunge* (W. Harlen ed.) London: Heinemann.

Osborne R.J. & Freyberg P. (1982) *Learning in Science Project (Forms 1–4): Final Report* Science Education Research Unit, University of Waikato, Hamilton, New Zealand.

Osborne R.J. & Freyberg P. (1985) *Learning in Science: the Implications of 'Children's Science'* New Zealand: Heinemann Educational.

Osborne R.J., Biddulph F., Freyberg P. & Symington D. (1982) *Confronting the Problems of Primary School Science* Working Paper No. 110, Science Education Research Unit, University of Waikato, Hamilton, New Zealand.

Oxfordshire County Council (1983) *Primary Science: The Oxfordshire Experience* Oxfordshire Education Department.

Paisey A. (ed.) (1983) *The Effective Teacher* London: Ward Lock Educational.

Piaget J. (1929) *The Child's Conception of the World* New York: Harcourt, Brace.

Richards C. (ed.) (1980) *Primary Education* London: A. and C. Black.

Richards C. & Holford D. (eds.) (1984) *The Teaching of Primary Science: Policy and Practice* Lewes, Sussex: Falmer Press.

Rogers C. (1983) *Freedom to Learn for the Eighties* Columbus, Ohio: Charles Merill.

Rogers V.R. (ed.) (1970) *Teaching in the British Primary School* London: Macmillan Education.

Science, a Process Approach (1966–1976) Rank Xerox Services.

Science 5/13 Series (1972–1975) *Teachers' Guides* London: MacDonald Educational (26 titles).

Showell R. (1979) *Teaching Science to Infants* London: Ward Lock Educational.

Straughan R. & Wrigley J. (1980) *Values and Evaluation in Education* London: Harper & Row.

Symington D. & Osborne R. (1984) *Towards Professional Development in Science Education for the Primary School Teacher* In *European Journal of Science Education* Vol. 7, No. 1, pp. 19–28.

Thier H.D. (1973) Content and approaches of integrated science programs at the primary and secondary school levels. In *New Trends in Integrated Science Teaching* (P.E. Richmond ed.) vol. II, pp. 53–70. Paris: UNESCO.

Thomas N. (1980) The Primary Curriculum: survey findings and implications. In *Primary Education* (C. Richards ed.) London: A. and C. Black.

Thurber J. (1945) *The Thurber Carnival* London: Hamish Hamilton.

Tyler R.W. (1949) *Basic Principles of Curriculum and Instruction* Chicago: University of Chicago Press.

UNESCO (1983) *New Trends in Primary School Science Education* (W. Harlen, ed.) vol 1, pp. 187–199. Paris: UNESCO.

INDEX